KNOWING JASPER

THE FIRST BOOK

First published in the United States of America
by Lillie Whittle
2010

UNEDITED PROOF COPY.
NOT FOR RESALE

ISBN 978 0 9566229 0 7

For Billy and Tommy

KNOWING JASPER

THE FIRST BOOK

'HELLO. MY NAME IS JASPER. I AM PUBLISHING THIS BOOK IN AUGUST 2010, FOR ONE REASON ONLY.

THERE ARE SOME THINGS YOU ARE GOING TO NEED TO KNOW.'
Jasper (1781-1853)

Hello. My name is Lillie and I'm going to help Jasper tell you what it is that you are going to need to know.

I'll do my best to make sure that all of the information in this book is written in plain and simple English without the long Latin words and fancy jargon which many 'experts' use to impress you, confuse you, or make themselves seem more important than they actually are.

By now you will have worked out from the dates of Jaspers life (1781 - 1853) that Jasper is dead and talking to you from the etheric layer. He talks through my husband Ernest. I record the words that he says and then put them on paper. It's that simple.

Many others also speak to me through my husband Ernest. Jasper brings them to speak, they do so and I record, word for word, what they say. They all have something to say to you. Later in the book I'll explain more fully who we all are and how we do this.

I am as alive as you are and I am well aware that it is not me that you are interested in hearing from – it's those who have left the solid side of existence and wish to talk to you from where they are now that you are most interested in. So I'll leave the technical details of how we do this until later and start by giving you the transcript of one of these conversations. Throughout the book you will see the date on which these people spoke to me. Any additional information which you may need will appear as notes before the transcript.

Billy the Baker's Boy

[On 10 May 2008 I heard the voice of a young boy who spoke with a bright and lively working-class cockney accent. To be able to date when this boy lived - Queen Victoria reigned 1837-1901.]

B: What's your name?

L: My name is Lillie. What's your name?

B: Billy. How old are you then?

L: Ooh, I'm very old. I'm really old.

B: How old is old?

L: Over twenty.

B: That's old.

L: Over thirty.

B: [Getting interested] Really?

L: Over forty.

B: No, I've never seen anyone that old.

L: I'm over fifty. I'm fifty five. How old are you?

B: Nearly twelve.

L: That's quite old.

B: Well ... yes.

L: Where are you from Billy?

B: Me?

L: Yes.

B: Here and about really. Where you from?

L: South London.

B: Oh, I don't know that.

L: Tell me about yourself Billy.

B: I work for Mr Charles, The Baker. I take bread.

L: You deliver it?

B: Big basket.

L: I bet you can smell it, can't you?

B: Lovely.

L: Lovely smell, new bread and warm in the winter.
B: Nice. At the end of the day he lets me take some home and my Mum toasts it. Lovely.

L: Do you get butter on it?

B: Sometimes, depending on how much money we've got.

L: Yes, of course.

B: But it's good because I don't have to pay for it. And I get paid as well. Tuppence.

L: Bet you give all the money to your Mum though, don't you?

B: Yeah. Tuppence I get.

L: Is that a week?

B: [Sounding surprised I had to ask that] Of course. How much more would it be?

L: No, no, not at all. Sorry.

B: Hmm.

L: What time do you start work, do you know? First light or something?

B: Early.

L: Is it dark still?

B: Sometimes. I don't mind because I go and stand in front of the ovens and I warm me bum. It's lovely. It's nice. I like the smell.

L: Is The Baker a kind man?

B: Yes, and his wife. She's fat. I think she eats all of the bread. She makes all the buns and cakes. He makes the bread, all shapes and sizes. Do you know what though ....

L: What ...

B: [Lowering his voice] Sometimes I drop the bread. Nobody knows. I just brush it down and ... providing it doesn't break no corners or nothing like that, no-one knows.

L: No. Well I'm not going to tell anyone.

B: No. Who do you think delivers that Queen's bread? Do you think there's a boy goes and delivers to her?

L: No, I think she probably has five or six people who carry it to her and they'll be dressed in bright uniforms with shiny buttons.

B: Bet she eats a lot of it. She's fat.

L: Queen Victoria?

B: Yes. People must eat an awful lot of bread to be fat because I eat a lot of bread and I'm not fat.

L: Have you seen her then, The Queen?

B: I've seen pictures of her. Seen drawings of her, pictures, paintings.

L: She's not very pretty, is she?

B: [Lowering his voice and rather stern] Shh! Mustn't say that.

L: Well she's not, is she?

B: No ... get into trouble for saying that.

L: O.K.

B: Mustn't say that.

L: [Whispering] But she's not.

B: No, I suppose not. [Then changing the subject quickly] Baker says when I'm older I can have a horse.

L: Oh, really? To deliver?

B: Yes, he uses it now. He's got a big wagon with windows in the side of it.

L: It must be a big bakery.

B: Biggest one in the whole country. And he's got a cart and horse. I feed the horse sometimes. I give it buns. Gives it wind, I'm not supposed to do that. He makes ... he burps at me.

L: Is he a big horse?

B: Big. So, if I work hard, when I get bigger I can use the horse and I can deliver more bread then.

L: How many of you work in the bakery. Lots?

B: Oh, there's ... there's some older than me. No boys.

L: Right, so you're the only boy are you?

B: Yes. I run faster than the others.

L: You're special then.

B: Yes. Baker says that he's going to get me some teaching, he says.

L: For what?

B: [Once more sounding surprised I had to ask] So I can read and write. He says I'm not going to be any good to him in the bakery if I can't read and write. He says I can read the orders then.

L: He sounds very kind.

B: Yes, he's a kind man. He's got a daughter. She's nice.

L: Is she older than you or younger than you?

B: Older, not much. Not much older. She doesn't talk much.

L: Is she shy?

B: Don't know, doesn't say much. Do you like buns?

L: I love buns.

B: Do you know how they make them shine?

L: No. How?

B: Do you not know? [Sounding pleased]

L: No. I'd like to know.

B: You won't tell no-one?

L: No.

B: Sugar and water.

L: Oh, is it?

B: Seen it.

L: Do they brush it on?

B: Yes. Makes it shine. I think it must be a secret.

L: Must be. Well I'm not going to tell anyone.

B: Tastes nice. I like fruit buns. And Mrs. Baker, she puts some stuff on it that makes them yellow. What's the name .... I don't know what it is.

L: Maybe saffron, or something.

B: Maybe, I don't know, but it makes them look yellow. Looks nice. I like them when they're hot.

L: I do. What sort of cakes does she make?

B: Well, I don't know what they're called but she makes cake with fruit inside, in like a ... looks like a loaf but it's not. People have it sliced in pieces and they bite pieces off it. And pies, she makes pies with apple with lots of sugar. Sometimes I get one of those.

L: Do you? Do you get a full one?

B: [By now thinking I am a little simple] They're not big ones! Big enough for me. Depends what sort of mood they're in really. If they've had a good day ... and I think it's when there's some left over. Sometimes I get some to take home to my Mum as well.

L: I bet your Mum's pleased.

B: Well, she said that it's a big help because she doesn't have to pay for it.

L: Have you got lots of brothers and sisters?

B: A few. She cleans. My Dad, he works with coal. He delivers coal. He comes to The Baker.

L: So you both deliver, you and your Dad.

B: Yes. Baker says 'Tell your Dad that I'll be in my office after work.' He hasn't got an office.

L: So he's a friend of your Dad's, is he?

B: My Dad smiles when I tell him, 'Mr Baker said he'll be in his office after work.' My Dad puts down his paper and he smiles and he goes out. He says it's urgent business.

L: [Laughing] Nice. A few beers together I think, don't you?

B: Camberwell. That's where I live. Sorry, you did ask me. [Then in a quieter voice] Fell in the canal.

L: Oh, did you?

B: Yes.

L: Were you delivering bread or playing?

B: I was playing. I'd finished work and I was going home and I thought I saw something in the water. I thought I saw a frog. Never seen a frog. But you can't get frogs in canals. I thought it was a frog. Just a leaf really. And I got a big stick and I reached out and tried to reach it, but it wasn't long enough. I fell in. It was cold. Freezing cold it was. Left the bag with the bread in it on the bank ... wonder if my Mum got it. Do you think so?

L: Maybe. But you know she'd be so upset that you'd died I bet she didn't feel like eating.

B: I reckon the birds had it.

L: Maybe. [Crying now] Ah, Billy, how sad!

B: [Sounding surprised to hear me sad] I'm alright.

L: I know you are. Did you see your Mum again, and your Dad?

B: Yes, course.

L: And The Baker and his wife?

B: Yes ... yes.

L: Are you still all together now?

B: Yes. I love the smell of warm bread .... oh, yes, it's cinnamon.

L: What is? Oh .... right, that's the yellow stuff she puts on the buns, the secret.

B: Smells very strong. Nice, yes. Don't tell no-one.

L: I'm not going to. I won't. Thanks for telling me.

B: And sometimes you get big pieces of sugar on top. Do you know what I did when they weren't looking?

L: No, what?

B: [Whispering] Put my finger in the sugar water. Licked it. ... it's nice. Didn't get caught.

L: Well I'm not going to tell anyone, am I.

B: No. Do you make bread?

L: Sometimes, and I'm going to try the sugar and water on some buns.

B: It shines. I don't like brown bread. It looks dirty.

L: I like white fluffy bread.

B: I like to pull the middle out. Soft.

L: And that smell, it's lovely.

B: Bye.

L: [Surprised] Oh ... are you going now, Billy. Nice to talk to you. Thanks for coming.

B: OK. Bye. [ENDS]

And just like any eleven year old little boy who had become bored or who had spotted something else to do which was more fun, he'd gone.

We selected Billy, and Tommy (who follows) to start Jasper's first book and you will see this book is dedicated to them. It is just a coincidence that they are both from the time of Queen Victoria when child labour was common, they start the book simply because they were two of our favourite people to meet. I love talking to the children. They are so matter-of-fact about what happened to them, and they are always so cheerful.

Tommy the Sweep

[On 27 March 2007 I heard a young boy with a bright, cheery cockney voice. Toffs were what the lower classes called the upper classes in the reign of Queen Victoria - 1837-1901.]

T: Hello.

L: Hello, I'm Lillie. You're very welcome.

T: My name's Tommy and I was a chimneysweep's boy.

L: That's interesting, Tommy, where are you from?

T: I lived with me Mum and me brothers and me Dad. Five brothers and a sister. Used to live in Nunhead [South London] by The Green. Used to work as a sweep's boy. We worked at big houses in Dulwich. Toffs. I used to climb up the chimneys with all the soot. Dust and dirt. Bloody awful.
    It was dark. We used to go up with a candle. If you was lucky you went up with an oil lamp. From the fireplace to the top, so you'd climb inside the fireplace. Them big houses is all clean, mustn't get no dirt on them, no soot.
    You'd go into the fireplace with a lamp. Big ones those fireplaces, you could live in them. Big as my house, some of them fireplaces. The chimneys had ledges inside where you could sit and dream. You'd climb up with your brush and your bag to collect the dust in, then you'd make out you was sweeping and have a rest.

L: How old are you?

T: Eight. I was little. They only wanted the little ones. The big ones couldn't get up, they was too fat. It was a bit scary at first, but me Mum needed the money. It was smelly and I coughed a lot. When you finished you'd go home and when you coughed it'd come up black, and when you blew your nose that'd be all black too. You'd just get it cleared ready to do it all again the next day.

[Becoming more serious now as he explained his job] You climb up into the fireplace and you're up there till you've cleaned it. The Governor, he puts a sheet over the back. He puts up his brushes. Big ones which push all the way up and out onto the roof. They come out at the top like a bird's nest. You have to be careful in them old houses because you could push the chimney pot off. If you cause damage it'll cost you a lot of money. The Governor, he does the brush thing, I didn't like it if the brush got stuck because I had to climb up and get it unstuck.

You'd go up with your brush. Them chimneys are rough inside. They look all smooth on the outside, but when they make them they don't care what they look like on the inside, and so you can climb them. You have to brush out all the crevices.

L: How long did it take you to do a chimney?

T: Sometimes you'd be up there hours. You'd climb all the way to the top and then clean down. You have a bag, like a sack but with a bit of straight wood and you'd hold that against the wall while you put the stuff in it. Sometimes you take an extra bag, you don't want to keep climbing up and down. You can't drop it or it would burst. You let it down on a rope. You work your way down from the top to the bottom.

You'd have to make sure it all cleaned and you had as much as you could get into the bags and then you'd tell the Governor to take the sheet down. If I got the room dirty I'd get a clout and me Mum didn't get no money. You'd stand there and he'd wrap you in another sheet and carry you out.

L: How many hours a day did you work?

T: Hours? I don't know. I just started when I started and when we finished I went home. Some days we didn't have no work. The only way I could know what time it was outside was to look up the chimney, see if it was dark or light.

L: I'll bet your Mum was really proud of you.

T: She didn't say. She was always too busy. I had a younger brother, then one who was about the same size as me, then two bigger ones. And a sister. The bigger ones, they used to go out and deliver the coal with a horse and cart. I used to think it was funny because most of the soot I cleaned out was probably from their coal. They used to make the mess and I used to clean it up.

On Sundays I got cleaned and scrubbed and taken to church. It was the only time I got clean. Rest of the time I used to have bread and something to drink before I went out. If I was lucky the Governor used to give me something to eat, he'd give me a bit of what he had. If I was working I wasn't allowed to come down and I wouldn't eat until I got home.

L: You must have been hungry.

T: That weren't the problem. It was the taste, it was horrible. I never used to clean me hands when I did eat. It didn't make no sense to me because I was already full of it.

Sometimes in a good house the servants would give you something to eat or drink. The Governor would sit down and have a chat with the man who looked after the house, or the lady, and I'd sit on the step outside. Sometimes the ladies would give me milk. They said it was good for the dust.

I wanted to be like the Governor one day and have boys of me own. He was clever. It always surprised me that he did all that and never got dirty.

L: And did you get your own boys?

T: No, I fell down the chimney. I don't remember nothing else. It was me own fault. They can be very slippery those chimneys when it rained. The rain comes down those big chimneys and if they haven't had a fire for a while they can be a bit slippery. If you're not careful, and I wasn't, you fell down it.

L: How old were you when you fell? [And died]

T: A bit bigger than I was when I first started. I can remember it being two summers because it was really hot in there. They had the chimneys swept in the summers when they weren't using them. Sometimes the people in the houses would go away in the summer. They was Toffs.

L: What year was it? Do you know?

T: Don't know nothing about that. Didn't go to school. I wasn't posh. We weren't Toffs. Queen Victoria, it was her time. Mum used to bake bread. I liked the smell of it. It used to smell nice. It was funny really, I didn't see much daylight when I was there. [ENDS]

In this book you will meet more children like Billy and Tommy and after certain segments within the book Jasper will comment. Anything in this type face has been written by me and anything in italics has been written by Jasper. It will always be obvious where others speak.

Jasper says ...

It is appropriate that this book starts with the words of simple folk, children who tell their stories as they were, without any need for sensation or shock. Children are innocent and speak from what they have seen and observed. The time that Billy and Tommy spent in the solid layer was short if compared to most life-spans, but the simple truth spoken by these two boys is refreshing and should give hope to all. Death came to them both, but that has not changed them, they are still what they are. They still exist, filled with their individual experiences they have been able to recount their stories to you. Although they left their individual lives behind them and moved on, they were both happy to share what they had experienced, and in doing so should comfort us all as we make our own journeys.

We all exist as individuals, but to exist is not enough. If we just exist there is nothing to look forward to, nothing to raise ourselves up for, to enable us to achieve our true and full potential.

What lifts us higher in our existence? It is knowledge. It is knowledge and our thirst for constantly absorbing and understanding this knowledge that makes us all what we are and decides what we will eventually become. If we just exist then we have already condemned ourselves to oblivion and nothingness.

I exist to bring knowledge to you and in so doing I am constantly increasing my own understanding. Each and every one of us comes from the same beginning. We have learned along the way, we have learned love and hate, compassion and greed. Be that is what it is, it is all knowledge.

But certain knowledge has left mankind wanting and fearful. Death is the most feared and to many the end, the final barrier. But I can tell you from experience and my own knowledge that it is not. Life is eternal, existence is forever. But it is what we fill our existence with that makes the difference.

Through the words in this volume you will hopefully learn many things from me and from those that I choose to bring to you. Some that speak are simple and happy with their existence, some have a message or a warning.

It is up to you as an individual how these messages are taken and received. For that you must draw your own conclusions.

LAUGHTER AND TEARS

Jasper brings many people to speak and they come because they have something to say. Some make me laugh, many made me cry and they all make me think. Thanks to the people who speak death holds no mystery for me, I have no fear of it and I know a lot about it. I think of it as part of the cycle of life now and for me it is as natural as the cycle of all living things. We don't mourn the leaves which die in the Autumn because we know that come the Spring we'll see them again.

So, here are some more of those wonderful people who came to speak and made me feel that way ...

Charlie The Night Watchman

[28 September 2008. A gruff, working-class cockney voice. 'The City' is the financial district of London.]

C: Hello.

L: Hello, I'm Lillie, you're very welcome.

C: Lillie. I'm Charlie.

L: You sound bright and cheerful.

C: Yeah. I'm a caretaker. Big house. Big Building. Not house ... big office block. Used to be a house before they turned them into offices. Up in The City, it was.

L: I like The City. I like it when all the bankers and the business people have gone home and it's all quiet.

C: Best time. I used to look after it at night. I'd come in and everybody would go home, stay there all night and make sure it's all alright. I used to go round and make sure it's all locked up. And in the morning, make sure everything's alright before they come in, and go off home.

L: Gosh, on your own. How big was the building, how many floors?

C: Eight floors.

L: Just you?

C: Well sometimes had others in there, but I liked to do it on my own. I found plenty to do. Had cleaners come in at night. The women, you know, chatterboxes ... H'm ... you just listen, don't you. Just listen and just nod and say 'Yes' and 'No' and you just let them get on with it really. Big place. Big houses. Solicitors they were. Toffs. Didn't see nothing of them mind you. They went home, didn't they.

L: Nice place though, I bet it was nice inside the building.

C: Yes, it was old. I used to have the run of the building. I had all the keys, big bunch of keys.

L: Very atmospheric, aren't they, those old buildings.

C: Bloody creepy.

L: [Laughing] Yes, you can hear every sound as well can't you.

C: Frighten the life out of you sometimes. You can really frighten yourself.

L: Yes, of course you can. You can really work your mind up into it, can't you.

C: You think 'If someone breaks in I'll go and .... I'll go and really give them what for,' and then you think 'Sod it, I'll hide.'

L: Did anyone ever break in?

C: No, nothing to steal, was there.

L: No, that's right, just a load of papers.

C: Had a few drunks come rattling on the door at night but you just see them off, don't you. I wouldn't ever open the door to them though. Sometimes you get the local bobby bang on the door to see if you're alright. They was alright. They keep an eye on you. Come in for a cup of tea sometimes. Someone to chat to.

L: How long did you do it for, Charlie?

C: Twenty five years.

L: Gosh, in that same building? I'll bet it felt like your building at the end, didn't it?

C: It was my building. I used to go and sit in all the big chairs. Had a conference room, didn't they, and I'd go and sit at the top of the conference room and the business I used to do there! I used to buy and sell ... whole towns. And I used to sue people and represent people and all of that. All with me mug of tea. Making sure not to leave tea-rings on the table. Get a bollocking for that when the cleaners come in. Cor I did get a dose if they thought I'd been making a mess. I had a cat once, but he went away.

L: What, in the building?

C: Yes, well, keep the mice down, see. And there was a load of stuff in there. There was boxes and boxes of papers. Bleeding great rats in the basement. Needed a cat in there really, but I suppose, really, too much for the poor old sod. Suppose he took one look at them and thought 'I can't do that.' Off he went.

L: So what year was it Charlie, when was it?

C: Well I was there just after the war. I finished me stint in the war, come home from the war, and they wanted a Night Watchman, so I thought 'That'll do me'. Mind your own business, you know. 1946. It was alright and as you say it's quiet.

L: And I love those old buildings.

C: Yes, they rattle about a bit, don't they. I used to get in there just after half past five, and I'd come out gone seven o'clock in the morning. [Whispers]: I'd have a kip in the night time, you know. Sometimes I used to go down the pie shop before I went in there and have me supper before I got in there. So I'd have me pie and mash and some eels, and wash it down with some tea, nice sweet tea, and that'd keep me awake through the night.

L: Then breakfast as you got out in the morning?

C: No, I used to wait till I got home for that.

L: Where was home?

C: Home? The other side of the river. Quite a way, down in Lambeth.

L: What a nice job. So you obviously weren't married?

C: No! Thought about it now and again but ... no, I was alright. I had me mates. Have a few pints on a Saturday. Someone else done it at the weekends. Used to fill in when others went away. Used to be over there at Christmas as well.

L: Did you get a good Christmas present?

C: Few quid and a bottle. But it was alright. I was in the warm. I didn't mind that because it saved my fire, didn't it.

L: Yes, of course. I think it's a nice job, owning your big building in the city.

C: Yes ... Right, well I'll be on me way.

L: Next time I go into The City I'll think of you sitting at that boardroom table, in your building, with your mug of tea.

C: With me feet on it. With me bleeding great boots on. If only they'd known.

L: Did you have biscuits?

C: Course I did. Well .... they had biscuits. Well you've got to make the most of it. You've got to make yourself comfortable while you're there. Can't have you being uncomfortable. Mind you I never touched nothing.

L: Well, of course not, or you wouldn't have been there twenty five years, would you.

C: Moved a few things around, but didn't take nothing. Apart from the odd biscuit.

L: Well they wouldn't begrudge you that.

C: Well they never found out, did they. I'm sure they never counted them. Sometimes, when they had ... I don't know, people came in, they'd have food brought in, see. I used to have that, what was left. Wasteful, some of them. Funny bloody sandwiches, all sorts of things in them. All goes down the same hole though, doesn't it. Still washes down with a mug. Well I'm off then.

L: Thank you Charlie. It was a real pleasure. Bye for now. Bye.

C: Yes, bye.

Sheila and the Chelsea Flower Show

[24 May 2008. Every year there is an event in London called the Chelsea Flower Show. Keen gardeners from all over the country attend and it is a popular event in the social calendar of many people from all walks of life. The show was taking place around the time of the following conversation. A bright cheery, well-spoken, friendly voice.]

S: Hello.

L: Hello, I'm Lillie.

S: Hello Lillie, I'm Sheila.

L: I don't believe that I've spoken to a Sheila before, you're my first Sheila.

S: I hope I don't disappoint.

L: I'm sure you won't.

S: I've been to London, to the flowers. I love the flowers.

L: Really? To the Flower Show? Chelsea?

S: Yes. Every year I went to the flowers. I used to bring my mother, until my mother passed over. And now, of course, we come again.

L: How lovely, you can come together again.

S: Yes, it's wonderful. It brought us such comfort when we were here, and now it does the same to so many others. Wonderful. I'm afraid I was a bit of an armchair gardener and although my mother loved the gardening, I paid others to do it for me.

L: [Laughing] That's my type of gardening, I agree with you, not your mother.

S: But it doesn't mean to say that I didn't get so much enjoyment from it. I used to enjoy my garden. Once a year, yes, I used to come up to London and look at the show.

L: It's very nice to know that you do that still. How nice.

S: Yes, I try to bring my husband, but even now he doesn't come.

L: [Laughing] So he wasn't interested then, and he isn't interested now.

S: No, no, he's always been one for his own pursuits, you know.

L: It's nice to know that no-one changes when they go across.

S: I thought that perhaps I could persuade him, but of course no. No, he likes his golf and his horse-racing, which he still watches. I don't think I would ever make a gardener of him. But we're all together now. It's good. So, I'm happy and he's happy also. I left him behind and I waited a long time for him to come. He behaved himself though. [Chuckling]

L: You kept an eye on him then?

S: Yes. Yes, he was a good man, despite what everybody said. They all said that he was a rough diamond but ... he was different. A good, kind man. I saw the side of him that others didn't. We married late because we had both been married before. He had some family, baggage you know. I didn't have any, apart from my mother. And he was a good man, he took all of it on.

We led a good life really, we never wanted for anything. Too late for children, of course. We travelled the world and we saw everything we wanted to see. And I didn't want to lose him. When I found out that I was ill I couldn't bring myself to tell him. I knew that I was very ill and there was no cure for what I had. I kept it going for nearly a year and I wouldn't go to hospital and I kept a brave face, for him really. And I couldn't hold on any longer, finally I was taken to hospital and it was all over very quickly, and he didn't know until that day.

L: Until the day? Gosh.

S: I kept it from him. I kept my medication secret and I carried on with my life.

L: Were you in pain Sheila?

S: Yes.

L: I don't know how you did that.

S: Because I couldn't stand to see him worry and I would much rather it had been like that.

L: And you got an extra year of just being together normally.

S: Yes, we carried on, we still travelled and we holidayed away and ... up to the end really. I kept it from him, I had to pretend I was tired, and it was ladies things maybe, getting older, and I kept it from him. I know I did the right thing.

L: Well, of course you've been able to ask him since.

S: Yes, of course. I didn't want to leave him ... I wanted to spend that last time together in happiness, not in sadness. I couldn't stand the thought of him falling to pieces over me. I didn't want it to happen. So I chose to live with it. But I'm pleased I did the right thing. And he lived for five years after my passing.

L: You're very brave.

S: He was never the same of course. I watched him all the time, waiting. I knew he'd come, we were never parted really. I think he must have known I was there. He spoke to me often.

L: Oh, did he. Good.

S: But I don't think he expected an answer. But he spoke to me and I answered him. He didn't hear me but the fact that I did brought comfort to me, and for him I hope. We're happy now.

L: And did you come and get him?

S: Yes, I met him.

L: Oh, how lovely.

S: Yes, he was older than me so I suppose it was a matter of time really. But I think .. I know ... I did the right thing.

L: You were very brave.

S: Well I think that we all have our time to go and I knew that nothing I could do would change that. So I made a decision to make it as normal as possible. Why should he suffer my illness as well? So I chose to be that way.

L: You're every brave and I'm very pleased to meet you. What a lovely story, Thank you. I like to think of you and your mother at the Chelsea Flower Show.

S: Yes, but Barry doesn't come. He never really did like champagne.

L: [Laughing] Well, that doesn't make him a bad man, does it.

S: No. He was more at home with a pint of beer.

L: Thank you so much Sheila. What you have told me was very special and it will be a great comfort to others.

S: Goodbye Lillie.

Daisy the Cleaner

[25 May 2008. Rough working-class Cockney accent. 'The City' is the term for the high-powered financial and banking area of London. ARPs are the civilians, usually old men who couldn't go into the army, used for air raid patrol in England during World War II, 1939- 1945. They would watch for any lights which might attract the enemy bombers in darkness.]

D: Who are you then?

L: My name's Lillie and you're very welcome.

D: Oh, thanks.

L: What's your name?

D: Me? Daisy. A daisy and a lily that's funny isn't it.

L: Yes, two flowers.

D: Two flowers, yes. Daisy ... Daisy Jones, not Davy Jones.

L: You haven't got a locker then?

D: No, wouldn't have nothing to put into it anyway. What do you want to talk about then?

L: You. Tell me about you. Where did you live, what did you do?

D: H'm ... where did I live. I lived in Rotherhithe down by the docks but ... [With a dramatic pause as though she was going to announce something important] I worked in the fine City of London. Very prestigious job that was.

L: [Laughing] Yes, of course.

D: I had to prepare offices [Posh voice now] for when the important people came.

L: Did you just. [Sounding suitably impressed] Oh, that is a very important role, Daisy.

D: [In a very grand voice] Everybody who walked into the building walked over the step that I had cleaned.

L: [Laughs]

D: Every doorknob they touched, brass one or otherwise – I had polished. Every doorplate - I had spat upon and cleaned it. Every floor - I had swept it. Every toilet – I had cleaned it.

L: [Giggling] You made your mark then. Didn't you.

D: Everything was down to me. If they looked through a window and it was clean, I did it. If they looked through a window and it was dirty, it wasn't me, I didn't do it, but I'd get round to it. I mean I couldn't do it all.
L: Of course not. Big Building.

D: There were a few other women worked with me. We had a Lil with us you know.

L: Oh, did you?

D: She was Big Lil - Big Lil we called her.

L: Oh was she? Well I could be Big Lil as well.

D: Oh, she was bigger. Bigger Lil I suppose. So, we cleaned and that was it. It was good really because we came home when everybody was going to work. The buses going home were empty and there were all the people crammed on the buses going the other way. I wouldn't want nothing to do with that. We used to start at five o'clock in the morning. We used to get the night bus to get down there and we used to do three hours till eight o'clock, then we'd finish. Sometimes if they had special meetings on we'd have to go back afterwards, we'd have to go back in the evenings. Then we had to get there at six o'clock at night and then work until midnight, but then we used to get money for a taxi or train home.

L: Yes, that's good because it could be dangerous going home at that time.

D: Yes, with all the massive money that I'd earned, and of course I might be carrying my cleaning stuff. I mean I wouldn't want anybody to steal my rubber gloves! But it was alright. I did alright there, it wasn't too bad. It was nice coming and going at different times of the day. The old man, he worked on the railway, so he worked odd hours which meant I didn't see him much, which suited me. Had time to myself, you know. Listened to my radio, had my cigarette and my glass of stout – suited me. I was alright. I cleaned all the house up, kept that tidy, did all the cooking, did his washing. That was it really. We were happy. Used to go down the pub together at the weekends. It was alright, just had a couple of glasses of stout. I had a chat in the corner with the other women, let the men get on with their business.

L: What year was this Daisy?

D: 1942. Well, that's the last one I remember anyway. Used to go to work when the bloody bombs were dropping. Well, I had to go to work, didn't I? I mean, Hitler wouldn't pay my bloody bills if I didn't go to work, would he? I thought 'Sod him, I'm going. He's not stopping me, air raid or no air raid!' I got told off no end of times, mind you, it was my cigarettes that did it. Well see, if the buses didn't run I had to walk, so I used to walk all the way along smoking my cigarette and I used to get these bloody ARP's shouting 'Hey, put that light out!' I thought sod 'em, I'm not putting my fag out for no-one. I told them that as well. I said 'Sod you. I'm not putting my ... if he wants to bomb me he bombs me, I don't care. You and your bloody airs and graces!' Bloody ARP's - they were all the old boys who couldn't go to war. Anyway if I'd have run they couldn't have caught me. So I used to go to work when the bombs were dropping.

   Didn't go down the dug-outs. Sod that. No, I figured that if it was going to hit me it was going to hit me, wasn't it. Too damp down there, full of bloody creepy crawlies. Why should I go down there when I'd got a bloody good home, I can sit in that. Anyway, the way I figure it, this is all I've got, my home, and if I go out of my home with all my furniture and stuff in it and a bomb drops on it, I haven't got nothing left anyway. So I might as well stay with it and have another cigarette. The old man was at work when the bloody bomb dropped. He must have had a shock when he got home.

L: Oh dear.

D: I wonder who made his tea that night?

L: [Half laughing now] Stop it!

D: I'd gone, me. Well, it was going to happen, wasn't it. I suppose they found someone else to clean. I was alright. Didn't hurt none. Quick. Made a bloody mess everywhere but still, I didn't have to clear it up, did I. Left that for him. He's here now.

L: Yes of course, he caught you up did he?

D: Yes, he did. Bloody long time coming! I wondered what he was up to. Kept my eye on him.

L: Did you? [Laughing] Were you waiting for him with a rolling pin?

D: Too right I was. Mind you, he behaved himself, because he knew what he'd be for if he didn't. Knew bloody well being the other side of the grave wouldn't stop me from coming after him!

L: Was he pleased to see you?

D: Well he didn't have a choice really, did he?

L: Not really.

D: Yes, he was a bit, I suppose. He didn't show it much, but he was. I was pleased to see him as well I suppose. My son came over too, he fell, poor boy.

L: Ah, did he? In the war?

D: Yeah. [Sounding serious for once]

L: How sad, Daisy.

D: [Bouncing back] Anyway, we're all together now, so cheer up and all that! I don't care, nothing to polish now. It's alright. Still have a look around – my old building's still there. They don't look after the step now though. Some bugger's taken the brass plate I should think, well, it's gone anyway. They've got a big stone step now with no brass plate on it. I like to think I rubbed it away with cleaning so often, that's what happened. Big modern door with glass in it where the big front door used to be. No brass knobs on that. These cleaners don't know they're born now, do they? They don't have to work hard.

L: I love cleaning brass.

D: Spit on it, that's the answer. And if it's really bad you've got to take some salt with you. Bit of salt and a rag. Wet the rag, bit of salt on it, rub it – it gets all the dirt off. Then you polish it, see? Clean anything, salt will. Gets all the dirt off. Don't do it too often though, if it's fancy it wears the pattern off eventually. That's it. Right ... time for a cup of tea. Enjoyed the chat. Bye Lil.

Molly's New Nurse

[27 February 2008. A tiny, faint voice. Queen Victoria reigned 1837 – 1901.]

M: Hello?

L: Hello, I'm Lillie and I'm pleased to speak to you.

M: Molly. Are you the new nurse?

L: No, Molly, I'm just a friend.

M: My Mummy said the nurse is coming, you sure you're not?

L: No, sorry Molly. Why do you need a nurse? Are you a bit poorly?

M: Yes. The old nurse was miserable. She wouldn't tell me stories when I wanted them. Mummy says she's getting me a new nurse – one who will make me laugh. I like laughing, laughing is good. Mummy and Daddy don't laugh much now, they're very serious. They smile, but I see them put the smile on when they come to see me and I know they only do it for me. I think they're sad.

L: How old are you Molly?

M: I'm eight years old, nearly nine.

L: Are you very tall?

M: Yes, very tall, very tall and my hair's very long. I have a big dolly. I have a big doll's house with smaller dolls in, and furniture, just like our big house. Big dolls house and sometimes when I feel sad I put myself in the dolls house. I imagine I'm a doll in there – and I live in the house and I look at the books and I sit in the chairs and I sleep in the beds.

L: That's clever. How many people live in your dolls house?

M: Oh, lots of people from time to time, depending on who's visiting. Sometimes I have royalty come to visit and they stay in the house with me - Dukes and Earls and Princesses. Princesses come to stay, but they don't stay when I'm there, because I'm the only Princess who's allowed to be in the house. And I have a footman who's a bear.

L: I bet he looks grand in his uniform.

M: Yes he does. Cuthbert. Very grand bear with a uniform.

L: Does he have a lot of braid?

M: Yes, he's like my Daddy, my Daddy was a soldier. He is a soldier but he doesn't do soldiering any more. He doesn't go to be a soldier.

L: What's your Daddy's name?

M: [Surprised I needed to ask] Daddy.

L: What do other people call him?

M: Mister.

L: Yes, of course, silly me. Sorry.

M: I don't eat much these days.

L: Don't you have much of an appetite?

M: It all tastes funny. Tastes horrible some of it. Not allowed to go out of bed. Mummy says when the nurse comes we can go walking in the garden. And we can go in the big park again and look in the river. It's where the big boats are.

We had a dog, but he had to go away. Every time he came near he made me breathe funny. He had to go away but Daddy says he's gone to a good home, where people will love him. And we had a linnet in a cage, but he had to go too. They made me cough so I couldn't keep them anymore.

But the toys all come to life at night. The dolls and the bears and others. I've got a wooden soldier who plays a drum. And they all come out when the grown-ups go. And there's a big fire in my room and it's always full of logs burning. It's always warm and Mrs ... Mrs ... Cook, I don't know her name, she's Cook. Cook comes and puts big logs on, sometimes I think she can hardly lift them, they're so big. And she puts logs on the fire and she wipes my head for me, puts cold flannels on my head and I feel good then. She tucks me in and my Mummy comes and tucks me in and some of the dolls sleep with me – but they fidget so much.

L: Oh, they're a nuisance, aren't they.

M: Yes, they fidget.

L: Do they chatter as well?

M: Oh, they never stop. And they have to go to bed in their own house and Mummy reads me a story some nights.

L: What's your favourite story Molly?

M: Fairies. I like fairies. Stories with fairies I like. Daddy reads serious stories, he reads stories of soldiers and I think he would have liked me to have been a boy. He reads stories of big adventures and I make out I'm interested, he seems to like them. He puts the voices on and he gets quite excited sometimes when he talks about the different things.

L: What can you see out of your window Molly?

M: Trees ... trees ... they have pink flowers on them. Lots of trees, lots of pink flowers and I can see trees with white flowers on them and big trees that reach right up to the sky, big pointed ones. And birds, I can see birds sometimes. I don't walk very well, so I crawl down from bed and I go across on my knees and pull myself up onto the window and then when I hear someone coming I very quickly crawl back.

I had a brother once, but I never saw him. He went away long before I did. And I think he went where I am now and ... Where am I now? .... Sorry, I know where I am. And where I met my brother, he said he didn't know me before. But he talks to me now. Robert. But Robert went before I did. I didn't see Robert when I was little, don't remember Robert.

L: So you met him for the first time when you got to where you are now?

M: Yes, Robert went through the same ... he kept coughing a lot ... and it's ... I heard the doctor when he came, nice man, but very serious and he said, when he was telling my Mummy, he said it was what my brother had. I don't know what it is, I just know that sometimes it makes me feel weak and I cough and breathe funny. Sometimes I feel that I can't breathe and it makes me feel sad because I can't talk when I want to. I just want to go out really, I miss going out, I like the sunshine. And I don't go downstairs, I think that lots of things go on downstairs and I miss them.

L: But also Molly everyone downstairs misses your toys coming to life.

M: I don't tell them. I don't tell them this happens. My Granny comes. She only comes when no-one else is here. My Granny comes and she looks and then she goes away again. She smiles and she says 'Not yet.' And she says she's getting things ready. And she did come.

L: [Crying] Did she, Molly, did she come and get you?

M: Yes, yes, and she gave me cakes. Yes [As if she's suddenly worked it all out, what had happened] .. she came ... yes, she did come! She did come and I walked away with her.

L: And you could walk properly again.

M: Yes, I didn't want to leave Mummy and Daddy and I was still waiting for the nurse who didn't come. And I sometimes go back and see if she's come. She hasn't come yet.

L: But you know why she hasn't come, Molly, don't you?

M: No.

L: Because you don't need her now. You don't need a nurse. You've got your Granny.

M: No, [Sounding disappointed] I suppose not.

L: You've got your Granny and you've got Robert and I imagine now you've got your Mummy and Daddy. What would you need a nurse for?

M: Could be fun to play with.

L: You must have lots of people to play with, but also Molly you only needed a nurse because you were ill and you're not ill now.

M: Cuthbert's with me. Sometimes I am back in my bed and I can imagine what it was like and I'm still there. I go sometimes, I come back. I wanted to see Queen Victoria because I've never seen a Queen before. She's very old though and I was told, some said, she didn't like children.

L: I have heard she was a bit bad-tempered as she got old.

M: Oh, miserable. I think it's because she didn't have dolls to play with. But then I didn't want to see her anymore, didn't worry, wasn't so important I didn't think.

L: So, you can go outside now any time you want and you have your Mummy and your Daddy and your new brother.

M: Old brother, but he's new.

L: And you have Cuthbert with you, that's awfully good.

M: And Daddy can read boys stories to Robert.

L: Well I'm sorry you didn't get your new nurse but isn't it good that you don't need one now?

M: Yes. [Not sounding convinced] ... wonder what she would have been like?

L: I think she would have been very funny and very kind. And I think she would have kept your secret about the toys coming alive at night, and I think she would have helped you to the window.

M: She must have gone to another little girl.

L: Yes, because of course you didn't need her.

M: I had my Granny.

L: And the cakes. And Cuthbert. Please give my kindest regards to your Granny, tell her that Lillie said hello.

M: Does she know you?

L: No, tell her that you have a new friend called Lillie.

M: I will. Yes, I will. I must go now.

L: What are you going to do?

M: Play.

L: You go now. Give a little hug to Cuthbert and say it's from your new friend Lillie.

M: I will. Goodbye.

Maisie

[26 October 2008. A tiny voice, a child, sounding very inquisitive.]

M: What's your name?

L: I'm Lillie, what your name?

M: Maisie.

L: Hello Maisie, I'm glad you're speaking to me.

M: Yes.

L: Tell me Maisie, tell me about you.

M: Me? H'm ... I ... I ran off.

L: Oh, did you.

M: Nanny's. I was at Nanny's.

L: Oh, yes. How old are you Maisie?

M: Old. Four.

L: Oh, gosh, that's a big girl.

M: Nanny had the big garden. I ... I ... ran into the garden. Away from Nanny and Mummy and they were talking. I didn't understand what they were talking, I wasn't happy with what they were not doing. So I ran to Nanny's garden. Nanny ... nice garden ... big flowers ... lots of stones. Fish.

L: Ah, there was a pond was there?

M: Big pond. Never seen a pond, before. Saw a fish.

L: Yes?

M: Nice. Pretty. Orange. Funny.

L: Yes, funny things aren't they, funny shape.

M: They look at you, then they hide. Funny. Big pond. Fishes all over it.

L: Interesting if you hadn't seen them before, Maisie.

M: Funny. Kept disappearing. Magic really. And ... I went to pick one up, hold it, see what it was like. Didn't know what it felt like. Not like a cat, not like a pussy cat. Never seen a pond. So I thought I'd catch one. And I waited ... and then when it ran away I ran after it.

L: Yes, into the pond?

M: Yes. It was cold.

L: Yes, it would be cold ... it would be really cold.

M: Cold and horrible. Tasted horrible.

L: [Distressed] Yes I'm sure it did, you must have been very afraid.

M: I shouted for Mummy and Nanny. [There was a short silence] And then my Granddad helped me out. Granddad came. Never seen Granddad before.

L: Did he say 'I'm your Granddad?'

M: I knew he was my Granddad. He said 'Come on' ... and he ... said 'Come on I'll take you and show you some fish you can touch.'

L: Oh good.

M: And I said 'What about Mummy and Nanny' and he said 'Don't worry', he said 'They'll know'. And Granddad held my hand and he took me and showed me animals, lots of them. And other children. I still look at

Mummy and Nanny and I sometimes hold my Mum's hand. I think she knows I'm there ...

L: I bet she does.

M: She cries. And Nanny looks at Granddad's picture. Granddad laughs. He laughs and he smiles at her. I like my Granddad.

L: Aren't you lucky. Did you get to touch a fish?

M: Lots of fish.

L: They aren't very nice to touch though, are they?

M: They're wriggly.

L: I don't like them to touch very much, they're funny things, better with a pussy cat.

M: Rabbits, I like.

L: Oh, yes, I like rabbits.

M: They've got funny ears.

L: Yes, they have, haven't they.

M: My Granddad sings to me.

L: Oh, does he?

M: And he tells me stories. And he says when Nanny comes he said I'll be old enough to look after myself. I've got lots of friends now.

L: Have you? Oh, good.

M: And he said Nanny's coming soon.

L: You and Granddad will be able to meet her. You'll be able to show your Nanny all of your new friends.

M: Yes. Going now.

L: Lovely Maisie, lovely to talk to you, and Mummy will be there one day, too.

M: One day. Granddad says she's busy for a while.

L: Yes, she's busy for a while and then you'll all be together. But you're alright, aren't you?

M: Yes. Yes. Bye.

Molly the Servant

[8 November 2007. Before this next person spoke Jasper warned me that I was about to speak to someone who was very timid and very frightened. He described her as a little girl, painfully thin with legs which were misshapen (as though she had something like rickets) and her knee joints were badly formed. He said he had seen her life as it had been and that she had been cowering in a corner, rocking and he wasn't sure if it was with cold or fear. She was wearing a long skirt with a pinafore over it and she was wearing a mob cap. These were servants clothes from times gone by. Jasper said that she hadn't been allowed to speak normally when she was alive, but that he had persuaded her to speak to me. I heard him say 'Come on, we won't hurt you. We are friends. Come and speak ...' and then she spoke for herself. A tiny, timid voice, hesitant at first.]

M: Yes. Hello. I was a maid servant to a big house, I mustn't speak too loud. I was taken from the streets as a girl, a child. They say that they gave me a home when there wasn't one, in a big house. Big house and big gardens, but I'm not allowed to go out of the house. I'm never allowed to go out of the house. I'm not allowed to go upstairs, I'm never seen upstairs. I know the house is big because others tell me where they've been. There are others who work here. Some are good and some are not so good. And some people come and go, do not stay.

I was happy at first to be inside, from the coldness of the roads and the streets. I do not know how long I have been here because all time seems to be the same and I do not have much spoken to me. People do not tell me much. They think because I'm like I am that I'm not intelligent enough to speak to them.

I cannot remember where I came from. I know that I was child in the streets, begging for something, whatever they would give me, and then a fine lady and man stopped their carriage one day, and they seemed very kind. They seemed very nice, fresh and clean. The man was tall and had whiskers and a tall hat and the lady wore a silky dress that made her look big, like a bell. She was pretty and she smelled nice. They said that they would take me as their own child because they had no children of their own and they would look after me. And the man gave me a coin to hold in my hand, a small silver coin, and he said that he would make sure that I was always cared for.

I saw the house. It was a fine house. A fine house that towered into the sky. It had many windows and gates and railing around the front. As we drove along in the coach I could see the green fields in front, the heath lands, and I looked upon this house that I thought was going to be my home and be comfortable.

They took me into the house and an old lady came. A big old lady. A big lady, and she was much older, she seemed kind, she was kind, and she helped me a lot. She took me and she took my old clothes away and she bathed me. I felt the warmth of the water and I felt clean. My hair was clean and somehow the heat from the water didn't hurt, my legs didn't hurt so much. She gave me clean clothes and I felt special. And she gave me lots of bread to eat and she gave me milk. I'd never tasted milk before and she gave me pieces of crusty bread and a small piece of cheese. I ate until I felt as if I was going to burst. And then we sat around this big table and I felt small amongst the others. They all came down and started to eat around me.

There were men in their uniforms with shiny buttons and there were ladies in their uniforms. They were chambermaids I was told, and they were all in their different uniforms and clothes. And I was sitting next to the old lady who was kind and she felt warm. And she put her arm around me and she said she would look after me.

I was given some work to do because the old lady said that if I wanted to stay in the house I would have to work for my keep there And she gave me spoons and knives and forks and other pieces of table things and she gave me some polishing rags and some funny polish in a tin. And I used to sit and polish these things until I could see my face in them. And then when they were finished there would be more.

I did not mind because the old lady was kind to me and she would tuck me into a corner with a blanket, in the corner of the fire in the kitchen, a big warm fire with all sorts of pans and pots and things. And things were steaming and smelling and giving fine smells.

She would get me to help some of the other girls who were older than me. We would clean the saucepans and the pans, and we would clean them until they shone. We hung them back onto the walls, on hooks all in a line, and they gleamed.

The others didn't speak to me because they thought I didn't have much to say, so just the old lady spoke to me. The old lady seemed to have authority, she told the others what to do and she did all the special things. She made all the food that was special, and they seemed to respect her because she would tell many of them off and they would go away sulking that she had told them.

Sometimes the lady I had seen in the coach would come downstairs but she would never speak to me. She would ask the old lady, the cook, about me because I could hear her talking about me but she wouldn't speak directly to me. She never did. She hardly ever looked at me.

It was not so bad at first when the old lady was there. There was another lady who worked in the kitchens and I didn't like her and she was mean to me when the old lady wasn't looking. She would push me and poke me and slap my head. She would say nasty things and told me not to speak to her unless she spoke to me.

I began to explore this world that was mine. I found that past the kitchen there were rooms with lots of food in, more food than I had ever seen before. There were animals hanging from hooks – big animals, I had no idea that animals could be so big. And there were sacks full of all kinds of vegetables and fruit. There were all manner of things in sacks and barrels everywhere. There were big rooms full of bottles of wine and different kinds of drinking things and barrels.

This world was quite fascinating. It was big. It went for a long way and I could look out through the window. There was a pathway on one side where I could watch the coaches come in and bring fine people. And on one side of the building there were windows which looked out onto trees and grass. Sometimes when the windows were open I could smell the grass and trees and I could hear the birds.

The old lady was kind but I was never allowed to go outside the doors and I was told that there were bad people outside that would take me away from where I was safe. So I didn't go there. There was a staircase that went upstairs to a different world but I was never allowed to go there. Everyone else would go and carry things up and down the stairs and I wanted to go with them and see what the other world was like above the stairs.

The old lady was very kind but she was becoming slow and she quite often dropped things on the floor and she couldn't lift heavy things. I tried to help her lift because I was getting stronger and I felt that I should help her. Then one day the old lady became ill and she went to her bed. She had a room next to the kitchen, as did most of the other servants live in the rooms in the basement of the house. The old lady was ill and she didn't get out of bed again, she stayed in her bed. A man came to see her who the lady from upstairs brought with her and he looked at her and he listened to her and he looked in her eyes and her mouth and he looked at her and he shook his head. He didn't look very happy.

At first I would take a bowl of some soup and I would feed the old lady, but then she became so ill she wouldn't take that any more and she wouldn't take anything. Then one day the rooms seemed quiet, nobody was talking and the old lady had gone. I couldn't find her anywhere.

Then this other lady I didn't like, she pulled me by my arm quite roughly and she said 'Now you belong to me and you work for me and I'm going to make you work for your keep or I'll throw you out onto the streets where you belong.'

She made me work harder and she made me carry these big heavy pots with hot water, boiling water, sometimes they were too hot to hold and they would burn my hands and I would almost drop them, but I knew I mustn't drop them because if I did she would just hit me again. She hardly ever spoke to me and always found some reason to beat me hard. And I had to do all of the jobs that the others could not do, all of the dirty jobs and the heavy jobs. When my clothes got dirty she made it my fault because I shouldn't have got so dirty. The lady from upstairs would come and speak to her and I wanted to say to the lady that I wasn't happy but I was frightened to do so. I didn't want to.

Then one day the cook told me to take off my old clothes and wash myself and she put some new clothes on me, some clean ones. She said it was time for me to be more useful. I kept the old clothes in my corner, I had a basket I kept my clothes in. And then when there were lots of people upstairs who would come and sit and eat at the big table I would have to carry trays and put them in the room. I would carry them upstairs. My legs really hurt, they were really painful. I would take all the things that were not as important as the others – I wasn't allowed to carry the food because cook said I was too dirty to do that and nobody would want to eat food I had taken them.

So I would take trays with serviettes and other things that were important but not as important as the others. I would take them and put them onto a table. I would make sure that I didn't look at anybody there because I was told not to. I was told not to show my face to them, just to keep my head down. I did this for some time and then the cook said that I could carry heavier things because I was not working as hard as I should be, and she gave me a tray to carry with some silver dishes of some special chutney she had made in dishes, and there were many of them. There were lots of these fine silver dishes with small, tiny spoons in them. They were all of these colours of different fruits and spices. I could smell them as I carried them upstairs into the room where all the people were eating and laughing. They seemed happy, they were laughing and joking and I did not look at them.

I carried the tray into the room and somebody spoke to me and as I turned to look at them I lost my footing and I fell and the tray went to the floor, and all over the floor and the people at the table laughed. I started to try and pick the things up and one of the maids pulled me by the arm and dragged me out of the room quickly.

I was taken back downstairs and I knew there would be consequences to pay because the cook had spent so much time preparing these special things and now I had dropped them all over the floor. She hit me so hard and it really hurt and my arm stung from where she had slapped me and pulled me. And she said I would never be allowed to go upstairs again because I was useless and I had been a disgrace and an embarrassment. She said that my life now was to be below stairs and never above them again and she took away the clean clothes she had given me and I had to put my dirty ones back on again.

She made me scrub everything, she made me scrub the floors and the tables and the chairs and she made me scrub the hearth where the cooking oven was and it was thick and dirty. I scrubbed and scrubbed until I couldn't scrub any more and still it wouldn't get clean. And she would come and beat me and make me do more. I would scrub with cold water and it was never ending, I would clean the floors and then the others would come and walk all over it and I would clean it again.

Then when everybody else had gone to bed and they were sleeping I would get into my corner and sleep for as long as I could because I knew that as soon as it was light again cook would make me start working again, cleaning everything. I've never cleaned so many things, she said it was all I was good for – I'd be no good for anything else.

Nobody spoke to me much, if at all and usually it was only to make me move away, out of their way. The others didn't have the time to really speak to me and I wished the old lady was there and that I could have seen her. I wished I could have spoken to her again.

I don't know how long it was, the time just seemed to be endless and I thought it would never end. I hated the time that I was there. I had to do everything special because if there was any dirt or anything left cook would beat me and be horrible to me again, she shouted and she was awful. When the lady from upstairs came she would change and then she was always nice and spoke to me nicely and made out that she was kind to me. But she wasn't, she was horrible.

And then I went to bed one night and when I woke up the old lady was there and she said 'Come on, it's time for us to walk in some fields now. And we walked out into the fields and I could feel the grass beneath my feet and I could smell the air and she said that she would look after me now. She said 'No-one can hurt you where I'm going to take you.'

And I'm happy now, but I still won't forget those times. But now I'm happy. We can't go back now. We never need to go back.

Anne

[31 May 2008. The voice of a young girl, well-spoken.]

A: Hello.

L: Hello. My name is Lillie and you're very welcome.

A: Hello Lillie, I am Anne. What can I say for you?

L: Tell me something about your life.

A: I wasn't around very long. I had an accident. Silly really. Bicycle accident.

L: How old were you?

A: Ten.

L: Oh, very sad. Sad.

A: I was showing off and I went shopping for my Mum and ... it was different times, I didn't know much about the roads and I always rode my bicycle around the streets from home. I went on an errand for my Mum and I put the shopping bag on my handlebars. I'd seen others do it before. Grown-ups do it. But of course when you try to turn it's heavy.

I kept in the side of the road, the kerbside and there were lots of cars and big buses and I tried to go along the inside of a lorry and he didn't see me. He pushed me into the kerbside and I tried to turn away and I couldn't get onto the kerbside and I had the bag on my right side and the weight pushed me over and it was a big lorry. It was frightening.

L: Oh, Anne, it must have been ... it must have been. Oh, I'm so sorry, how sad. You must have been very scared.

A: Yes, my friends at school cried. I watched them when the teacher told them what had happened. I was very sad for them, and my Mum and Dad were sad.

L: I bet they were.

A: And it was a silly thing to do really.

L: Well you didn't know. It was just an accident. Are you with your Mum and Dad now?

A: Yes, and my sister.

L: Oh, good. I'm pleased. Sad though ...

A: My sister was older than me, she thought of me often, I know. I felt sorry for her because she didn't live her life, she felt that she needed to think of me constantly.

L: Oh, what a shame, yes.

A: And she was alone in the end, and I waited for her and welcomed her.

L: Ah, did you?

A: Yes, because I knew how lonely she had become.

L: Was she pleased to see you?

A: Yes ... yes ... long time ago. Children learn better now. The lorry driver was very upset. He was very sad but he didn't see me. It was my fault. I must go, thank you Lillie.

Jethro and His Leg

[3 February 2008. A jaunty, gruff, common voice, bright and cheery. The sea Battle of Trafalgar was 1805.]

J: I was at Trafalgar. I lost me leg at Trafalgar.

L: [Sympathetic and concerned] Ah, did you?

J: It was alright. It made me a living.

L: Well that's a nice way of looking at it.

J: Well, you've got to look on the positive side, because the way I looked at it I lost me leg but I found a new life.

L: Not many could turn that into something positive.

J: Well I did. I was a bit of a character. Still am. I thought about it for a while and I thought how am I going to manage? But I thought, you hear tales of sailors with wooden legs, so I suppose it goes with the job. The only thing I wanted really was a parrot, then I really would have been a character, wouldn't I? But ..... [Voice changes now to something theatrical]: I was no pirate! I fought for my country. I was with Nelson. I was on the Flagship see. [Low Voice]: I wasn't really, I was on one of the lesser ships. [Loud again]: I was on The Victory, I saw Nelson get his mortal blow! [Low]: I didn't.

L: [Laughing] So this is your business is it?

J: Of course it is. [Loud]: I saw many fine men fall under the cannons of the French. [Low]: I was a cook, don't tell no-one.

L: I don't suppose I use the same inns as where you told your stories. Is that where you told them?

J: I might have done. I might have done that. There are many likes to listen to the story of a hero. They never let you put your hand in your purse ... you does it slowly ... you put your hand in your purse slowly and they says 'Put that away' and the ale appears in front of you, as if by magic.
   See I learned to live with it. I had a wooden leg, but I only put it one for special occasions. You see I found that you get more sympathy if you goes along with the crutches and no leg. Then it looks better, don't it. I makes me living, or made me living, or still makes me living, I don't know, round the docks, round the old sailors, you see, the ones that's still got their legs, they feel guilty. But I know, old Jethro knows, how to play on their sympathies.

L: Is that your name? Jethro? Ah, Jethro, I'm Lillie and I'm really pleased to meet you.

J: Hello Lillie, yeah. I got married too. Had six children and all with one leg. No, the kids didn't all have one leg, what I mean is I had one leg.

Mary, big woman, looked after me. Used to clean for people and they used to feel sorry for her too, having six children and a p-o-o-r disabled old man. [Laughing and low]: I wasn't so poor!

So, all in all you could say it done me a favour. I wonder if I'd have done so well if I'd had two legs.

L: [Laughing] I'll bet you wouldn't.

J: And do you know, I didn't miss it. Wasn't vital was it? Wasn't a part that I needed really. Got used to it really, it was alright. Hurts at first but after a while it goes away. What's a leg anyway? Still got me arms, that's the main thing. I mean, if I'd have lost me arms or something like that I'd have been a little bit more different, but a leg – I mean it's not that bad is it? There's some people makes so much of it. I saw people whose whole life was ruined because they'd lost something in wartime and instead of turning it – the way I look at it you've got to turn all things to your advantage. You mustn't be disadvantaged by nothing and if you're going to be worried about losing legs and arms and things you might as well be dead completely., you know what I mean.

[Loud again]: You see, I always say I took my inspiration from the old man, from Nelson himself, when he stood upon the deck there I admired him, the way he put his telescope up to his bad eye and he said 'I see no ships' or something like that he said, but I heard him say that, I heard the very words he uttered! [Low]: I hardly ever saw him really. [Loud]: And I was there when they was gathered around him and he took his last breath. I saw all of that ... [Coughing a little] ... me memory goes a bit when me mouth gets dry. And I find that me memory comes back more vivid when I've got alcohol inside. And a fine brandy – oh, the stories flow forever with a good brandy. I could talk all night really. I could talk the leg off a sailor ... [Both laughing] ... that's a funny one, isn't it. Anyway, I came to the con ... con ... what's the word?

L: Conclusion?

J: That's the one, you know all the big words, I came to the ...

L: Conclusion ...

J: ... long time ago that life's what you make of it. It don't matter whether you've got one arm, one leg or .. I don't know, one ear I suppose ... you still make the most of it. I reckon that's a good lesson in life really, because you could take it two ways – you could either sit and mope around about what you ain't got, or you makes the most of what you has got. And the way I looks at it, I still had the one leg, I didn't lose both of 'em.

Still wished I'd got myself a parrot though, a parrot and an eye patch, I think business would've really thrived. I did alright, though, because I did have a good wife, I had six kids who looked after me and I didn't want for nothing. And I think my storytelling must've chilled a few on a cold ... oh ... warmed a few on a chilled night.

L: Or chilled a few on a warm night.

J: Oh, that as well. Bloodcurdling stories! How we was boarded and ... ooh ... terrible stories ... how I fought and me leg was taken off by a cutlass of a pirate on the high seas ...

L: How was it taken off?

J: [Low]: Blown off by a cannon. It's out there somewhere. Didn't bother going looking for it. Sometimes I wondered if you could make one up out of all the bits ... [Then loud again]: I remember when I had me leg cut in two by the cutlass, it cut me to the bone and how I struggled to hold me leg on as I carried on fighting at me position. I had to hold me leg with one hand and with the sword in me other hand I had to fight to defend me country. My fellow countrymen and I fought to the last. And then when me leg finally came apart I couldn't fight no more and I had to admit defeat. And as I sat there I prayed to god himself and he took pity on me and they left me alone. That's a true story, as true as I'm sitting here. [Still theatrical]: Where I am now we're good friends, me and the governor, Nelson. We quite often down brandy together and talk of old times, when I defended him on the ship.

L: I don't pay more for this story, you know, even if you've met him where you are now.

J: I haven't, but I can't spoil me storyline. [Loud again]: As the ship was sinking ... going down ... me leg was trapped in some of the rigging and I was trying to save some of me poor, fallen comrades and I had to slice off me own leg so I could swim after 'em and save 'em. I saved many a poor soul from the sea that day. The pain of me leg was numbed by the coldness of the water and I managed to save twelve men that day, pulled 'em up on a piece of driftwood I did. But I stayed in the water myself because I knew they needed it more than me.

L: [Laughing and joining in] I'm just so honoured and pleased to meet such a hero, Jethro, it has really warmed me ...

J: Yes, but I like to be humble about my escapades. I don't really like to tell of what went on, because, you know, I don't like to be thought of as a hero really, because it doesn't do much good ... no, it wears a bit thin being a hero, all this hero worship and everything that goes with it.
I couldn't imagine what it would have been like with two legs after a while. I felt sorry for people with two legs – they had to buy their own ale.

Anyway I'm glad I've been able to tell you the tale. [Chuckling] Now you know the truth ...

[Theatrical once more]: How the ship was burning around me. It was terrible, terrible, my leg caught fire in the battle and it was caught in the deck of the ship and it was me or the leg and I had to get away. Fighting as the ship was going down and the flames was all around me. I had to cut it off, so I could survive, and the leg went to the bottom of the sea with the rest of the ship.

L: Thank you for .... [Trying to say goodbye]

J: [Undeterred] I suppose a monkey would have worked as well as a parrot. Always wished I'd got a parrot and an eye patch. I'd have done well. Mind you, they might have dragged me off and hanged me for a pirate – wouldn't have wanted that really.

[And off again]: They wanted me again after Trafalgar. They would've given me a commission in Portsmouth. The navy actually came to get me. But I said 'No, I got a life and children to support now, and friends around me, I couldn't possibly leave them.' They begged me to come back because they said with all the knowledge that I had of warfare, of survival ... when the sharks was all around me ...

L: [Giggling] Sharks now!

J: And the navy wanted to fit me with a proper leg, they said it would look like a real one and I said 'No, I'll manage.' So I had to turn the navy down and I stayed with me friends. Just remember, if you want a good story – brandy loosens it up. Well ... I'm off now. I'll be around.

L: Thanks, Jethro, I loved it.

J: Bye.

George's War

[3 June 2008. An older voice, sounding friendly. He actually named the small coastal fishing village he is discussing here but I have withheld it.]

G: Hello.

L: Hello, I'm Lillie and you're very welcome.

G: Hello Lillie, I'm George. How are you?

L: Well, thank you. What about you?

G: Not too bad at all. What shall we talk about?

L: You, George. Tell me about you, Id love to hear it.

G: Me? Well, I don't know where to start really ... Spent most of my life working on the land, lived down on the South Coast. Did a bit of gardening and free range farming, going and helping farmers out. I didn't have a farm, I'd go and do farm work and gardening work, that sort of thing, fencing and mending. Then when the war came along I was too old to go away, couldn't go to war, so I joined the Home Guard to do my bit.

It was a funny old do really, we didn't have any uniforms at first, we just had to go in our normal clothes. It was funny, there were about thirty of us altogether, but we did different shifts. We didn't have any uniforms and we didn't have anything to fight with so if the Germans had turned up on the shore I think we would have had to have fought them with broom handles or pitchforks. We didn't have nothing else. As it went by we got given bits from the Ministry. Army lorries came round and brought the stuff round for us. I think they didn't take us seriously at first, if you ask me.

L: But you could so easily have been on the Front Line, being on the South Coast.

G: Yes. We had a shed down there. We had a shed right down by the harbour. We looked out. I don't know what we'd have done if anybody had come. When we first had it we didn't have nothing. We didn't have a radio and we had to run quite a way for the nearest phone box.

L: [Wanting to laugh] To phone and say we'd been invaded.

G: Yeah, so I don't know what we'd have done really. I mean we got a flare pistol from somewhere, but I don't know what we would have done really, because if we'd have sent a flare up, most wouldn't have known what it was.

Anyway, it was alright because we made ourselves comfortable down there, see. As I said there were thirty of us altogether, so we used to take turns down there. There was a big shed, we had like an old boat shed, it was right down on the seafront. Blooming cold! Anyway, we made it comfortable, we took some old furniture down there and we had somewhere to make a cup of tea and, you know, do a bit of toast. It was alright really.

And we had binoculars, we had bits from everywhere, people gave us bits, you know. Binoculars and telescopes and bits to look out. We had to look out to sea, you know, and see if anything was coming. We had to look out for aeroplanes as well. And then, what they did, they gave us a radio. They gave us a radio and they gave us some uniforms. I think they were old ones, I think they were ones that they didn't use any more, they looked like First world War ones to me. So they gave us some uniforms and

[Sounding proud now, yet slightly surprised] we had some rifles too, eventually.

L: Oh, did you?

G: Yeah. Oh, yeah we had some rifles. We had some rifles and ... that was it really. We had some old Enfields, you know old Enfield rifles. And ammunition. So we had a radio and some guns and that was how we sat the war out really.

L: Did you have to use them at all?

G: No, well ... no we didn't, I mean it's a good job we didn't really. There were only like ten or twelve of us at a time. I don't know what we would have done if there had been an invasion force.

L: [Laughing now] I'm sorry for laughing George.

G: I was ready to stand my ground but I don't know what I would have done with it really.

L: [Laughing still] Oh, dear me ...

G: But we had to improvise really because nobody really told us what we had to do. But they did come round and they had some officials come round and they wanted us to watch for aeroplanes. They gave us loads of pictures to put on the wall, like posters.

L: So that you would know what sort of plane it was.

G: There was all the posters of the aeroplanes, which was ours and which was theirs. They gave us outlines of the boats as well. But I tell you what – if a boat had got that bloody close I wouldn't have been there by then I don't think!

L: [Laughing quite openly now] No ... no, not really.

G: I mean, of all things they gave us the shape of battleships. Battleships and cruisers and all the different boats. But I mean we'd have seen it coming a long time ago, wouldn't we?
So they gave us all of that and they ... [Sounding puzzled now] they gave us lots of plain paper to write on, I don't know why. We were supposed to write down everything that we saw.

L: [Chuckling] Oh, yes, that would have been useful.

G: They said there were a lot of Fifth Column operating you see, so they said we had to write down all the movements of all the boats that we saw go past. So, every time we saw a boat go by – we knew most of them anyway ...

L: There's Ted out fishing again ...

G: Yeah. So we had to write them all down. We had to write down all the movements of all the boats, where they were going, we had to write down their numbers and just write ... nobody ever came to look at them.

And then what we were supposed to do, we were supposed to ... if we saw any strange boats or any strange aeroplanes coming over we were supposed to get on the radio and tell 'em what was coming. A couple of times we did that, I mean we saw some aeroplanes coming over, I mean we did see some German aeroplanes because they all came down that way, but the thing is they probably knew they were there anyway. They'd already spotted them.

We saw a couple of our boys backwards and forwards now and again from the airport down the road. We didn't know really what went on down there, there was all sorts of planes flying out of there, we knew the shape of 'em so we knew they was ours, because [Laughing] they were going out, they weren't coming in. Anyway, it was alright, we took it seriously and we had our radio and we thought in a way we was doing our bit really.

And so we improvised, as I said, and we got a bit of a patrol going. We got bloody bored to be honest with you, just sitting looking. So what we did ... as I said there was like ten or twelve of us at a time and we'd take two of us and we'd walk up and down the shoreline. So we'd patrol a bit, we'd go up and down with a torch and our rifle – feeling a bit special I suppose. We'd walk up and down and sometimes we'd do the old 'Halt! Who goes there?' routine. That was good practise that. But we didn't see anybody we didn't know really. We didn't see any strangers, if there had been they'd have stood out. So ... we did our bit there, and ...

L: You did do your bit. I mean, you were just fortunate that you weren't needed but you might very well have been.

G: As I said, we had our tea and toast and some biscuits, and a bit of cakes the wives had made for us and we were alright really. On occasions we had a bottle of beer if we could get one. But that was it .. and all we did really was write things down. Writing things down and writing things down and when the war was over we kept 'em, but nobody ever came and asked for 'em. Don't know what the bloody hell they was for really. I suppose it made us feel useful.

L: Well you would have been useful if you'd been needed.

G: And we had to do fire-watching and blackout patrol as well. And we had a different lot come down for that – the police had the air raid wardens attached to them, A.R.P's they called em, and they came down. They came in for a cup of tea and we used to have chat. We used to tell each other what we'd seen, and what we hadn't seen. That was it really.

I was quite glad to get down there to be honest with you. Gets away from the nagging at home, doesn't it. I'd get down there and as I say I'd have tea and toast ... sometimes we'd get bits and pieces people had given us, cake and biscuits, anything they thought we might need really, and the odd drop of beer.

And we used to get bits from some of the fishermen. They used to come at night and walk by, and they'd give us some fish to take home. That was alright, a bit of fresh fish, it just added to the table. Not a lot, mind you, because the poor buggers needed enough to make a living. But they'd give us a few and we'd take a few home. Quite often I used to go home with a bit of fish wrapped in some newspaper. It was good for the next day.

It was alright, I suppose. We had nearly four years of that, yeah we did. But when – I suppose I shouldn't talk about it – but when D Day came along there were boats and things everywhere, we didn't get a look in then, we still did our work but then the real army came in. There was army lorries everywhere. A lot happened then and there was lots of boats building up. They went from all along the coast, see, and there was big boats then and we didn't get a look in.

Some of the regular soldiers was good to us really. I mean we were old lads, you know, and some of the regulars would come along and have a laugh and a joke and a cigarette with you. Because they had to put on proper patrols then, see, because when the real army came in and the navy and all that and they had all the military stuff building up I suppose it was a bit sensitive. So they had proper sentries posted and we used to have a laugh with them really.

And that was it really. When it was all over it was a bit funny knowing what to do with yourself really. I used to like going down there at night. I used to get a good sleep there to be honest with you, we'd take turns keeping watch and we used to get a decent sleep in the armchairs. And it was peaceful and I'd take a book down there or a newspaper and have a read. And as I said I got away from the old woman as well. But afterwards I didn't have nothing to do. It was funny I found, at home in the evenings. I'd sit and listen to the radio and have a chat and go down the pub and have a beer, you know, but it wasn't the same really. We got to be real comrades you know. We all slowly dwindled off and they popped off, you know, and of course then my time came – course I'm back with them all now.

L: I was going to say I bet you've met up with them all now.

G: But we ain't go nothing to watch for now.

L: You still all get together though, don't you?

G: Yeah. Wouldn't mind that old shed back. That was alright. Draughty as it was, it was quite cosy. It was home for four years. So, yeah, we're all back together now. We get together and we get away from the old women, you know. Still can. Yeah, we can look back on it and say we did our bit. Anyway, so that's it then. That's me.

L: Thank you. I really enjoyed that.

G: I like to have a chat, if anyone wants to listen.

L: Any time George. Give my regards to the boys. Look after each other. I'll think of you all sitting together.

G: Alright then, I'll see you. Bye now.

Jasper says ...

People come and speak to us for a number of reasons. Sometimes there are deep messages and lessons, some tell of their lives and regrets but others are happy for the "audience." They recount their lives emphasising the moments that were most important to them. The preceding 'speakers' were selected because of the content and meaning of their conversations. Some are sad, some are amusing, but all had a right to be heard.

Charlie the Night Watchman could have led a lonely and boring existence but when the doors were closed on his private world he ceased being the night watchman and lived out his imaginary existence and he was happy. Never once do you hear him complain. He was ruler of his own domain. He did not have much time for people, perhaps he had seen enough in the war he had just safely returned from. Charlie has of course progressed since those times but he still reminds us of the cup rings that he left on the boardroom table. Like life itself really, you can remove the evidence but that does not detract from the knowledge that it has still been there.

Sheila who loved her flowers continues to do the things that she enjoyed when she walked the earth. Although she has left behind what must have been a time of pain and suffering, she is happy to have the ones who meant the most to her still around. For her, existence has not changed, life continues, but she is safe in the knowledge that now what she has will not end.

Some people spend their whole lives complaining and always seeing the down-side of things. But not Daisy, she was determined to 'get on with it' in spite of what wartime did to stop her. She did her duty and took pride in what she did, it may have been just cleaning to others but to Daisy it was her way of life. When the war did catch up with her and took her away through the curtain she still did not change. Daisy kept a watchful eye on her husband until he joined her. She has not lost her sense of humour. Her family are all together now, but Daisy is still happy to give out her cleaning tips from where she is now. As always, Daisy is getting on with it.

Molly, who loved her dolls so much, passed over as a child. The time that she spent in her bedroom must have appeared long sometimes, and although her world hardly ever extended past the four walls, she filled her time with a kind of happiness that only children can make. Her toys took on a whole new existence in Molly's mind. Her last expectation before leaving the earth was the arrival of her new nurse, one that she hoped would be better than the last one. Children are very perceptive and her parents could not hide their sadness and even at her young age Molly knew that she was going to move on. When a child dies it is hard for the parents to accept that their loved one continues on, and that they grow and learn. Molly's grandmother came to take her hand and although Molly is with her family now, no longer a child and needing childish fantasies to ease her troubles, she still playfully talks about the coming of her new nurse. But of course she has long passed that time of needing, it is just that as she recounts for us her life in the solid layer she reverts to the feelings and emotions she felt at that time. She re-lives it for us, as the child that she was then.

Maisie again recounts her life and death through the eyes of a child. Children tell their stories as they see them with the truth of their observation. Maisie's passing was a sad one and must have been devastating for her mother and grandmother and although it would not have changed the fact that this little child had gone from them they would have been comforted to know that Maisie was safe with her Grandfather and that their separation was only a short one.

Molly the servant girl told the story of her terrible existence and how she was used and abused by so many. There were then (and still are today) many willing to exploit those who are down and defenceless. There are those who treat others with such cruelty because they are different. Molly had trouble walking and instead of helping her and taking pity on this poor girl, those around her simply added to her suffering. This was the way life was for many devoid of the privileges of their birth. But from this story comes kindness. Molly helped and tended for the old lady who had been the only one to show her any kindness, the only one to acknowledge that she was a human being, with her own feelings. Molly had no family on the earth but the old lady came to take her away when it was her time and together they share a bigger family than either of them could have imagined. But what of the ones who made Molly's life such a misery? I can tell you that by now they will have been made to experienced all of the scorn that they poured upon Molly and those others like her. In the etheric layer as part of their punishment they will have felt all the pain and despair that Molly felt - I hope that they will have learned that you should be careful how you treat others less fortunate than yourself. It is worth remembering that in your next life you may well be born into a privileged situation where you want for nothing and have all the happiness that such a life can bring, but there are no guarantees, and, as it is pure chance where you next walk, you may just be in such a position as Molly, and then you would wish for a kind old lady to help you through.

Again the story of Anne and her bicycle is a sad one, but not for her. After her death Anne progressed. Not so for her family. This is often the case, a loved one passes and those left behind mourn for them with the exclusion of any further consideration for their own lives. If only they could understand that life does not end at the graveside. But for those still walking it sometimes does, as they spend so long grieving that they forget to live. If only Anne could have let her sister know that she was safe and well. Yes life did end prematurely with the accident that took away Anne but for Anne it was the beginning of the rest of her existence - but for others left behind, it was their end. Those that wait for their time of crossing should make the most of the time and experiences that they have remaining in solid form. Grieve for the 'temporary' separation from your loved one but then lock the grief inside you and get on with existing, it is what those on the other side would most want for you.

I am sure that everyone has met at least one Jethro. For many, an accident or a deformity causes a bitterness that twists and distorts an individual and drives many away. But Jethro made a life and a living from his disabilities. He could have given up on life and begged for handouts, but Jethro was a true showman, a clown to his audience. It is such humour that helps us through. A smile can drive away many a depression. Yes he was truly a rogue and I am sure that no one really believed any of his tall stories, but next time you are feeling low think of Jethro and those like him - and whatever life has dealt you things may not seem so bad.

Humour is a very strange thing as I have said it helps you to face up to whatever life brings to you. But often it masks something else. In the life of George, who spent his wartime in the shed, it must have been fear. If George and his friends had stopped to consider the true seriousness of their situation they may not have been able to carry on the way that they did . They were at war, ill-equipped for what they would have to face if the enemy landed on their beach. What chance would these old men really have had? But again they shut out the real world and made the most of a bad situation. But do not be mistaken in thinking that these old men were in any way cowardly, they would have given their all to defend what they had. George is with his friends now and they are free to carry on with whatever their next step on the ladder of existence may be. But I hope that they will continue to tell their stories.

As I have said many people come to speak, some have long stories to tell but have very few words. What they do say speaks volumes for the lives that they left behind and made something special to take with them on their journey. Here is one such story ...

Jack's Hat

[27 March 2007.]

J: I'm Jack. Worked on the farm. Mending fences, mucking out, feeding the animals.

L: Have you always done that Jack?

J: Farmer took me in when I was a kid. Don't know how old I was when I died. I just got cold one night and didn't wake up. Used to sleep on the straw in the barn. Nice and soft. Had the horses for company, and the dog, farmers dog.

L: Was it a good life, Jack?

J: Yeah, not bad. I've still got my cap. It were the only new thing I ever had. Bought it at the fair down the village. They buried me in it, in the church down the road.

THE PARANORMAL INDUSTRY

I really hope everyone takes great comfort from the information contained in this book and from every other piece of information that we provide. We want to show that life continues, even after death, and that you will never be separated from a loved one forever. We understand that when a loved one dies you must mourn, you miss the closeness, the interaction, we all do.

But there are many who prey on that time of loss and great sadness. There are many look on the death of another as a way to make money, to profit from it. There are also those who enjoy the sensationalism of death, who see a graveyard as a place for play and excitement. Neither of these groups have respect or morals.

There are those who exploit the industry of death, and there are those who use the unexplained to make their fortunes. There are many misconceptions which can be used in this way and we would like to set the record straight.

In our usual no-nonsense style we would like to pass on the following information. We have categorized the various areas of the paranormal industry and tried to simplify the terms so that there can be no doubt as to the facts.

Fortune Telling

This is not possible. No-one here in the solid layer can predict the future. None of the standard etheric beings in the etheric layer can predict the future, including those who charlatans call their 'guide'. Your future is shaped by a combination of your actions in the present and the direction you decide upon if you are faced with a choice.

Tarot cards

They cannot predict the future. There is no paranormal intervention to aid the reader and tarot cards cannot predict the future. It is chance how they are shuffled, chance how they are selected. They have no relationship with the sitter or the reader. Most tarot readers use vague terms which are often what the sitter wants to hear. Any predictions which come true are pure luck. The words used often follow the same pattern as horoscopes – vagaries which could fit many eventualities.

Crystal Balls

None of these toys have special powers. Genuine mediums do not see those in the etheric layer with their eyes and so what their eyes are looking at has no significance. A crystal ball is a piece of theatre and just like the magicians use stage props to perform their illusions, so some charlatans use a crystal ball.

Fairies

They do not exist. You can add elves, pixies and many other very pleasant childhood fantasies to the list of the many mythical creatures which do not exist. These were used to entertain and delight children. Add also the less-pleasant fantasies which were often used to scare and control children, such as bogie men. All do not exist and frankly adults should know better. Adult horror fiction brings us vampires and werewolves which can also be discounted.

Angels

They do not exist. They do not exist in any form. We are not each given a guardian angel and most certainly do not have a team of angels who surround us and keep us safe. If this were so there would never be any accidents. There is no angelic realm.

Do Ouija Boards Work?

[23 March 2010. A broken man with real, genuine horror in his voice]

X: I'm not so sure you would want to speak to me.

L: It is very rare for me to have anyone I do not wish to speak to.

X: I have a terrible story to tell. I am paying the price now but I now know the reasons for what I did. That does not make them acceptable.

L: Please tell me your story.

X: Well, mine is one of abomination. When on trial they said I was the devil himself, the devil incarnate and I let them do that because it was what I wanted, the notoriety. From very meagre beginnings it became possession and I know now that I was used, but of course I was too stupid to realise that I was. I did some terrible things, I took the life from people, I tortured and humiliated, I degraded and defiled them. I am not proud of what I did. And I will face what comes to me. I have been judged and I am waiting now for my sentence and whatever is meted out to me I will accept. And now I am free of that which held me.

L: So you were possessed? A spirit attached to you whilst you walked here?

X: Yes. It was my own fault, it's coming. I toyed with things that I should not have done and I invited something into my body that should not have been there.

L: I have seen many with the same.

X: I tried many times to kill myself but it would not even let me do that. I know now it was not a devil, of course, there are no such things, but it was an entity of a long-gone spirit that held me and guided my every movement. Every time I took the life of another I tried my hardest to fight it, but it was stronger than me and I was physically sick every time. I looked at what I had done and it laughed at me, I could feel it's laughter inside my head. The devil was there all of the time, for that is what I called this spirit of a man, the devil. I even built an alter to worship it, such was its power over me. Even the court, the police, said that I was the devil incarnate. The things that I did were so appalling.

L: What is your name?

X: [He told me his name and details of where he 'operated' and these check out. I will not reveal them]

L: OK.

X: By way of a warning I come to you. As with all young people they seek excitement and ... adventure I suppose that you would say that it is. And I found it exhilarating when I felt the possession first of all. First it gave me a power over people, I found that I was able to acquire females, and both sexes and the depravity just grew, and I enjoyed it, but it was not a natural enjoyment, it was a sickness, it was disgusting [showing the disgust in his voice here] ... I ... am appalled at what levels I fell to. I could not remove this thing that held me.

L: When you say you toyed with things, as a lesson to others ...

X: It was a Ouija board.

L: I thought so.

X: At first it was a fascination and then it became an obsession. I became a devil worshipper, I moved with those who thought they worshipped the devil. But I realise that I was the devil, all that epitomises the devil was within me. It was as though it was gripping into me, every time I tried to shake it loose it held on tighter. I could almost feel its hands around my neck choking me, and it wrapped around my chest and arms. I wanted to be rid of it. I plied myself with drugs and alcohol to try and numb it.

L: Feeding it. It would enjoy that.

X: It made it worse. I killed many. They did not find all that I killed. I am so sorry. Such was my possession I did not even find their names, I did not even know them. I know that you are capable of warning people, there are many things that are not understood still, many ancient things that should not be disturbed and they prey upon the weak. And I was weakness itself. I am not the devil, there is no devil, but the devil can be in all of us if we let it. I had no-one like you to take it away from me. It left me at the point of my own death.

L: It would move to another.

X: I blame the church in every way because I wished to turn my back on such things, I looked for alternatives. I couldn't understand this lie that they perpetuated, I did not want to believe in this ... story that they told us. I blame my mother also who made me god-fearing. It is not god that I needed to fear – there is no god, there is no devil – there is just man's weakness. I hope that I am never free of this memory, because I let it use me and I should be punished eternally for that. There is no other to blame but myself. I let it take me. I enjoyed what it did for me. But it was wrong. I know this now. You must warn others not to tamper with that they do not understand. Even now there is danger for those unwittingly playing with what they do not know. Heed my warning. Do not let this happen to anyone. You must all be strong, it is weakness that these things play on, the weakness of mankind itself. Do not pity me, you must be sickened by me always. You must use the warning. If I can help others with my wretched story, then this is what I must do.

Spirit Guides

They do not exist. It is true that our loved ones and friends in the etheric layer keep a watchful eye on us, but they cannot intervene in any way. If they could there would never be any accidents. If you are thinking of a loved one who is in the etheric layer and you feel an overwhelming feeling of love then he or she is standing beside you comforting you through the curtain, but they cannot guide you. You make your own decisions and you make your own mistakes. You have no-one to thank for your progress but you and you should congratulate yourself if you're doing well. In the reverse you have no-one else to blame for any misdemeanour. Events and circumstances beyond your control in the solid layer effect you and those in the etheric layer cannot change that. You make all of your own decisions and are accountable for your own actions.

Heaven and Hell

Neither exist. There are two layers. One is solid and the other is etheric. Those who commit crimes on the solid side still go into the etheric layer, to the same place as the others, but if their crime is terrible then they are immediately separated and dealt with. Heaven is not up and hell is not down. The curtain between the two layers is so thin that for all intents and purposes the etheric layer and the solid layer are in the same place. No crime goes unpunished and there is no such thing as being able to 'get away with it'. There are no secrets.

Ghosts

They are not actually there. A ghost, or apparition, can never speak to anyone or do anything to harm or help anyone. It simply is not there. There are certain events which have had such an extreme effect on the atmosphere that they have left an imprint there which is detectable by those who are very perceptive.

Sometimes it is fear which causes the imprint. It could be the mass feeling of fear of a group of people who were in an accident, or the fear of one person, for example, as they faced a hangman, but the feelings of the person or people was so intense that it etched itself into the atmosphere and stayed there.

Sometimes sadness leaves its mark, maybe from a widow grieving at length for a lost soldier and her grief was so intense that it stayed. She is now with the soldier and happy, but her emotions stayed behind. Those who are perceptive might 'see' or 'sense' a sad woman still pacing the floors, or walking around where her garden was, but she is no longer there.

Happiness and contentment too etch themselves into the atmosphere. You may have noticed this when you are buying a house and you step into a place that feels welcoming and friendly. Generations of happiness and laughter have etched into the atmosphere itself to create an overall feeling.

So, ghosts are no longer in that place. Ghosts cannot speak to anyone. They can never harm anyone or interact in any way. Ghost-hunting will never find anything spectacular. There is nothing there to find.

Photographic evidence

The camera sees the same as you. People see something on a photograph which they say was not there when the photograph was taken. The lens of a camera can only see the same as the lens of the eye. It won't find something etheric that you couldn't see. If you can see it the camera can see it, if anything else comes out later there is always a scientific explanation, a fault or a blemish and often a mock-up fake.

Physical Signs as Messages from the Other Side

They won't come. Many people have been told that our loved ones can send a sign from the etheric layer. There are many examples including tilted pictures on walls, phones ringing and no-one there, white feathers, rainbows, cloud formations, strange sounds, footsteps, knockings, doors left open or unlocked, appliances working, water running and objects (large and small) which have mysteriously moved. None of these are possible. There is always a scientific explanation.

Those in the etheric layer can no more make something happen in the solid layer than we can make something happen in their layer.

Messages in Dreams

Dreams are just dreams. It would be lovely if all we had to do was fall asleep and we could immediately all converse with our loved ones in the etheric layer. Sadly it is not the case. We do not visit the etheric layer when asleep. We are not visited by them in our sleep and we do not see them in our dreams other than the way we see everything that we dream about. It's our imagination. Dreams of the etheric layer and etheric beings are not real. They are just dreams. Dreams are never sent, dreams are not messages and analysis of them is a waste of time.

Those in the Etheric Layer

Can you see 'spirits?' Once someone dies and goes through the curtain into the etheric layer they are etheric. These people are all the same as each other and they talk and interact with each other in the same way that they did in the solid side. The only differences concern the body, which of course they left behind – so they are never cold, never hungry, never tired and never ill – all of these are symptoms of the body and thus do not apply.

Just as we cannot see the curtain between the layer with our eyes, so we cannot see the people in the etheric layer with our eyes. No-one has ever seen an etheric person, on this side, with their eyes. It is not possible. There are many who do not understand why they have never seen a 'spirit', or why their loved one who passed over has not appeared to them – because they cannot do it. It's not possible.

The very few genuine mediums that there are see our loved ones with a receptor which has no connection to the eyes and they hear them with a receptor which has no connection to their ears. So real evidence of eternal existence is possible but you have to find a genuine medium who can give you that evidence. There are many fakes, many charlatans and many who claim to be a medium for financial gain. There are some genuine mediums who can provide real proof, but they are rare and great caution should be taken when consulting any medium or business practitioner who claims to be a psychic.

Past Life Regression Therapy

This doesn't work. There are two layers – the solid and the etheric. We start in the etheric and we then enter the solid, in the ongoing cycle of reincarnation we then pass again into the etheric and the cycle continues. We always move forward in time, never back. That's the law of time and it's logical. When you fall asleep tonight you will awake tomorrow. You'll never wake up and find it is the day before.

There are business practitioners who will tell you that by discovering what happened in a previous life you will have some improvement in this one. This isn't possible.

Any information pulled from a sitter in past life regression therapy is pulled from a long-forgotten memory in their present life. It is often taken from a work of fiction they have read, a movie they have watched, a school history lesson where they were barely paying attention or a story they have been told by another. They are often jumbled fragments from many sources, like our dreams tend to be. But all of the 'memories' are false and not from a past life.

In extreme cases Past Life Regression Therapy can also be dangerous.

Healing

This is not 'divine'. There are many forms of healing and many who confuse the realignment of energy lines within the solid body with something spiritual or divine. Realignment healing is an ancient art performed by many civilisations and it did work – the Chinese and the North American Indians in particular knew how to do this. One of the current trends is Reiki. Reiki is of the solid layer and although it is based on an ancient art there is no intervention from the etheric layer and there is nothing spiritual or divine about it. The practitioner has learned how to redirect energy lines around the body. It works in some cases and as in all business practitioners there are good and bad exponents of this.

In very rare cases there are Elevated Beings in the etheric layer who work in partnership with a solid person to provide healing. The healing they provide comes from the Elevated Being in the etheric layer who is using the healer in the solid layer to direct the healing energy to the one who has asked for healing. The healing energy does not come from the healer in the solid layer, it just passes through them. Nor does it come from a god or any divine source. It is rare to find a genuine healer and even rarer to find one who will work for nothing, and the title 'healer' allows some the opportunity to prey financially on those who are afraid and scared. There are many charlatans.

There are genuine healers who do work with the etheric layer. Please be aware that they cannot perform miracles and they are there to comfort more than cure. I believe 'healing' is the wrong word and creates the impression it can do more than it actually can but a genuine healer who is working from the right motives can help to sooth and calm an otherwise desperate individual and give them the strength they need. I am wary of any healer who charges a large sum for his or her services. Healers, like mediums, should not think of their gift as being their profession. It was never intended to be so.

Mediums

There are many fakes. Some have a genuine gift but are incompetent. Exceptional genuine mediums are rare, but they do exist.
Etheric beings exist in the etheric layer, and they can all see and hear those in the solid layer, but they cannot be heard by them other than if they speak via a genuine medium. There are mediums in the solid layer who can see and hear through that curtain and communicate with those in the etheric layer. They do not see with their eyes and they do not hear with their ears, the receptors are different and that is why not everyone can do it – not everyone has the working receptors.

Those who have the receptors have a gift, an ability and would be able to practise and train themselves to become fully interactive with those in the etheric layer. They should be able to give real evidence that they are passing on information from the etheric layer. It is not enough for them to tell you they have 'a woman' who wishes to speak to you, they should be able to tell you they have your aunt and they should then go on to tell you firm details which leave you in no doubt that you were in contact with your aunt. If you wish to ask a question of your aunt you should be able to do so and your aunt should be able to respond via the medium. It is possible for a medium to practise and perfect this skill to completely interact with the etheric side. Sometimes they stop trying to improve and operate on limited skills which can cause doubt and make people suspect trickery, which is not necessarily present. They could be a perfectly honourable medium who just has not worked hard enough at gaining real evidence for those who go to them.

Those who consult mediums should also be prepared for people to come through to them who are not necessarily those they wish to speak to. They might go to a medium and be desperate to speak to their father who died recently and have a disinterest in someone who speaks to them through the medium. It could be someone, for example, like an old friend of their grandfather who they barely, if at all, remember. Do they not realise that evidence of one is evidence of all? There are two layers, here and there. If they are not here then they are there. And if you hear from one who tells you they are in the etheric layer and they give you enough information for you to have no doubt, then you have your evidence and you know they are all there.

I have seen people who consult medium after medium to try and speak to one special person, and even after they do get their message from that person they still go, over and over to see mediums. Once you believe and have your evidence you should not need to go again. Don't forget - if one is there they all are.

There are many who use the title medium who are not. There are many fakes, many charlatans and many who prey on the desperate and grieving.

Mediums were never given this gift to sell and the price you pay to consult a medium is a good indication of whether they are genuine.

Dangers of the Paranormal

The dangers are very real and the consequences more severe than you can possibly imagine.

A genuine medium works in a certain way which is safe and they cannot be harmed but there are many individuals who play around with the paranormal and they are playing with fire. Although there are rules of the two layers and what can and cannot cross the curtain there are still very real dangers in playing around with the rules. Rules are broken by the bad not by the good and so it is on both sides of the curtain. However exciting it sounds to fool around with a Ouija board or séance it is highly dangerous, and this has been made quite clear by our previous speaker. As I have already said it is not possible to see a person from the etheric layer and what you cannot see can harm you in ways that are not obvious. Some of those who are in institutions for the mentally ill hear voices, and in some cases where they have dabbled with the paranormal those voices are very real. That is one of the costs of dabbling with the laws of this.

There are many dangers and the best way to avoid them is to stay away from it. Ghost-hunting, séances, working with outside energies or forces and invoking the spirits in any way is dangerous for you and those around you.

Many try and become mediums without the correct protective training and open themselves up to all manner of dangers. There are many ideas on what can protect you such as saying a prayer or 'surrounding yourself in a white light'. These do nothing. And don't forget angels don't exist so they cant protect you, either.

If you feel you have the possibility to become a genuine medium and have the right non-commercial motives for doing so, then the only safe way is to study under another genuine medium and learn the correct procedures and protection. Someone in the etheric layer will work with you once you start to develop, if you are truly genuine. An Elevated Being would come to work with you as a mentor if your motives were non-commercial, but any hint of greed or the need for celebrity status or fame and they would quickly move away. This has happened frequently in the past and when their mentor moved away - that's when so many mediums who had real potential had to resort to faking it!

Jasper says ...

Keep your hand on your purse and your money firmly inside it, for there are many who would wish to relieve you of your hard earned coins and more, maybe even your sanity itself.

There are two kinds of people - those who know and those who do not. The magician keeps the audience transfixed on his act and the audience gasps and applauds at the 'miracles' that he performs. There are no miracles, just tricks, tricks that the conjurer has practiced and perfected. The magician is the one that knows, the audience are the ones who do not. A simple trick with the right dressing and delivery can appear to be a magnificent spectacle, but it's still only a trick.

A person will usually see and hear whatever they really want to see and hear, but one who is suitably skilled can manipulate this understanding and truth so that you will believe that it is your own.

There are many who claim to practice this magic and manifestation of miracles, but I can tell you that, but for a very few gifted individuals, they are all fakes. It does not matter what stage props these charlatans use, be it crystal balls, tarot cards or other toys - they are lying and deceiving you. Look at how filled their purses are at the end of each sitting, yes you may be happy for the moment with that message or prediction and maybe you didn't even notice as the money left your hands, but you have been lied to.

These parasites prey on your grief and inadequacies. You could say that it is only a bit of fun, that would be so if you wanted to know if you will meet that tall dark stranger or if you will win that fortune you have been waiting for. If that was all, I would say more fool you for crossing that palm with silver. But when it comes to death and grieving there are many leaches that will suck away your money, along with any real hope that you have of contacting your loved one on the other side of the curtain of existence.

The human mind is very complex and constantly seeks stimulation. This morbid fascination with the unknown is as old as time itself. That which frightens you also excites you. Often those who are discontented and have too much time on their hands waste their lives seeking excitement.

But often this need for excitement opens doors that should be left closed. The lesson should always be that if you do not understand do not experiment.

There are as I have said a very few gifted individuals who truly can connect those who are grieving to their departed loved ones. You will know who they are, they will be more concerned with the message and the comfort that it will bring to you and not how much you are prepared to pay for the information. Those who are truly gifted have the knowledge that will comfort and benefit others and give it freely.

The gift of understanding cannot be marketed or sold to the highest bidder, we all have a duty of care to each other to share what we have learned. Unfortunately the number of those with the gift has been further depleted by the seduction of those old enemies fame and fortune. Many a gifted one has fallen into the trap set by materialism.

HOW WE DO WHAT WE DO

Let's be quite clear here. Anyone who claims that they have heard a ghost speak or heard a spirit talking to them with their ears is mistaken. It isn't possible. We would all be hearing them all of the time. I smile when I watch paranormal programmes on television with their recording devices. They can only record anything which the ear could hear. Communication from the etheric layer uses a form of telepathy and the person who genuinely can 'hear the dead' from this side uses internal receptors which are very different from the ear.

On 5th June, 2004 Ernest was in our kitchen making coffee. He 'heard' someone saying 'Jasper … Jasper … Jasper' over and over.

Jasper says …

How do you communicate with someone who does not even know that you exist? What would be your first words? Ernest and I are old friends, we have been together for a long time, I will explain to you one day just how long and where. But at this time, in this material existence, Ernest knew nothing of me until that very moment.

I was hesitant, if the approach was wrong Ernest would just ignore me. I knew that the time was right, he was becoming more aware and open-minded to all things around him. His life had changed dramatically and he was free to think freely for the first time in his fifty years of walking the earth.

It had to be now, time was moving on and I had much that I needed to share with others. Ernest was my one way through the curtain that separates me from the solid layer, no one else would do, and this was how it was meant to be. I just knew that once I had made the first step Ernest would accept me and his inner being would once again know his old friend.

I had watched Ernest grow as he walked the earth. I looked on and thought of his family as my family. I thought of his friends as my friends. I chose to present myself as my last solid incarnation, Jasper the Harlequin - an incarnation that I hoped Ernest would accept.

So the moment came … 'Jasper, my name is Jasper'. Ernest stopped what he was doing and listened, but his ears could hear nothing, it was his inner perception that heard me loud and clear. 'My name is Jasper, hello old friend.'

He told Lillie straight away, I knew he would and I knew that she would understand. As we grew more comfortable together Ernest and I spoke of many things, I made it clear what we had to do. I brought him knowledge that he shared with Lillie. I trusted them both without any doubts whatsoever. I knew that if I had approached any other that by now I would be used as a tool for financial gain. All things strange have become fashionable and profitable and there are many charlatans.

We had a job to do and I was eager to start. At first Lillie could only listen to Ernest recounting my conversations with him. But in time it became necessary to speak directly to the one who would record everything that I and my invited etheric guests had to say to the world.

Now we speak and Lillie records our conversations. Ernest is the key - without him there would be no way of recording so precisely what is said. He sits quietly and lets me speak through him. We trust each other and that is how we will continue until our work here is done.

The first time Jasper spoke to me through Ernest I was nervous. I didn't know what to expect. Paranormal programmes, ghost and horror stories had not prepared me for how little there was to see.

Ernest had told me that Jasper wanted to try and speak to me. Ernest sat quietly, eyes closed, with his hands resting on the arms of his armchair. At first Jasper struggled a little to speak ... 'Jas - per ... Jas - per.'

But he (and I) soon got used to it and then we started to get to know each other. Since that day we have become good friends and often, even when there is no-one in the etheric layer waiting to speak, Jasper and I have long discussions (again through Ernest.) Jasper has taught me so much, and he teaches me still. I never tire of it and I always have more questions.

If Ernest, Jasper and I wish to all speak together it's obviously more complicated. Then Ernest has to speak for himself and then also interrupt with 'Jasper says ...' to make it clear who's speaking. We manage. Although now I can still only see one of them with my eyes I feel as though I am living with them both and talk to them both quite freely.

Jasper is the one with the knowledge and he is the one who decides who speaks through Ernest. They soon developed a way for other people in the etheric layer to speak through Ernest. They all use Ernest's voice box and so there is a similarity to all of them, and yet the accents and voice patterns are very different for each one. I have become used to hearing the different voice types and so it no longer surprises me, but the first time I heard, for example. a very young girl speak through Ernest it did sound a little strange. As I said I am now completely comfortable with how they all sound and never get shocked.

Ernest and I do not dress in long flowing clothes embroidered with stars or surround ourselves with the smell of incense and the sounds of Tibetan bells to do this work. If you met us without knowing who we were you would have no idea of what we do. We look like an average couple as we go about our daily lives. We introduce ourselves as writers and many people who meet us do not even know what we do or that Jasper exists.

Most days we sit down to allow people to speak through Ernest, usually in the early evening. It is easier in a dim light simply because it allows Ernest's eyes to rest and there are no distractions, but it is not essential. Ernest settles into his favourite armchair and I sit close to him. I switch on the digital voice recorder, and wait.

After a very short time someone will start to speak through Ernest. I record every word they say on the machine and I hold a full conversation with them. It doesn't look scary, it doesn't look like anything other than my husband sitting with his eyes closed, hands resting on the arms of his chair, his mouth moving in the way it does when he speaks for himself.

After the period of work and a number of people have spoken, Jasper will decide when it's enough and usually says he feels we should stop. He monitors Ernest and knows when he's getting tired. Then I put the machine somewhere safe and Ernest and I get on with our evening. I prepare dinner whilst Ernest walks the dogs. After dinner I often sit with a book and listen to classical music and Ernest is quite happy to go off and play one of his guitars in his small music studio. We both love music of all types and when we're not working there is usually something playing somewhere in our home.

The next day I transfer the voice files we recorded the previous evening to computer storage and transcribe them word for word with an exception. As instructed by Jasper I sometimes take out a surname or place name. The messages in this book are so important that we do not want people wasting their time checking up on the irrelevant details, and we don't want to waste our time answering 'historians' who might tell us that a certain bakery did not exist in 1759 in a certain street. It is what the people say that's so beautiful, not how they appeared in the census's and other records.

But other than the name or place I do not change the words that the etheric people say (unless I make it clear in the book that I have done so, maybe to protect a living relative) as I feel it is not up to me to do that. I will often omit some of what I say to them because I can't see that what I say would be of interest. Then I catalogue the voice file and leave it there ready for when we need to use it in a book or on the website. In the future we will release some of the voice files so that you can hear the differing voices.

And really that's all there is to the mechanics of how we do this. No special effects, no drama, no magic tricks, no theatricals. Nothing to be afraid of and nothing to see really. No trumpets, no ghoulish ectoplasm, nothing spectacular. Except of course the information that comes from those wonderful people who choose to speak.

Why do we do this?

I feel very privileged to have been trusted with all of the information that I have been given and all of the knowledge that I am still given on a daily basis. I know that this knowledge was not given to me to keep for myself, it was given for me to share it and I am so pleased that I have been trusted enough to allow me to do so. I do not feel 'chosen' in a spiritual sense and most certainly not in a religious one, I just feel very privileged to be trusted.

Jasper says ...

Ernest and Lillie are my trusted friends. Through them I am able to communicate with you. The words are my own, Ernest and Lillie relay the knowledge that I have for you. I hope that you understand and benefit from what I have to share. The knowledge is for all and if only one small part of these written words make you think beyond that which you currently know and understand, then my work for you is just beginning.

Who speaks to us?

When we first started we lived in London and Jasper brought many English people to speak who had also lived in London. London was bombed heavily in World War II and many died there. Many came and told us of their times in the war. Many were sad stories, but just as many were amusing and I met some real characters.

When we went away, on holidays or trips, we carried on doing the work and I met many locals who had lived in the other areas of England that we travelled to. I met Cornish pirates and Lancashire witches and many figures who had framed English history. All had played their part.

Then our work broadened and Jasper started to bring those who had lived in different countries. Many were from recent times but there were also those who had lived long ago. Some were famous people from history but many were ordinary folk whose lives were just as interesting.

Some have become special friends and they come often. For example a very famous deceased English Prime Minister might be followed by my dear friend Morag, the 'so-called' witch. Morag was tortured on the rack many centuries ago. Jasper always leaves till last a very dear friend, an English comedian, very famous in his day, who calls in most evenings at the end of our work sessions. He always starts with the words 'Am I on?'

Ernest and I often joke about how it would be wonderful to have all of these special friends around our table at a dinner party. They would make such a lovely mix and it would give Morag the opportunity to pass on some of her poultice recipes to the Prime Minister.

These wonderful people come to speak for a variety of reasons. Some come because they simply wanted to talk and are curious. The children seem to come from that category. They just come through and speak with such confidence and I love to speak to them. It must be devastating to lose a child, it feels somehow as if it's the wrong order of things, and I cannot imagine the terrible pain parents must go through when it happens. If only they knew how matter-of-fact the children are about death, how they seem to understand it all and have accepted that they are now where they are. They talk of being with other children and having many friends, and I have yet to speak to one who is sad. They know their parents will join them when it's time and they seem to be nicely occupied until then.

Then there are those who want us, here in the solid layer, to know what really happened to them. They may have been murdered, disappeared or wronged in some way and they know that we on this side do not know the truth. Many famous people have spoken in this way and there are many mysteries which have now been solved for me. In time I will publish them all, and I have promised those who have trusted me with the truth that I will do so.

There are those who want to set the historical records straight. Maybe experts will no longer need to pontificate on what may have taken place long ago in faraway places, such as, for example, ancient Egypt. How better to learn of those times than from those who were there.

Then there are those who have come to us and unravelled many famous puzzles from the past. If we were to include them all in Jasper's first book we would be accused of sensationalism and profiteering, but I have to say that it is rather nice to know how they made Stonehenge and who Jack the Ripper really was. But for now let's put aside most of these solutions to puzzles, which really do no more than show how historians and experts have managed to tangle themselves into such a knot over so many things.

It is rare for me to refuse to speak to anyone. At the time of writing this book it has happened only once. In October 2007 a notorious criminal wanted to speak. She was an English woman who died in prison where she was serving a life sentence for her part in the abuse and murder of a number of children in the 1960's. I had already spoken on a number of occasions to one of her victims and thought it would be disrespectful to the victim to speak to her, nor did I have any interest in what she would wish to say.

There are also just a few that have spoken where I would not publish what they said, simply because I found the speakers so distasteful. One of these was Belzoni, the Egyptian grave-robber. When I asked who I was speaking to, he said 'The Great Belzoni' with the emphasis on the 'Great.' When I jokingly said 'I can't call you The Great Belzoni,' he said 'But Great is what I am, Madam' and went on to tell me just how very great he was. He was obnoxious and full of his own self-importance. He spoke of the gold, the money he had made and of his great, and much-deserved fame. I will never publish it because we all feel that The Great Belzoni is quite great enough. He is, so far, the most repulsive of our visitors.

As we continued to work our knowledge expanded, and I learned so very much about true history. I am also lucky to be able to discuss the present state of the world with deceased politicians, scientists and philosophers which makes me think on a much larger scale than I did before. My mind is expanding constantly and I hope yours, with the reading of this book, will do so too. You would be surprised just how much knowledge you can fit in there.

Jasper says...

When I again began to speak to Ernest we had so much to speak of and so much 'time' to catch up on. The reason that I am here is not to make polite conversation with Ernest and Lillie, although I do enjoy our exchanges. I am here to bring knowledge. I have much to tell but I cannot tell it all on my own.

Many wish to speak, many who have not been able to make themselves heard for a long time. Some who are recent crossings who wish to bring comfort to their loved ones and some who bring with them a message

My time with you is short and there is so much that I have to bring to you. Ernest and Lillie work as long as they can but they need to rest, where I do not.

I opened the door through Ernest. I speak through him and those visitors I choose to bring through do so also. I protect Ernest at all times I would never allow anyone to cause him harm or discomfort. So no-one speaks unless I am sure that all is safe. Those with the most important message are given priority.

It started off simply at first, but as Ernest gained in strength and confidence more and more came. Our most knowledgeable visitors are the Elevated Beings and Higher Beings who enlighten and tell of their experience. But sometimes someone of simple existence has much of interest to tell. In the etheric layer none are more important than the next. Politicians, great thinkers and small children can all speak up and be heard.

We have gained many friends and renewed many acquaintances since we have been working together. The doorway is narrow, the time is short and many wait their time to speak. I will bring through as many as I can to share what they have to say with you.

All that you have to do is listen to what they say. Through the words of these pages the hard work has already been done for you. They have made their respective journey to the doorway - now listen and learn.

LIFE LESSONS

You have already heard from many who came to speak to me through Ernest. Jasper and I selected Billy the Baker's Boy and Tom the Sweep to start the book because they made such an impression. Tom's phrase 'The chimneys had ledges inside where you could sit and dream,' has a place in my heart forever. This book is dedicated to Tom, and to Billy who was so stern when I called Queen Victoria ugly and who shared with me his secret of the shiny buns.

Then you heard from a selection of people who told such emotional stories. Jasper and I selected them together and we thought that these were such a good cross-section of those we speak to. How lovely to think of Sheila and her Mum still attending the Chelsea Flower Show, and what a delight to speak to Molly as she told me that her dolls came alive at night. How brave of the other Molly to re-live such a terrible life, her time incarcerated in the servants quarters of her rich masters, so that her story might be told.

In this section we decided to use those whose stories contain a lesson for us all. Jasper selected the following group of speakers, and he has commented on each one.

The Woodman

[23 January 2007. Jasper told me he had a Woodman with him who had lived in woods close to where we were at that time. Although at that time there were a few parks around the area of South London where we lived, the idea that you could live in woods nearby meant that this man's story came from a time far distant. He spoke in a strange, high-pitched voice which was faint. His voice held the quiver of age and his words held a great wisdom which often comes from someone who has never had any form of formal education. I call him 'W' for Woodman.]

W: It was all country round here. I worked in the woods. I used to go picking up all the sticks, all the branches and things. People used to buy them for kindling, for firewood. I used to go and collect all the branches, the trees, the windfalls. Then I makes them up into a bundle. I didn't do much chopping. I was too old for that. I used to pick up all the ones that'd fallen. Twigs, kindling, sticks, and I used to cut the logs up. I'd have all the bits and pieces. I worked for the man who owned the big house. He used to own all this round here. All this was his land.

L: Did you live here all your life?

W: Yes, I had a little ramshackle thing that I built in the woods for the governor. I used to keep his woods tidy. Pick up the fallen trees, keep it tidy. He used to give me some money when he wanted to. Not much, but he let me live here. I had everything I wanted. It was cold in the winter. I used to do the charcoal. People used to buy the charcoal. Everything I had was my own. It weren't no good giving me coins. I didn't know what they were for. There was a village nearby. I used to go down with my sticks in a bundle. I'd bundle all the stuff up. I'd got a thing I used to drag. I'd drag 'em along. I made this thing to drag, I don't know what you'd call it. It was like a wagon without wheels.

They'd have my sticks and I'd get some bread. I used to like their cheese but they wanted a lot of sticks for that. I'd get my bread and some ale. People used to grow things like vegetables and that. I could cook 'em up, in my pot. The man in the big house, he used to hunt and if he had more than he wanted he used to give me something, like a small deer. I'd hang it up and it didn't matter if it went off - you could still cook it.

There was a little stream where I could get my water from. It was cold in the winter. I didn't like the snow because it meant I couldn't get out.

There were some travelling people who would come by and they'd stop and talk. They'd get some stuff off of me and they'd give me bits of food and things I'd never had before. There was plenty to eat in the summer. Berries, nuts, apples. All you had to do was make sure you had enough to eat in the winter.

Around here it was all woods. In the wintertime you had to keep warm. You keep your fire going. I had my shelter made out of branches, I put skins on the outside and then covered it with mud. You keep the fire lit inside and you keep your pot going. It was always on. Then you always had something to keep you warm.

It was nice when the sun was out. The leaves on the trees. When they were hunting you could see the people coming by in their finery.

L: I think you had the better life than the one's in the finery. Do you know what year it was?

W: I don't know nothing about that.

L: It's really nice to meet you and talk to you. What's you name?

W: I didn't have no name. I don't even know how I got there or where I came from. One day I was just there.

L: [Trying to find the date] Did you hear anyone talking about the King or the Queen?'

W: Someone said Charles, or was it Charlie?

L: I have really enjoyed meeting you and you're welcome to come back at any time.

W: I might. I don't speak to many. It was a good life. I didn't mind.

[The Woodman's memory of a King Charles puts his time at anywhere between 1625 and 1685.]

Jasper says ....

The Woodman led a very simple life. Although he was uneducated he gained so much from his existence. Some would say that he did not know any better, but then if he had all that he wanted why should he have looked elsewhere? Although they were worlds apart the landowner and the Woodman had a respect for each other. The landowner sometimes gave food to the Woodman who looked after his land and let him live there in freedom. In return the Woodman cared for the land that he was so much a part of. There was a complete awareness by the Woodman of all things around him.

The lesson here is that no matter how little one has it is sometimes enough. For the Woodman the earth provided everything. Times have changed so much now. Have all of the simple values and sustenance gone from the earth? Or has mankind just forgotten how and where to look for it? The Woodman still loves the old land that he was so much a part of, he still visits the area. Although the landscape has changed out of all recognition, to the Woodman the images are permanently etched in his existence. He has moved on as we all must do, he is not trapped, but he frequents his old home from choice - no one can ever deny him that.

Not Quite Enough

[23 November 2007. Strong, almost sharp, upper-class, well-educated voice. Wellington 1769 – 1852.]

D: David. That's my name. David. Pleased to meet you.

L: Hello David, pleased to meet you. Tell me of your life.

D: My life was colourful if you look upon it in that way. Yes ... I suppose you could say I was a bit of a waster in my younger years, because my parents, god bless them, had plenty of money I didn't have to do much for my keep really. Just be around the place. There are ways of keeping yourself occupied [Laughing] when you're a young man with money, I don't think I need to explain, because there are many who wish to keep you company. But it's not that satisfying when you come home to empty rooms. It's all very well putting on the show and the façade but it's sometimes a lonely life when you're young and own your own. I had a sister but she was away and married. Fine house, fine family, good name – father's a banker, don't you know. Plenty of income there.

I took up the law. Yes, well, I felt I needed to do something. Did interest me, as such, and I was pushed to move into some kind of profession. Took a long time, mind you, and I sometimes wondered if there was enough business in the area that I'd decided to settle. Property – it's not as involved as people. People are more complicated in many ways but, you know, preparing paperwork and deeds and transfers and ownerships - it's good, it's interesting enough but it doesn't get on the ground really, if you understand. Looking back now it's not what I would have chosen really. I think I would have chosen more to be working with people. But you can't go back, can you.

Business grew quite well where I was situated, I lived around Greenwich. Yes, we had a large house overlooking the park, down by the river, very pleasant indeed. Yes, very pleasant, and I carved a reasonable existence for myself. I had a wife and a son and a daughter and happiness. Mother and father left me all when they died, and so I was not without means.

There was always something not quite there, something missing. I still really never found it. There was always something missing from my life and I was never sure what. Although I cannot complain, I made a reasonable living and had a good lifestyle but I did feel empty from time to time. There was always something not quite right.

I would sometimes feel that life was passing me by. I would watch the ships passing through the river and the carriages passing by and although I was not without means I do feel that I missed so much. I was never a patron of the arts, I was never really that refined, I didn't even have a religion. Had a family of course, my family were everything to me and I love my family, but I cannot help thinking that something was missing.

Sometimes I would look at the sailors down at the docks and I wished I could be one of them, but of course I couldn't have been one of them because they wouldn't accept me into their circle of people. I suppose it's a matter of upbringing and class, which I find somewhat distasteful at times. I think a man should be able to do what he wants no matter what class he is. I feel that those who are low-born should be able to climb to heights, I also feel that those born into substance should be allowed to look beneath themselves. I would have loved to have been a sailor, I would have loved to have sailed the seas and seen foreign lands and foreign people. We are so insular in our lifestyle here, we are not without comforts but we are without knowledge and experience. I sometimes feel that these people who travel the world and have no money have a wealth of experience which is worth more than the money itself. Being able to meet people from different lands and speak to them and listen to their stories would be wonderful. Although I executed my works well it was never that satisfying, do you understand my meaning?

L: What do you think actually stopped you from doing these things do you think?

D: [Rather surprised by the question] My class of course! Can you imagine? I would have been an outcast. My family would have disowned me and I'm afraid you just have to come to a compromise really. Although your mind is telling you, and your heart is telling you to do one thing, you know from a sense of duty that you cannot – you know, your family, you cannot move away from your family and your friends. Takes a very brave man indeed to do so.

The lesson to be learned is that they say that money buys everything, and it doesn't. I think money buys any material thing but I think money doesn't buy happiness. You can be happy, but I think you have to really work at happiness and contentment. It's not something you can buy. It's not something you can be born into. I see the soldiers going off to war to fight for Wellington and his men and you know I'm even too old for that. If I had been younger I would have been more of a mind to enlist, if I had been allowed to of course. But even that's away from me. It's not something I can do.

I don't mean to sound ungrateful, because I never wanted for anything, but I do feel that life could have been much more exciting. I don't feel like I've actually achieved anything, I've never left a mark. The papers that I cast my legal eye over have long since been archived and lost, so there's no mark for me. There's nothing that ... I don't wish to have been thought of as a great statesman but I feel sad that we all have this opportunity and not all of us are able to leave our mark. I feel that I wasted so much. I could have done so much more but I still don't know what I could have done to have made a difference.

I did think once of giving it all away but what's the point of that because even if you give it away there are those who if you gave away all of your wealth and you had nothing, you would still not be accepted. The way you speak and the way you act would keep you worlds apart. I often tried to mix with the common man, I did frequent the inns, places of drinking, and it was always a situation where they would try to rob me or they didn't trust me and they wondered why ... you find even those of the different classes who tried to make your acquaintance usually had some different kind of motive, they either wished to profit from you or use your experience. There are many who when they knew that I was in the legal profession tried to use me for their advice, but when they found that all I could really give advice on was what property to buy they really didn't show much interest.

The lesson to be learned is that money doesn't buy everything. Not only doesn't it buy you everything – it doesn't buy you anything ... I'll go and watch the ships now. The time has passed now and there are so many of them, but they still have a fascination. A sailor I should have been ...

Jasper says ...

When he walked the earth David had everything that he could have wanted. Many would have given much to have been born into such a privileged position. But for some to have it all is just not enough. He longed for the romance that he associated with the ships that sailed the seas, but in reality he could not have lived in such a way. He would not have had the strength and courage to exist there. From his privileged position of birth he really looked down upon those classes beneath him. He still does.

David still cannot understand the true values in life. Wealth and position are not foremost in importance, it is accepting where you are and what you have. What others have is theirs to maintain and enjoy. Perhaps if David had taken the time to share what he had with those he considered to be beneath him he would have been accepted, and in this acceptance he could have shared the life that he so longed for without taking a step outside of his comfortable surroundings. David still has many lessons to learn. Maybe he will never learn them. One thing is for certain - he will never find happiness until he lets go of his "position" in the life that has now long passed him by.

Sir Archibald Rodwell

[20 April 2008]

B: Found a body. It was horrible.

L: It would be. Where was it?

B: Just in the road. They said it was run down by a carriage. A gentleman he was, I think he was done to death. Didn't look like no running-down wounds to me.

L: Horrible thing to find though, for you.

B: Yes it was. No, it was nasty, didn't like it.

L: No, I wouldn't like it.

B: I was just foraging around, see what I could find, and I was just out with the early morning light and ... there he was. I couldn't tell no-one though.

L: Oh, couldn't you?

B: No, they'd have said I'd done it. So I just picked up my bits of wood and moved off. I often wonders who he was. Never did see him again. I've looked for him, mind you.

L: Oh, have you?

B: Yeah. Tried to find out who he was but I didn't hear nothing, so I made up all sorts of things about him, you know. I just imagined he was a gentleman who'd lost his way in the dark. I don't like to think that he died violently, I like to think that he was walking along, having had a few drinks, and he was hit by a carriage in the dark, and he didn't feel nothing.

L: No, because he'd had so much to drink that it would make him numb. That's a nice way of thinking. Nice way to go.

B: Yes, so I like to think that's how it went really, and when I thought about him, years later, I sort of thought perhaps that was right really.

L: Well, we know he's alright now, don't we.

B: Yeah, I know he's alright, I'm not even going to bother trying to find him, but if I come across him one day I just want to say I'm sorry I didn't do nothing.

L: But what could you have done?

B: Well, nothing really. No, if I had have said something they would have thought it was me, especially with it being a gent. They'd have just thrown me in the jail.

L: You did the right thing. My name's Lillie, I don't know your name.

B: I'm Bill. Hello Lillie. I'm just so sorry I didn't do nothing for him. It was the only one I ever saw.

L: Which road was it Bill?

B: Dulwich, road through the village.

L: Oh, yes, a carriage road, wasn't it?

B: Yeah, lots of greenery.

L: Did you live around there?

B: Well, a bit of way from there really, on the common land. Had a little ... little abode, you know, how I like to think of it. I used to go out gathering sticks and things in the morning. Course, as the carriages used to go through they'd knock some of the branches off, some of the branches that I couldn't reach. So I'd just pick them up and break them and bundle them, and take them home and have them for firewood. That was when I found him.

L: Gosh, you must have been really shocked.

B: Frightened me really.

L: It would frighten you Bill, it would do.

B: I'd never seen a dead body like that before. I've seen them since but I haven't seen one that died like that. I've seen some that have just died, you know, where all the wind went from them.

L: Yes, the natural way.

B: I never seen none that died like that.

L: Also it's not what you were expecting to find there, is it.

B: No, but he was my gentleman who died in his sleep, having had a few drinks.

L: Yes, had a few drinks and just fell over.

B: Even gave him a name once.

L: Oh, did you? What was it?

B: Archibald. Thought that ought to be a gentleman's name.

L: Archibald ... nice name ... Archibald. I wonder what his second name would be?

B: Don't know.

L: What about Rodwell. We could say Rodwell, Archibald Rodwell.

B: Lord, do you reckon?

L: (Laughing) Lord Archibald Rodwell.

B: Lord Archibald Rodwell, late of Dulwich village ... yeah, that'd do.

L: And what was his profession?

B: He would have been a doctor or something, wouldn't he. Perhaps he'd have been a gent that never had no job.

L: Yes, probably had enough money and didn't even need one.

B: Yes, let's say that shall we.

L: And let's have him buried, with some ceremony in Dulwich Churchyard in one of those big mausoleum places.

B: Would he have a gun salute?

L: I think so.

B: Have to be military for that, wouldn't he?

L: Well, he might have been military when he was younger ... and they might have taken his coffin beneath those crossed swords.

B: Poor widow grieving at the graveside. Half a dozen kids around her. Poor woman ... poor woman.

L: Shall we make that she was already in love with another?

B: Oh, I don't know about that.

L: Bit of intrigue ...

B: Yeah, but then that could've been the one that run him down.

L: Oh yes ... no, then we're back on ... no, no ... let's just have her not with any problems because ...

B: She's got his money. All his money.

L: And a fine house.

B: And she married a poor old woodman who was collecting wood.

L: [Laughing] And he got the big house.

B: Oh no, I wouldn't want no big house.

L: I think you do alright as the poor old woodman, I don't think we'll change your role. I think you're alright just as you are.

B: Yeah, I reckon. Anyway, look, nice to talk to you. I'll be off then. What's your name?

L: My name is Lillie and you're welcome any time.

B: Well, bye Lillie, I'll speak to you again.

L: You take care.

B: I'll see you around. Bye.

Jasper says ...

Bill was so concerned for this unknown person that he found beside the road. Although he was a simple soul Bill knew that it was wrong for this body to be just lying there. He carried this care past his own death and pondered over what the unknown man would have been and invented a whole life and existence.

Has Bill been searching for the answers because he feels that this unknown needs them, or is it really Bill who needs answers? This is commonplace with death, sometimes we forget that the deceased has no longer any need for such answers and that the grieving that we bestow upon them is misplaced.

Bill was undoubtedly very caring, but he must learn to come to terms with his find and look for his own destiny and not for that of the nameless one.

Gerald the Surgeon

[16 November 2008. A well spoken, strong voice.]

G: I am Gerald.

L: Hello, Gerald, I am Lillie, and you're very welcome.

G: Hello Lillie. What would you ask of me?

L: Tell me a little about you, Gerald. I would be most interested.

G: My name is Gerald, I was a surgeon, a skilled man some would say. My speciality was children. But in the early days I was not so good, I was not good at my craft. I was slap dash I was careless, I perhaps did not care so much for those that I worked upon. I had spent long years on university, and training and college. It's a long road to becoming a doctor and even longer to become a surgeon.

I assisted many, many eminent surgeons and then I was on my own. All of sudden. And I was qualified, I had the experience, and I was on my own, I had my own team. But I hadn't realise that a team is what it is, you depend on everyone. I was young. I was pig-headed. And I wouldn't listen. Minor operations were not a problem, I had performed so many, I performed thousands of operations on children.

But there were three in particular ... that it was my fault that they died. And it was through my own carelessness and I think those around me knew it was my fault, but they never spoke of it. But I still remembered those three children. You do become somewhat desensitised when you do this kind of work. At first you see it with every waking hour, you see these children with terrible illnesses, these terrible things that grow upon them, and deformities. It's very difficult. But I was responsible for killing three children.

At the point of the third one I was about to give in. I was about to admit defeat and realise what a useless person I was at my trade. But then I thought that I owed it to those three children, and their families, to carry on.

It was a turning point for me. I know some would say that they saw the light and suddenly found religion, let me say that I found the medical profession. I suddenly realised why I was there. I suddenly realised that ... I always thought I was special, but I wasn't special in that way. The speciality was that I had something that could help people.

And I lost all of that selfishness, all of that brashness, all of that pomposity. I was going to give in, I was going to stop, but I realised that it had all meant nothing if I had given up. And I decided that if I was going to do this at all, I would do the best I could ever do for these children. These children, after all, who didn't ask to come and certainly did not ask to come with such illnesses.

And I decided to go on, and I've lost count of the amount of children I worked upon. I decided that to repay the debt of these three children I would, with every last breath in my body I would help others.

I spent some time in Africa on voluntary service. I took semi-retirement towards the end of my life and I helped children there. These children were far worse off than anything I'd ever seen here. Then I came back to England as a consultant, as a professorship actually and I tried to instil this enthusiasm into my pupils. I hope that I did.

So I suppose the moral of the story is that if you're going to do anything, you have to do it to the best of your abilities. You can't ... if you sweep roads you do not endanger anyone by sweeping them badly, but if you have someone life in your hands you cannot do such a thing badly, there is no second chance. You have to be one hundred and ten percent all the time, you have to give all. And more. You have to give your life because there's no time for anything else.

L: And how did you feel at the end. Did you feel, on balance that you had done all that you could?

G: I still felt sad for the three that I lost, as indeed any doctor must do.

L: But you made a difference. How many people can say that?

G: Well, it was my intention. I needed to. And as I have said you must, whatever you do, make sure you do it to the best of your ability. There is no room for half measures.

L: May I ask you, have you seen the three children?

G: Yes, I have. And their families. And they bear no malice against me. Carelessness, yes, but it was not premeditated. Not intentional. I suppose every operation I performed after that I could see those children beneath me, under my knife, every one I saved was a re-enactment of the ones I had lost.

I am going on to heal from this side now. I have decided that I must find a way to put this knowledge back into something. I do not know when, but I will give gladly.

L: That's wonderful. Good luck with that.

G: Thank you for listening.

Jasper says ...

Everyone comes to a point in their lives where they can either admit defeat and give up completely or pick themselves up, learn by their mistakes, and carry on. In some professions it makes little difference which direction we take, it does not have much effect on the next man. However, in the position of a doctor there must always be an unwavering duty of care. To be given the gift and skill to heal others must not be taken lightly.

Life in solid form is comparatively short compared to the whole picture of existence. Without exception all human beings deserve the right to exist as best they can with those in trusted positions easing all of the pains that living can give. This doctor made mistakes but he did all within his grasp to repay the debt that he felt he owed to the three children and their families. His achievements did not cover his 'crime'. He knew that this would never be so.

We all make mistakes, but it is how we act upon this discovery that makes the difference. This doctor went on to help many and will continue to do so from where he is now. But he will never forget his mistakes. Rightly so, because without such mistakes how will we ever know that what we are doing is wrong and correct it?

Tom

[9 November 2008. A tiny voice, cheeky.]

T: Hello.

L: Hello. I'm Lillie.

T: I'm Tommy. Tom, my friends call me.

L: Can I call you Tom?

T: Yes... Lillie.

L: Tell me about you Tom.

T: Well ... I used to pinch things.

L: Did you?

T: Nothing bad. Only to eat. Times was hard, see. And I used to sneak out in the night, in the big estate, see. Big wall around it.

L: Were you hungry?

T: Yeah. My Mum used to say 'Out you go, boy, go and bring us back some apples for a nice pie'. And I'd sneak over the fence, with my sack. Didn't bring too many, just those I could carry, with my sack. The wall was high, but I knew where there was branches hanging over and I could climb over and I could get up and down easily. If I didn't take too many apples I could get back over again. Only a few – like the fingers on my hand, that many, no more than that. 'One for each finger', that's what my Mum would say to me, cause I couldn't read, didn't know what ... you know ... to count, so she'd say 'Just bring one for each finger, and that'll be enough for us'.

L: One hand? That's five.

T: No, both hands. I knows five isn't enough.

L: Oh, ok. Ten.

T: So, I climb over the wall with my sack, and get some. Sometimes I'd venture a bit further and see what else there was. Sometimes I'd bring back berries. They was a bit mess though ...

L: Oh, yes, if they squashed.

T: No. Not that. If you was caught and you'd been eating some, they could see them around your face. You could drop a bag of apples and run away, but if they caught you and you had juice around your face, it'd give you away, wouldn't it?

L: Ah, yes.

T: It was a big estate. Belonged to some Lord, I don't know his name, big place it was. The house was miles away from the wall. I used to sneak down there at the night at look at it flickering in the darkness. All the lights in the windows. Big house – you could keep loads of people in that! I used to wonder if it was really warm in there, and wondered what it was like to sit in front of a big fire. Sneaked right up to the window once. And I saw a great big table with loads of food on it, and do you know how many people were sitting round it?

L: How many?

T: Well, there was ... the old man ... then there was an old lady ... then there was a younger man. That's all there was!

L: Three. Not even the fingers on one hand.

T: And they had more food than I think I've ever eaten in my life! And they was just picking at it, you know, didn't look right some how. And there was ... don't know ... men in their suits ...

L: Giving them their food?

T: Bringing it round to em. They wasn't eating none of it, don't suppose they was allowed to. They was bringing it around and giving it them and I thought they had more people coming. But they didn't. And I thought 'how can you eat all that food?' More than I'd ever seen in my life.
And there I was with my bag of apples. Done me though, enough for me. And my Mum makes a good pie. Sometimes my Dad would come back at night and he'd bring back a rabbit, and Mum would make a pie and we'd have two pies – we'd have a rabbit pie and an apple pie. That was lovely. We wouldn't eat it all at once, mind you, because we had to ... sort of ... be careful in case it all went.
And then my Dad came back one night and he said it was getting bad, because he said people had been getting caught. They'd been taken away and not seen again. They get taken away and put in jail, I was told, and I didn't want my Dad to get caught, I was worried about my Dad. I was quicker than him, I could nip over a fence and get away, but my Dad wasn't as fast. So, I thought ... I ... 'I'll have to bring a bit more back', see, because if my Dad couldn't do it, well I'd have to do it. And I had brothers and sisters and they all needed to eat.
So I went out one night and I went over the wall, like I normally do, and I was rummaging around for ages, and I couldn't believe my eyes! There on the floor, on a big cloth, there was some fish, big fish, there was a couple of rabbits, and I thought 'Look at this! Someone's put this here for me'. And I thought, 'I'll take that home with me'.
So I gathered it up, and it was heavy. Then, it was dark, see, there wasn't no moon out, and somebody shouted 'Hey!' and I got frightened and I started to run, and ... and it was the gamekeeper and he came after me and he shouted. And he said I was a poacher and he said 'Stop where you are or I'll shoot!'
I couldn't stop, because I had to get home. So I kept running. Then there was a big bang. Big Bang! Ooh, and there was .... all this pain ... all my legs and back ... ooh, it was really painful. And I felt hot ... from

running ... I felt funny ... and ... and I dropped my bag and I tried to walk a bit more, but I couldn't. I thought I'd just have to lay down on the floor, because I felt a bit tired now ... and ... err ... I ... err .... I just 'went', you know?

L: Yes, I understand.

T: And the poacher ... was me! I was a poacher! [Sounding really shocked.]

L: But, Tom, you weren't a poacher.

T: Then the gamekeeper came along and he saw me, and I watched him. And his face! I saw his face go.

L: Ah, when he saw it was a little boy?

T: I saw his face go, and he fell down to his knees. And he cried. I'd never seen a big man cry. And he cried and he picked ... picked my body up, and he carried it, and ... he cried. And ... err ... he took me home to my Mum and Dad and he cried. And then my Mum and Dad was angry at first, then they were sad. Do you know what that man done? [Sounding surprised]

L: No, what?

T: Long time after I'd gone, well ... long time after they'd buried me, you know, he used to bring things round to my Mum and Dad.

L: Ah, did he?

T: He'd come round and he'd ... he'd give em things, a fish or a rabbit or something. Didn't say nothing, just used to have it wrapped up in a bit of paper. And he'd give it to em. And I suppose, really, I don't suppose my Mum and Dad was happy that I'd gone, but if I hadn't gone, they wouldn't have been getting that stuff, would they?

L: Yes ... you were still feeding them, in a way.

T: Yeah ... [Still sounding doleful, then brightening up quickly] Anyway, we're never hungry now.

L: No, Tom, I bet you're not. And are you all together now?

T: Yeah. [Sounding pleased]

L: And what about the gamekeeper, Tom?

T: He's alright. He's a nice man. He was only doing his job, I suppose.

L: I bet he was pleased to see you, wasn't he?

T: Yeah. Yeah. He was only doing his job. I seen that big old Lord. I don't speak to him. He got big and fat, he did. Anyway, my Mum's pies are still good.

L: Thanks for coming to tell me that, Tom, I really liked it.

T: It's alright. Good.

L: You enjoy your pies and your lovely family.

T: All right then.

L: Thanks a lot. Bye!

T: Bye.

Jasper says ...

Tom was a thief, as was his father. Although stealing cannot be condoned, who could say what they would do faced with such circumstances? The Lord and his family had more than they needed but were obviously quite unaware of the poverty that existed outside of their comfortable home. The gamekeeper in Tom's own words was just doing his job. But who was really responsible for the death of Tom? Was it the gamekeeper and his employer or was it the fault of Tom's parents for putting so much of a burden upon the young lad? There is enough for all if only mankind can learn to share what they have.

Billy's Handkerchief

[26 March 2007. A rough voice. The Great Fire of London was 1666. Blackheath is 7 miles outside London.]

B: Hello.

L: Hello, I'm Lillie. I'm pleased to speak to you.

B: Hello. Billy. There are some don't speak to me. I never killed no-one. I was a thief. I used to pinch a lot. They hanged me for it. Bastards.
All I did was pinch up on the heath, Blackheath. Up the heath, got caught in the heath cutting the pocket out of a gentleman. Well I couldn't help it. How was I supposed to live. I never hurt no-one though. Hang you for picking a handkerchief – 'cause the gentleman's handkerchief is worth more than the peasant. Never robbed the ladies. Liked the ladies.

Used to catch 'em coming out of the inns at night, when it was dark. 'Help you along home Governor?' and I relieves em of their pocket. Serves em right for getting so drunk.

I knew what was going to happen if I got caught, we was told that, but anyway it happens, don't it. Do you know I watched London burn. I stood up on the heath and I saw it. I watched it burn. It burned for days. I saw it in the sky. Yeah, you could see a lot from up there in the heath. It burned for a long time. I didn't go there, I could see it. I saw it burn and it was funny. All the sky was lit up. Because it was all diseased it was all bad. It was a rotten place so they said. It was bad. And it was dirty. Didn't go there. Didn't go that far.

The law was different because there was local law, in local areas. You could be tried and hanged in the same day. They soon strung you up. I gave a bit of what I stole away. Used to share it out between us. There weren't no jobs for me. Nobody wanted to give me work. Just a silly old beggar. But I was quick with the knife and the pocket. Only got caught once, but I had a good run.

Used to run fast when I was younger. They couldn't catch me. Market day was good. Good pickings. Lots of people. It was different then. I've looked at it now and there's lots of buildings there now. Wasn't like that then. There was nothing much and it was dark. There was some right villains on there, on the heath. Not that I was one of 'em. I wasn't one of them highwaymen who used to shoot people. I lived down in Deptford, down by the boatyard. I think I've told you too much.

L: Don't you worry. I'm glad you told me. I think what they did to you was too much.

B: It was quick. You could see a long way from there, you could see the river from there.

L: It's nice up there. [Meaning up on the heath at Blackheath]

B: Well it wasn't very nice looking down from a rope. I used to stash the stuff in a hole. Mustn't be caught with it on me. Never had no coins on me when they did catch me, when they done for me. Had an empty purse and a handkerchief. They said it was too fine for me, the handkerchief. They found me guilty. Still, I did it. I did pinch it. It's different if you're a gentleman, you can have fine things around you. But if you're a beggar, a poor man, you can't have fine things. They know you pinched em.

Suppose it's a good thing it was quick. I was only in the jail a day. I didn't like the idea of that, because of all the rats and all that. Well I've told you me story now.

L: [Crying and shocked] Did they really hang you for a handkerchief, Billy? Just for a handkerchief?

B: Yes. Because they said I shouldn't have had it.

Jasper says ...
The times that Billy recalled were hard ones. Luxury items, though simple, were valued higher than the lives of the poor. The punishment was harsh and final. All crimes have to be paid for eventually, but the scales of justice should never balance that of a life against a mere handkerchief. The world is still learning but the poor are still poor.

Danny and the Wall Street Crash

[15 November 2008.]

D: Hello. I'm Danny.

L: Danny, ok. Tell me a little bit about you Danny.

D: I jumped from a building. It's a warning I bring to you. Do you know the Wall Street Crash?

L: Ah, yes.

D: Do you know this?

L: Yes, I do, and something very similar is taking place right now.

D: It is about this I wish to warn. I had family, two young children and I worked for a medium sized brokerage. I feared being blamed for so many things, everything was falling around us. Men were being ruined with the stroke of a pen, everything they'd ever worked for, gone. And I was one of these. I wasn't as much as some of them, but not as little as others, but still had a lot to lose.
   But the stupid thing is, of course, the biggest thing I had to lose was my family. And this I did. And I still feel that I've lost them. I put all of my faith on money. A stupid thing, and I couldn't face not having any. I couldn't see how I could raise my family without any – but of course they managed without me.
   They survived, fortunately, in spite of what I did. So the stupid things is I could have lost everything and still had them, and now I feel I've lost them forever. Because I really didn't do right by them, I did the wrong thing. I know it's wrong. But at the time if you're so focused in the job that you do, sometimes you can't see further than the desk of papers.

L: I suppose sometimes it becomes the only thing that you know.

D: Yes ... but I had the picture on my desk and I should have looked more often. My warning is to those who are considering it now – I know there are many and I have watched what is going on. The situation is very similar, already some have done so. I believe there will be more, but they must realise this isn't the way. I know now that no matter what fortune I had amassed I couldn't have taken it with me. So, really they've got to look closer to home, they've got to look at the priorities.

L: May I ask you a question?

D: Yes.

L: When you were here, when it was happening, would you have listened to this?

D: No, I suppose not. It's all a matter of priorities, isn't it. You lose sight of it. When you're earning money and the greed sets in.

L: Also you are in an environment where everyone around you is the same, it's peer pressure.

D: It breeds it. It's the competition as well, it's the need to succeed. There is no place for failure in commerce.

L: But if looking at the photograph of their family on their desk doesn't stop them, I'm afraid your words won't stop them, sadly.

D: It didn't stop me. But they risk losing all, losing the money is nothing, money and wealth means nothing. It's what they lose later. And I believe that I have lost them, and I cannot say that I blame them. I had a good wife, good children – the children are all grown now and have children of their own.

L: I'm sad for you.

D: My wife married again. He was good man. He was a ... worked with his hands, he was a mechanic, and they were happy, and the money didn't matter. I watched them for a long time, and I was happy for them. I was pleased for them that they found comfort I others. The funny thing is that I lost all material wealth, but now I'm paying more.

Jasper says ...

It is strange how the human race have such short memories when it comes to certain subject matter. The Wall Street Crash is not exactly ancient history but the important facts surrounding it have been forgotten or are ignored. It is that old seducer of men, greed, that has brought the cycle around again. How many 'ruined men' will it take like Danny to jump from the ledge before mankind realises that the things that are the most important are not the figures on a balance sheet, it is the people themselves who are important - not their wealth.

Even if Danny had not lost all of his wealth before jumping I wonder if he would have expected to take it with him when he died. Instead he really did lose it all. But his biggest loss was his wife and children who would have loved him however he was, rich or poor. He had a picture on his desk to remind him, when he could pull himself away from his figures, that they were still there, but his family were not important enough to pull him back from the edge. He saw after his death that his wife and children carried on without his wealth, they found happiness where it mattered the most - with each other.

When the time comes to make the transition from life in the solid layer you will find that the money and possessions that have been weighing you down for so long are just too heavy and cumbersome to take with you. On the other hand you will find that life itself and the love that you have shared with others weighs nothing at all and it is these things that will be with you always. Mankind must learn that it is not necessary to jump – when your time comes just take your time and walk across the divide.

Adrian

[18 September 2008. A young mans voice and a way of speaking I recognised as having come from the 1960's but he sounded monotone, almost bored.]

A: Hi.

L: Hi, I'm Lillie.

A: Adrian.

L: Well you're very welcome Adrian.

A: Thank you. It's been a long time calming down. Everything's much slower now. Everything was so fast. Faster and faster. Everything moved too fast. Doing something, you know, never enough time. Always something going on. Parties and festivals and things. Summers were great. Sleep in the park. Yeah .. with friends. It was cool, you know. Drink with friends and share. Share the ... share things around, you know. Smokes and pills and the like.

L: Was it the sixties?

A: Yeah. Yeah .. peace ....

L: Peace and love.

A: Yeah, peace and love. We moved around, one party to another, it was a big scene. Big scene. It was one big party and everybody always knew someone else had something going on. One big scene. Chelsea. King's Road, you know, Carnaby Street. Clubs in Wardour Street.

L: Yes, and the Marquee Club.

A: Yeah, Marquee. Just one big long party.

L: Were you in a band Adrian?

A: No. I didn't have that ....umm ...

L: No, me too. Always loved the music though, didn't you?

A: Yeah, it was cool. I went to University and dropped out. I was at the LSE for a while [London School of Economics], I gave that up. Couldn't see much point really if we were all going to die young anyway. Never going to get old. And it was just fun. It was just crazy and ...umm ...... just mad really. Everything goes on. And your head's never clear and things spin and you see things and ... you know ... dots [Drug], you know, dots. Clubs, good scene, you get close to the bands there. I had a girl. Suzie. And we were sometimes close but we mixed around, you know. We didn't stay together that much. Drifted.

L: Free love.

A: Yeah. Drifted. Drifted. Yeah, and good friends but family were ... umm ... not happy. Lived in a squat in Clapham, back of the Junction, do you know? We painted all the doors and windows different colours and we lived there for a while. It was cool, you know. Everybody chipped in to get by and we had parties, and drinking, lot of drinking and it was just one big scene and just used to lose whole days, you know. Wake up, wouldn't know where I was, or who I was sometimes. And it all got kind of weird, and it just ... really strange. You get crazy, you can't see things straight. You see things climbing the walls and coming at you in the shadows. It's just madness really, madness. You think you can ... umm ... you think you can just do anything really. Yeah.
    I went to ... I went to the bridge one night ... Chelsea. Really late. And there wasn't anybody about. It was just .... I don't even know where I'd come from. Just wandering. Just wandering. Everybody had gone, I was just on my own and I just felt really alone, you know. Really alone. And I figured that if I was that alone I may as well not be here. And I ... kind of sad ... you get so sad and you just, nothing's going to get better. I climbed up onto the wall, you know like the wall thing on the bridge. It was warm, you know. The air was warm. It was so quiet. It was just ... just the breeze, you know. Nobody was around. And I thought 'if anybody really cares,

they'll come and stop me. They'll come and get me because they won't let me go'. I leaned forward, you know, and ... I kind of just half jumped half fell. And fell into the water. It was deeper than I thought. Any that was kind of it really. That was kind of it.

Jasper says ...

Adrian led a completely wasted existence. He lived in a time of freedom but he was a child who, like many, had been born into a world which followed a period that had seen the world at war, a time when his parents and elders had had no time to think of anything else other than survival. Adrian had become a man completely unconcerned with the values of the older generation that had brought him into the world.

Freedom is such a responsibility and living is just too much of a chore for some. Adrian just wanted to enjoy himself without any of the responsibly, and the age that he lived in, this age of freedom, made many things available to him in the form of drugs and drink that could further numb not only his responsibility but also his very life. He was unable to accept the responsibility that we all must have for each other and for ourselves.

Even in the end, just before he jumped from the bridge, Adrian wanted someone else to come and stop him. This was not a cry for help - just a continuation of his lazy and wasted existence. I hope that he has learned his lessons now and will not make the same mistakes next time he is given the gift of life.

Laku and The Rainforest

[17 September 2008. Jasper told me that this man was from the Peruvian rainforest and that he came from 'quite recent' times. This was a sad, broken man, quietly spoken. He spoke with such a big question in his voice.]

Laku: Laku.

L: Laku?

Laku: Yes.

L: I am happy to speak to you.

Laku: Tribe come. They have big monsters. New tribe. Not seen before. Tribe with big monsters. Men of tribe control monsters. Monsters eat the trees. They take the trees and they eat them. Many, many trees taken. They take them away. Many trees that my father and many fathers before him saw grow from small seed.

L: From your land of course.

Laku: Yes. Big monsters come. And take trees. Big areas where the sun now comes through and burns, where trees stop the sun. Many things die. Many food that we eat die. Many animal die. Many tribe die.

L: Very wrong. Wrong to do this.

Laku: Trees gone as far as you can see. They take them and take them and we cannot stop them. The monsters eat the trees and take them away. They kill them. They cut them from the ground and let them fall. And makes us sad.

L: Yes of course. Very wrong.

Laku: We hide away from this tribe. They are big men. With shining faces that reflect the sun. They are not like our tribe. They have weapons that can kill. They have monsters that do not walk, they move along the ground. I do not understand how. They roar and burn smell. Smoke come from them.

L: Yes, I understand.

Laku: And they roar. And bigger monsters come and they drag the trees away with them. They take away all of the leaves and all of the smaller pieces and burn them. We can see the sky. We feel afraid that people can see us now.

L: Yes. Danger for you now.

Laku: We cannot hide in so many places.

L: Very wrong. Very sad.

Laku: My people could not find food to eat. Because it had all gone. We wandered to find, but there was never enough. And my people slowly disappeared. Away. And I could not stay any more. I did not wish to stay where it was so broken. I am sorry.

L: Very sad times. Very wrong. I am so sorry that you suffered so much, you and your people.

Laku: Yes. [And he had gone.]

Jasper says ....

For any civilisation to grow they have to constantly move forward, this is progress. As the world's population grows the needs of its people has to be catered for and the natural resources of the earth have to be used to best advantage. *It would be a perfect world indeed if all mankind moved at the same pace. This unity and collective responsibility is a long way off yet. Unfortunately there have been many people like Laku. Some would call them primitive, even savages, but just because they have not progressed does not make them any lesser a man than the next. Until modern man and his progress touched them they were happy with their existence, living off of the land and only taking what they needed to survive. Laku's people probably never even considered that they did not own the land on which they lived.*

This constant need for ownership has been the downfall of many a proud and ancient civilisation who were trampled beneath this progress. I have said that mankind must progress, he must learn. But the most important lesson that mankind has not yet learned is that all men have a claim on this earth. We are all born and we all die. Perhaps if modern man and his tribe with its monsters of destruction had treated Laku's people like human beings and not just another type of animal to be driven from the forest and taken time to listen to the needs of others, supposedly less civilised, there would have been a place for Laku and his people. He and his kind could have been given time to catch up with the rest of mankind. The bulldozers are oblivious to that which they crush underneath them and are only focused on the way ahead.

The time will come when this progress will consider the needs for all and not just a few who think they have the ownership of this earth. Alas it was too late to save the earth for Laku and so many others like him. But Laku has his forest again now and where he is no one can claim it and take it away.

Jimmy's Cigarette

[9 November 2008. A chirpy, friendly voice.]

J: How are you then?

L: I'm alright, thank you. How are you then?

J: I'm not too bad at all.

L: I'm Lillie.

J: Jimmy. Just Jimmy.

L: I'm pleased to speak to you Jimmy.

J: That's alright. Have you got a cigarette?

L: No, sorry, I gave up.

J: Cor. Blimey. No-ones ever got one. Bloody rationing! You'd think I'd get one, wouldn't you! Cor, blimey, after what I've been through.

L: Oh, have you bee through a lot?

J: Yeah, well, you come to expect it. Goes with the job, really.

L: What job is that?

J: Me? Air crew, wasn't I. Course, you couldn't smoke on the bloody plane, could you, set thing alight, do Hitler's job for him. No, see I bailed out.

L: Oh, did you?

J: Thing caught fire, didn't it.

L: Tell me you had a parachute.

J: I did ... bloody thing didn't work, did it.

L: [Shocked] Oh dear!

J: Bit late to find out though, isn't it. We'd finished, see, we'd been out, done our job and it was all quiet. And ... it's nice, you know, apart fro the drone of the engines, it's quite peaceful really, you just hear the wind rushing past you. And I was settling down, see, I'd done my job,. I was the navigator, I was the one with the maps. We'd done our job and we was in quite good spirits really. We'd done so many of them, you just do it and go home and you just look forward to getting home, really. I suppose really you've got to numb yourself to it a bit, you can't think about what you're doing. I was looking forward to getting home to Rosie and my pint of beer. I don't know which I was looking forward to the most ...

L: Let's say Rosie in case she'd listening.

J: Well let's say a bit of both. So I was thinking about Rosie, and a pint and ... a cigarette, I was really looking forward to a cigarette ... and we was coming back and it was all quiet, and we'd done what we'd done and got away with it, really, as you quite often did, and then the bloody heavens opened up! There was flak all around us, all come from nowhere. That was one that wasn't on the map. Ugh, it was horrible! Exploding all around us. The old plane took a couple of hits, and the skipper told us to get out. 'Get out while you can, go on boys, off you go!' and we all dived out. I think we were somewhere over France, don't know exactly where, somewhere on the border. Well, I had to get out, didn't I. Funny, really. It takes ages ... when you ... when it's ... you know ... it just takes ages. To go from you.

And I was just looking up at the plane and it was burning and I wondered if my mates got out. You know? And I pulled the chord and the bloody thing didn't work.

L: Oh, [Horrified] I just can't imagine what that must be like.

J: I mean we didn't all have parachutes. I mean we was lucky if we had one, [Chuckling] in my case I wasn't lucky, was I. Anyway, nothing I could do, was there?

L: No. That moment must have been terrible.

J: Well, a lot goes through your mind then. I was thinking of Rosie. Thought of all the kids we could have had together, you know.

L: How old were you?

J: Me, twenty two.

L: Oh, that's young. That's young, Jimmy.

J: And I saw the ground coming up, really fast, really fast. And do you know, it didn't hurt!

L: No, I bet it didn't, actually.

J: Funny, didn't hurt at all. Bloody parachute!

L: And what about your mates?

J: Oh, they got out, didn't they. I've seen them since. Anyway, there I was, in a sorry state, looking down at my body and I thought 'Now I'll have that cigarette.'

L: [Smiling and chuckling.]

J: And I reached into my pocket and do you know, it was the best cigarette I've ever had! And I looked down at myself there and I thought 'That's it mate, that's your war over!'

L: Oh, how nice!

J: But that cigarette was lovely! It was the best one I ever had! I went back to see Rosie, you know. Yes, she married someone else – I was pleased for her.

L: Of course, you wouldn't wish anything else for her, would you, but happiness.

J: No. And I'm not unhappy, My mates are here, my Mum and Dad are here. And my little brother, little sod! He got through the whole lot, he did. He was aircrew, too. Went through the lot! Lucky sod! But … [Laughing now], what do they say? Smoking's bad for you? It's bloody good for me, I'll tell you.

L: [Really laughing now] … How funny.

J: Cor, yeah, I really wanted that! Don't tell Rosie about the beer, though. Funny how things go through your mind.

Jasper says ….

A soldier at war has to live with the fact that he could be killed at any moment. It can be considered in two ways, you either panic and sit cowering, waiting for the inevitable to happen, or you just get on with it and do what you have to do. Jimmy was a soldier and although his battlefield was in the air and somewhat removed from the hand to hand conflict of others, he was still a soldier. All killing is wrong and Jimmy knew that he had just returned from raining death on the 'enemy', but it was his duty and he had his home and loved ones to defend.

Even when death came to him Jimmy still refused to let death cloud his senses. It was luck for any aircrew to get home safely and Jimmy's luck had just run out. He did not waste his last moment on what could have, for all he knew, be his last glimpse of existence - he thought of his Rosie and the comforts of home. And then when his lifeless and now no longer needed body lay on the ground Jimmy calmly reached for his cigarette and accepted what he had now become. Yes his war was over, as he said to his lifeless body, but his time of peace had just begun.

John's Death

[27 March 2008. An upper-class English accent. Very well-spoken.]

J: Hello.

L: Hello, I'm Lillie.

J: I'm John. Had a bit of an accident, that's all. Dashed stupid really. Just a bit of a prang in the car. Didn't seem so bad at first, thought I'd get away from it really. I was just glad no-one else was in it really, no-one else was involved. Family now – we're back together again, so it's not so bad.

It was all very strange at first because after the impact I didn't see anything else – next thing I know I'm looking down at myself in hospital bed, you know, I didn't know of anything else between the accident and then. Takes a time to realise what's happened to you, it's very confusing but once you get hold of it it's not so bad.

L: Yes, I suppose it was just coming to terms with the fact that you'd died.

J: Yes, it's so far removed at first, it's like when you hear your voice on a recorder for the first time and you don't realise it's you. When you look at your face it's not like looking in a mirror, funnily enough. It's very different from that and you look at it and it's not as you imagined yourself really. But it's just a piece of material really, the body, it's just like hanging your suit up, if you understand, in your wardrobe.

L: Yes, yes, how interesting.

J: It's very odd at first.

L: Yes, yes, it must be.

J: I'm sorry I'm taking up your time.

L: Not at all, please tell em more, what an interesting way of putting it, like hanging up an old, comfortable coat that you've been wearing for a long time and no longer need.

J: Yes, of course, you don't need that any more do you. It's like all things, when the suit becomes too old and moth-eaten you throw it away. But the interesting thing is .... I'm probably telling you something that you already know ...

L: Tell me please.

J: Well the interesting thing is that now the girlfriend who looked so lovely when she was young is just like that again, here. And your parents, your mother and father who you saw grow old and withered away – they're suddenly full of vitality again now they're here. It's wonderful, really, because everyone seems to return to a point where they were at their best. And it's nice to be ageless and to be able to see people for what they really are. They are ageless and their age and wrinkles have all fallen away. They are as they should be really.

L: How nice, and how comforting that is. I will tell everyone on this side because it will comfort those who have just lost someone.

J: Yes ... I mean everybody grieves, but it's unnecessary really, but I suppose it gives them some release, doesn't it.

L: Yes, they still miss being able to interact with the material body of the one who left.

J: Well, not many of mine left on that side now.

L: Most of you together now?

J: Well I've got some distant relatives but of course they don't know me, so they won't miss me and I won't miss them. Anybody who's important is here – passed through – so it's not a problem. I'll leave you now.

L: Thank you for those lovely words describing that, it will be so comforting for others.

J: There's nothing to fear. I wasn't a particularly religious man, but that makes no difference, you can tell them that too – it doesn't matter whether you follow the church or you follow your own pathway really. It's good to know that there isn't an end, I suppose that a thing which crosses your mind. They say your whole life flashes before you, but it doesn't, you know, it doesn't. It's just like waking from a sleep really ... but of course the dream is here, the dream is here and the strange reality is left behind. The what you left behind seems like the dream and where I am now becomes the reality.

L: Yes, funny isn't it. And of course you're at home now – it's me that's away [laughing] that's nice to know, isn't it.

J: That's right, yes, and of course where we are we're free of any pain or illnesses that we had when we were there.

L: Yes, I'm so pleased to meet you, John and thanks for this, that was so kind of you and I wish you well. Maybe we'll speak again.

J: I hope so, Lillie. Goodbye.

Jasper says ....

We are very privileged to have had John tell us in such detail all about his death and the transition to where he is now. The way he described his vacated body as an old suit that you no longer have a use for is a very true comparison. The body is exactly that - an old suit that we grow out of. There is much comfort to be gained from John's words. He confirms that we take with us all the important things in our existence and that which has exceeded it usefulness is left behind.

Ernest's World

[19 January 2009.]

E: I ... I .... [Struggling a little to speak] ... Hello.

L: I'm Lillie, and you're very welcome.

E: Hello Lillie. I'm Ernie ... Ern .... Ernest ... Ern. I had such a headache you know. I was confused for a long time. I was ... I went off to war and ... early really, I was at Dunkirk. It was a bad lot there you know. We were pinned down on the beach. Gerry was shelling us. We managed to make the beach. And we didn't get much further, really.

There were shells exploding all around us. I saw some of my mates go down and ... it was a bad lot really. And then there was this big explosion. Big Bang. And I couldn't see or hear nothing. And I wondered if I was already dead. I was frightened really. Then I could feel, sort of, people touching me, you know. I could feel somebody took my hand and then I don't know how many but they lifted me around the shoulders, you know. And I still couldn't hear. I couldn't see. All I could smell was the smell of ... explosives, you know the smell it makes, and that's all I had – the smell and the touch.

And I wanted to scream out. Maybe I did, I couldn't hear it. I felt completely isolated I couldn't see, I couldn't hear and I didn't know where I was really. All I know is that I wanted it to stop. Or Start. Or whatever it was going to do.

And ... I was having my head bandaged, I could feel someone with a ... wrapping round my head, you know, I could feel it, I could feel the tightness of a bandage wrapping round my head. And I could feel pads on my eyes. I could feel all of that.

I could feel sometimes a bit of rough handling, a bit urgent, you know. And I could feel water under my feet. I was walking but supported on both sides. I could feel my boots filling with water and I could feel the bottom of my trousers wet. And I could feel wet patches on me and pain. I mean, I gathered that was where I was bleeding, I don't know.

And I was in this world of complete darkness and complete silence. And I could feel the water getting a bit deeper and then I could feel I was being held on both sides and supported under the arms. And then I was aware of walking up like a slope, do you know?

L: Yes, I know what you mean.

E: And it was moving so it must have been a boat. And then I was sat down and I couldn't hear nothing. I could feel the boat moving up and down and I could feel the throbbing of the engine. And I felt sick ... and I was sick ... I don't know what happened and then the boat was dancing around, it was rough and I could feel the throbbing of the engine.

Occasionally somebody would nudge me from one side when they sat next to me, and then somebody else would sit next to me, and somebody would trip over my feet. And all of a sudden somebody stuck cigarette in my mouth. And that was good, you know. I took a long draw on the cigarette. At least I could sense that. I could taste it and I could smell it. And occasionally someone would come along and take it out of my mouth and smoke it for me.

And it was a long trip really. It was up and down and rough and I felt sick all the time really. And I thought this must be what I've got now. Or haven't got. And I tried to think ... have I got a family? Have I got mates? Do you know I couldn't even think what my name was. I didn't even know where I was for a minute. I knew it was a boat. I could feel a boat. So I must have known something about a boat, and I knew what cigarette was so I ... I was running all these things through my mind. But my head did hurt, it was throbbing, it was horrible.

And then I could feel like a bump, a couple of big bumps and the boat didn't rock so much then, it was calmer. Then somebody came along again and they got me on either side and they helped me off and again my feet were in water. Then I could feel steps under my feet, a bit slippery. And I could smell fish, a fishy smell. All I could smell was the fishy smell and the diesel, from the engines, and the smell of bodies, you know when people are sweaty and dirty. I could smell that.

And then I thought 'I wonder if there's anybody going to come for me?' And I thought 'I don't know anybody. Who's going to come for me?' I don't know ... must have had a family I figured, everybody's got a family. And I figured, I don't know, someone must come for me.

So then I was helped up in the back of a something ... must have been a lorry. Funny how I could remember things like that.

L: Yes, to remember what a lorry was but not to remember if you had a family.

E: Yes. And I was helped into the back and I could feel it moving up and down and again I could feel people next to me, you know, pushing up next to me. And I felt like there was a lot of people in there. I couldn't see them, couldn't hear them but I could feel that there were a lot of people around me. I didn't feel so frightened. I felt that I was amongst people like me, you know, friends.

And then after a while it stopped. I was helped out again. This time I was put into a chair. A wheelchair, because I was sat down and all of sudden I could feel the gentle movement of the chair as I was moving along, And occasionally somebody would touch my hand and put their hand on my shoulder and all these things I could feel. And I didn't realise how important they were before. When You can see and you can hear it's different. Now this was probably all I'd got. I couldn't think of nothing else really.

And I thought ... it kept going through my mind that I couldn't think of anybody I knew. I couldn't think of any names. I couldn't think of any places. I couldn't think of anything really. I was trying to talk but I couldn't even hear myself talking, I couldn't think of what words I was saying, was I talking gibberish or ... what was I doing, so after a while I didn't bother. I couldn't see the point really.

Then I was in a bed, I could feel myself lying, half lying. Lots of activity going on, I could feel things going on around me. I could feel my clothes being cut off me. I could feel the coldness as the material went. Like when the air gets to you. Lots of attention, I could feel like washing, cleaning. Then I could feel this bandage on my head being unwound and I thought 'That's good, I'll be able to see something. See where I am.'

And I could feel the bandage being unwound and I couldn't see anything. And I put my hand up to my face and it was a mess. Yes, it was a mess. And I couldn't think what I had looked like, I couldn't think what this face was, I couldn't think of what it was. And it was wet ... they took my hand away quickly. I was trying to feel around, but I couldn't make anything out of it really. Just a mess.

And there was a smell now, you know,. Like a clean smell. I could smell fresh linen, like bed linen. It was nice really, it felt quite clean. And I touched it and I could feel it, it was to the touch. And I thought 'Well this is what I've got. I've got to really make the most of it.'

But I couldn't think of who I was supposed to know. I couldn't think of any names. I suppose they were asking me loads of questions but I couldn't hear them. Couldn't see them. I was poked about, had things poked in my ears and I could feel the cleaning and the dressing, and the stitching sometimes I could feel. Needles poked in my arm, pills in my face. Somebody would take a mug of tea and stick it in my two hands and ... strange that I could remember it was tea but I couldn't remember if I knew anyone. Didn't even know where I'd been to get this really ... 'Must have been in some sort of accident,' I thought.

I was always lying down. I wasn't allowed to get up much. I used to lie down all the time and you get used to it after a while. I used to ... I used need to go to the toilet .. you know .. you need to do what you have to do. It was a bit embarrassing at first, then you get used to it. But I could feel gentle touch around me, must have been the nurses, women I should think. These weren't the touches of a heavy man, these were a gentle touch. I just wish I could have seen them and heard them.

And it was just odd really because I tried and tried and tried to think that surely I must know somebody and I figured that somebody must know me. I went on like that and I just got used to it really. I don't know how long it went on for.

Then I was lying down one day and somebody picked my hand up. And this wasn't one of the nurses because the nurses just did what they had to do and moved on. And somebody was holding my hand, my left hand I could feel it. And it was smaller hand than mine. It was woman. And this woman, whoever she was, she was twiddling the ring on my finger and it was funny because I didn't realise I had a ring on that finger. And she was twiddling it around, you know. And then she put her hand into mine, in the palm of my hand and she got my fingers and she had a ring on her finger too. So I must have known ... this must have been ... was this my wife? It must have been, I thought. Must have been.

I wondered what she looked like. I tried to smell, to see if she smelled of anything but all I could smell was the cleanliness of what was around me. And this happened a lot, this unknown woman would sit with me. She's hold my hand and I don't know if she was talking to me. I couldn't hear anything. And she'd sit for a while and then she'd go away again. And I'd get a kiss on my chin and she's go away. I got quite looking forward to it, you know.

Then one day she came and she did like she always did and she put her hand in my hand. Then there was a small one. There was a small hand. And I could feel the little fingers on this hand. The little fingers were playing a little game, like tickling. So I played back. And this little hand was hanging on to my fingers and squeezing them. And next this little person was on me, holding me and cuddling me around the chest. And she must have been ... he or she ... must have been mine. I wondered what her face looked like or his face or ... and this little unknown had long hair in like little ringlets. A girl. It was a girl. I cried you know.

L: Oh did you. [Crying too, and finding it hard to speak]

E: Yes. But I still couldn't think of who it was. So I knew that I had a wife, a daughter and I didn't know anything else really.

Time just went on really. I was moved around occasionally, I was moved from bed to bed. Time wasn't really important really. I didn't know much about it. I just knew that I got fed, I had something to drink. Occasionally I got a cigarette. I had a bottle of beer once or twice. Strange that I could remember all of these things. I could remember what beer was, what a cigarette was ...

L: But you couldn't remember who you were.

E: Couldn't remember any of that. And they'd come around and they'd take the bandages off and they'd change me and put the bandages back on again and then one day they came round and took the bandages off and I was knocked back. There was like a light. I could see light. I could see light.

It knocked me back and I was frightened at first and then I could see bright light flashing backwards and forwards in front of my eyes and I could feel hands moving my head around. I could see this light. It was just light, but I could see it. Then they'd put the bandages back on And this went on and then they'd come and have another look.

Then after a while the bandages didn't go back on. I just had pads, soft pads on my eyes. And the light was getting better. The light was getting better. Next I could make out movement, shadows, shapes. I don't know how long this went on. And then one day I could see colours. I could see colours and this ... she must have been a nurse ... she came towards me and she had white and blue on. But the white was so brilliant white, brilliant white, it was almost painful the brilliant white from it. And I could ... if I really strained I could just make out black hair around her face.

And it slowly got better and then when this lady came in, this one who was my wife, she had a brown coat on. Long brown coat., blonde hair and a hat off to one side.

L: Was she beautiful Ernest?

E: Cor! Best I'd ever seen. And every time she came it got better. Every time she came ... and I could make out all of her features. Then the little girl came and she was lovely too.

And it got as good as it was going to get I supposed, I could see through my right eye, the left eye was just a blur. I was happy with that. And then one day I was got out of bed and I was walked out of the hospital. Big place, never really looked around it before. Lots of beds with people in. Some bandaged up, some with their legs up in the air. I was walked through that lot and I could see the nurses and some of them came up and shook my hand. Some patted me on the back.

And there was a man there, I don't know who he was. Soldier he was. He was in uniform, he had a khaki uniform on. And he put a big coat around my shoulders, great big heavy coat, didn't put my arms in it, big heavy coat. He took me outside and sat me in this car. I sat in it and it was all bright. I'd never seen such brightness outside before. He lit me a cigarette and I smoked it and we went along for a while. I looked around me but of course I didn't know what I was looking at really.

Then we came to this little house, red bricks, a nice wooden front door, a few flowers in the garden at the front. And when we went to the door, this soldier, this man walked me up to the door, and the door opened and there was this lady and the little girl. He shook my hand and left me at the door.

And the lady, my wife, took me in. Of course I still didn't know who they were, really. And I looked all around me, searching for something familiar. But I didn't know any of it, you know. I knew this woman must have been my wife and this little girl must have been mine, but apart from that I didn't know any more.

And I sat down and the little girl brought me a big cake and she cut me a piece off and gave it to me on a plate, and it was sweet, you know, it was lovely. And I had a cup tea, too. And I could see them talking to me but I couldn't hear them. Never did hear them, you know. Never did hear them.

And my eyes were alright, well one of them was and I got fitted with glasses and I could see a lot better. I couldn't see a lot of things but I could see a lot better. And I could see the face of this woman who was my wife and I could see this girl.

And they would write things on paper for me. Funny how I could still read though. So I learned that my wife was called Mary, because they wrote lots of things to me. Mary, and the little girl was called Susan. And that was it really.

People would come and see me and I used to get a hug and a kiss and a pat on the back, all of that, but I didn't know any of them. And then the biggest shock was when I looked in the mirror for the first time, I wasn't half the mess that I thought I was really, I mean it was a mess but ... didn't make any difference, I didn't know who it was anyway.

L: Ernest, weren't you lucky in your choice of wife.

E: Yes. I wish I could have heard them though, when I was there. And do you know that was my life then. But you know I thought of how lucky I was. Then we got old together and my daughter grew up and she had a family of her own and it was nice really. But I thought of how lucky I was and how all these things were so precious.

L: It shows what's really important, doesn't it.

E: Yes, it really does. It was a shock really when I finally died because then all of a sudden it was all there. I could see it and hear it and all of that came back. Really strange.

L: How old were you, when it happened, at Dunkirk?

E: I've no idea, it's one of those things that's not important. I've seen my mates since and they were young lads you know, all like me really. I went back and looked at it, you know. Well I had to see it. I had to see it. Sometimes you have to fill in the bits. I looked at where the beach was. I looked at where the boats came in on the other side. I'm glad I did but of course it doesn't matter.

But do you know what - I've got great grandchildren now, on your side, and I go and listen to them. I'm catching up on all that I didn't have, I listen to them.

L: Is Susan with you where you are now?

E: Yes.

L: So you can hear Susan now?

E: Yes.

L: And Mary?

E: Yes. And do you know it doesn't matter what you've got as long as you make the most of it.

L: You know, Ernest I really appreciate you telling me this. [Crying now, as I have been throughout] what a wonderful thing.

E: That's all right.

L: Please give my regards to the lovely Mary and the lovely Susan. What a wonderful thing that was.

E: Well I thought you'd like to know.

L: So beautiful, one of the most beautiful things I've ever heard. Thank you so much. Any time you want to call back and let me know how you're all doing I would appreciate that. You stay together and look after each other.

E: We will.

Jasper says ...

All life is so precious and it is very difficult to imagine that a body so broken or ravaged by illness or deformity still has a consciousness within it. Often the body is left and disregarded because the doctors and carers cannot communicate with the life inside and consider that the body is dead and they think that it is just the body functions that still function until their final demise.

Ernest thought that death had come to him. His senses were diminished, his sight, his hearing but most of all his memory had almost gone from him. But as Ernest became more aware of the senses that he still had left he began to build a mental picture of who and what he really was. The courage of accepting what he had and not grieving for what he no longer had, together with the love of his family helped him to carry on living.

Life continues under such extreme circumstances but it is coming to terms with what you have, no matter how little that may be, that makes the difference between living and just existing. Ernest has it all now where he is, but the experience of what he lived without for so long has made him understand what he now has and he knows that this time he will keep it all forever.

TRUE MEANINGS

By bringing you the words of those who have spoken to us from the other side, hopefully we can help you to understand a little more about the natural cycle of life and death. But in order to help you understand we need to unravel the tangled mess that a number of business practitioners have made with the jargon they use.

Life and death is big business. Many profit from it and many charlatans include themselves in the industries which surround it. Many involve themselves in the area of self-help, therapies, cures and analysis and there are a variety of consultants who claim to be able to perform the most astounding tricks and miracles, for a price.

These practitioners use fashionable words to impress. Many use perfectly good words which had a very clear meaning when they were first used, but now these people use them in the wrong way. They have changed their real meaning out of all recognition. Thus we can no longer use them to describe what we do. We can no longer use words like medium, channelling, spirit, spirit realm and veil.

To distance ourselves from others (and to make it plain what we mean) we have decided to use our own vocabulary in all of our work.

Our Vocabulary

As Jasper has said you will get as much, or as little, as you wish from this book and even if you are only reading it for its sensationalism I hope you still take something from it. By understanding our terms and what they really mean you will get a lot of knowledge from the book. It's up to you.

Our words and terms are in bold and below that are the [present day definitions] and finally an explanation, if needed.

The Solid Layer

[The earth plane, the earth, the material world]
Where you are now, as you read this.

The Etheric Layer

[Known as heaven - and many other religious titles, the afterlife, the spirit realm]
Where we go when we die. Where Jasper is speaking from.

The Curtain

[The veil]
This is the thin gossamer veil between the two layers.

Judgement

[Some man-made religions call this the day of reckoning. Most in the solid layer accept the fact that you have to pay for crimes committed in the solid layer during their lifetime.]

Explanation: Everyone is responsible for their actions and accountable for them. Those who have committed severe crimes in the etheric layer, when they die, are immediately taken for judgement and dealt with accordingly. For the majority, they join their loved ones and friends already in the etheric layer and await the arrival of the rest of the 'group'. Once all are assembled then each individual goes forward for judgement. This is a two-tiered process. Firstly they are evaluated on their actions in the solid life just gone, and then the other lives they have had are returned to them and the judgement is based on the entirety. A small misdemeanour in the last life could be overlooked based on their total lives, but also a small misdemeanour could be amplified by the fact that that person had repeatedly made the same mistake in other lives. Previous lives could never compensate for callously and without any mitigating circumstances taking the life of another in the last.

Crime and Punishment

[Added to this section by way of explanation, but the words have the same meaning in both layers. In the etheric layer it is more just and manipulation is not possible.]

Explanation: It is not possible to hide anything we did in the solid layer from those who make the decisions at the point of judgement. The punishments vary and are always just and logical. One example is that a serial killer would be made to face his victims and then he would be made to feel the same pain and fear that all of his victims had felt. His terrifying experience would not end as quickly as that of his victims did. Anything which takes place behind closed doors in the solid layer is seen from the etheric layer. There are no secrets and everyone is completely accountable for their actions.

Time

Time - one short word which means so much in the solid layer and yet it is irrelevant in the etheric layer almost to the point of not existing at all.

Time in the solid layer is defined by a calendar and a clock. Both are related to the rising and setting of the sun each day. The way we use time depends upon what we are doing with our life – time to sleep or wake, time to start daily employment, time to be at a pre-arranged appointment, time to take a form of transport or to watch something on TV. When you are not working then time does not matter so much – those who do not work find that time drags on and often are not even aware of what day it is. Time only becomes important if you need to be somewhere, or do something at a certain time.

In the etheric layer there is no 'time'. They are aware of a sequence, an order of events – more in a non-specific 'past, present and future' way, but they do not experience time. They do not need to sleep and so they do not need to wake, they do not need appointments and they do not need diaries or calendars. They watch us and so they are aware that our time passes for us and they see us aging, but other than that they have no real notion of it.

When a loved one dies and leaves the solid layer we are very aware of how the time without them passes. We mark the anniversary of their death and we note our own birthdays, annual festivals and specific dates, all of which remind us constantly of how long they have been away from us. But when it is our time to cross the curtain and join them they will welcome us as though very little time has passed since we were last together – and for them it is true.

And don't forget it is they who are 'at home' and you who is currently away for a 'short time'. We all started in the etheric layer and came here – so when we leave here we are returning home, where our loved ones and friends who left the solid layer before us will welcome us and help us to settle back in.

A Being, Beings

[Man, a person, a spirit, a soul]
Being is the term used for all intelligent life-forms, solid or etheric. Animals are of a lesser intelligence and not beings. Your loved ones in the etheric layer are beings, you are a being.

Elevated Beings

Although the majority of those in the etheric layer are standard, simple beings who are still very much part of the reincarnation cycle there are also Elevated Beings in the etheric layer who have much true knowledge and certain skills and abilities. They are mentors, knowledge-givers and sometimes healers. They work towards becoming a Higher Being.

Higher Beings

These are beings who have attained and shared much knowledge and whose actions have touched and helped many, whose motives are pure and whose actions are always compassionate. They have many skills and abilities. Jasper is a Higher Being.

The Cycle of Existence

To put these words into use and by way of simplifying the cycle of existence, I have used an average life cycle as an example.

A being leaves the etheric layer and is born as a being in the solid layer. He has no memory of his previous lives. Where he is born is pure chance. He has not pre-selected anything about his location or situation.

He grows from baby, through childhood and into adulthood. He walks as a solid being in the solid layer for the duration of his lifetime.

At his death he makes the transition to the etheric layer, passing through the curtain, and he becomes an etheric being in the etheric layer. If he were a serious criminal he would be separated immediately and punished - otherwise he joins his loved ones and friends already in the etheric layer.

Whilst getting on with his existence in the etheric layer he stays close to the curtain and can see and hear those still in the solid layer. In time the rest of his loved ones and friends will join him.

Once all of his loved ones are with him in the etheric layer they are together for a period. Then it is decided by Higher Beings at the time of judgement if he should be punished, or if all is well it is decided if he needs to return to the solid layer. (For this example let us say he returns.)

An etheric being then leaves the etheric layer and is born as a solid being in the solid layer. He has no memory of his previous lives. Where he is born is pure chance. He has not pre-selected anything about his location or his situation.

... and so the cycle of existence continues until, finally, during judgement the being could be raised to the status of an Elevated Being at which point he would work towards becoming a Higher Being. Existence continues and each level is always striving to better themselves by making a difference to others, and whatever the level beings have attained they never stop seeking knowledge.

Where We Stand

This would seem to be a good place to let you know exactly where we (Ernest and myself) stand on the subject of religious organisations, religious groups and the industry and commercial marketing of the paranormal. The following statement applies to all of our written work and makes it clear who we are and where we stand, for now and the future, even after our deaths.

Statement

Ernest and I are not members of any religious group or spiritual organisation. We do not follow any man-made spiritual guidelines or religious doctrines. We do not promote a belief system nor ask that any join with us or follow us. We do not associate ourselves with any mediums, paranormal or psychic groups or business organisations of any kind.

We are not associated with any religions, individuals, groups or organisations who are interested in the subject of Outer Space or UFO's, nor do we subscribe to any of the many conspiracy theories and fantasies which have come from over-active imaginations. We prefer fact and science to theory and supposition.

Jasper is not a god, he does not wish to be worshipped now or at any time in the future. Jasper is a provider of information. During Ernest's lifetime Jasper speaks through Ernest and during my lifetime I act as a scribe to get the information to you. When Ernest and I die Jasper will stop speaking to the Earth. Neither Ernest or I will speak from the etheric layer. We will never appoint others to speak on our behalf from the etheric layer and anyone using our names for validation should not be trusted.

Thus no-one in the future can claim to be channelling our messages and profit from it. All of the knowledge Jasper has to give will be published in my lifetime and any new information published after my death should not be trusted.

Only exact reprints of the original works should ever be trusted. If others in the future begin to re-write or revise the knowledge then it will change the information given to the presumptions and assumptions of others, who do not have the knowledge we are privileged to have. We have written all of our work in simple terms to avoid the need for 'experts' to re-interpret 'what we meant'.

Our words are simple, unambiguous and it should be obvious what we mean. Analysis should not be necessary.
Lillie Whittle.

WHO IS JASPER?

I asked Jasper to answer that question himself.

Jasper says ...

When I walked as Jasper I was born on a small farm near Lille in France, where I lived with my mother, father and brother. Life was hard enough but we always just managed to survive. I remember my last look back at the farm with its fields devoid of any useful crops or means to support us all. As did many others, our family went in search of food and employment. I was just a child.

The feeling of poverty and tension was all around us as we found ourselves in Paris. I did not understand what was really going on but the times became very uneasy with angry gatherings on many street corners. I later learned that I had lived through the time known as the French Revolution.

The following years on the streets, living by any means that we could, saw the disappearance of both my mother and father. They left us one day to go in search of food and they did not return. My brother and I were left to fend for ourselves, not knowing of their fate.

The coming of war was a turning point for us both. We both found ourselves in Napoleon's army and for the first time in our lives we had enough food, warm clothing and companionship. Sadly we were soon separated as we were both sent to separate units. I never saw my brother again in the solid layer, or knew of his fate.

I do not wish to recount my war years as I am ashamed of the total disregard for life that all wars bring, with this one as no exception. After the war the broken and beaten army returned to much the same conditions they had left years before. I found myself back on the streets again as a beggar, ignored by the very people that I had been fighting for.

After what seemed an endless time on the streets I was taken in by a kind person who owned and ran a theatre. I was introduced to the theatre that would become my home and the performers who would become my family for the rest of my life. The theatre was magnificent, it towered above in all its splendour. I very rarely left my 'home' as this was the best and safest place I had ever been and with the wonderful people who worked there I felt that I finally belonged somewhere.

I worked hard with whatever job I was given to keep my home in good order, scene painting, cleaning, mending, tending to the lamps and many other tasks. My 'family' were wonderful kind people all of who were like me, thankful to finally belong. Many hid behind their face paint and costumes and nobody ever seemed to want to talk about their past. What was important was now, nothing else. I made myself comfortable by sleeping on the piles of curtains at the back of the stage. It was often so cold but at least this was my private area.

We all ate and drank together. If the production had been successful the food and wine was good and plentiful. Mr Robert, the owner, was good to us - we had a little money for our efforts and we wanted for nothing. If the production had been less than successful we managed as best we could, knowing that the next one would be better. The smell of the bakery next to the theatre often filled the air with a wonderful mixture and even if we could not always afford to buy we were often given what was left over and could not be sold.

It was in the theatre I first noticed people Yes of course I had always noticed people but now I began to find that I really came to understand them. I could read their moods, their happiness, sadness, truth and lies - all of this came by looking into the faces of the audience. I came to love people and welcomed any time that I could spend with them.

My time had always been spent when the house was full, working behind the scenes, doing all of the things that were not noticed so that I had to look at my people from behind the closed stage curtains. Then one day (I have never been quite sure how I was talked into doing it, maybe it was too much wine the previous night) I found that I had been talked into taking the place of one of the performers who had hastily left the theatre. I was to take the costume of a harlequin.

I was Jasper, the harlequin with no experience, no confidence and an ill fitting costume. 'You will be great' they said,' just go out and fill-in between the scenes, you will think of something.' I tried to think of all of the things I had seen the other performers do.

Then all at once I was on the stage. I juggled, I sang ridiculous songs and generally made a fool of myself. It all seemed a blur and I thought what an idiot I must be. But then I looked out for the first time at the faces (this time from the stage itself with its curtains open) and people were laughing, smiling, children were pointing and sniggering into their hands. At the end of each performance the audience shouted and clapped. From this point on I really became 'Jasper the Harlequin' who filled-in between scenes.

I still managed to carry out my other work behind the scenes but for five or six times each night I was the one to hold the audiences attention. I never looked back. After making the costume a better fit and more comfortable I began to make the character my own. I must make it clear however that I was a serious artiste and never a clown.

The rest of my days in the theatre were as Jasper the Harlequin. Over the years the part grew and people actually came to see me and on a number of occasions artists came to sketch and draw me. My observation and love for people grew I became to think of them all as my friends and family.

After each performance, with all of the lamps out, I would return to my lonely existence and my pile of curtains backstage. I was the only one who lived in the theatre when everyone else had gone to their homes. But the monkeys and various animals that were used in some of the performances were company, even if they did not make great conversation.

Then I met Antoinette, a lady dancer who seemed lonely and lost. We became friends and then in what seemed to me great haste (again probably caused by too much wine the night before) we were married. I had a wife. But a few weeks later she was gone, I later found that she was a friend to most of the men in the theatre and probably a large part of the male audiences as well. She was gone. I missed her for a while but soon settled back into my solitary life with only the animals for company, but at least the monkeys treated each other better than my wife had treated me and their moral standards were higher.

The years went by and I was happier than I had ever been. I had everything that I wanted. The nights seemed colder and my body became slower, but I had the people that I had come to belong with, my friends all of them. I never lost my love for people and life. Each night brought restful sleep until the final night when the peaceful sleep brought me death.

I awoke from what seemed like a long sleep and the first thing that I noticed was that the pains of age and illness had left me. I felt refreshed and vibrant. I looked up at the figure standing over me and he was no stranger. It was the one who you know as Ernest in his current life, through whom I speak now. He held out his hand (as I had done for him so many times before) and we walked away together. Only once did I glance back at the lifeless frame that had served me for so long.

Ernest led me by the hand to a beautiful garden were we sat and talked, unaffected by time or any other influences. I felt at ease as we discussed my latest journey through the solid layer. I knew that he and I had done this many times before, but neither of us spoke of it at that point.

My 'new life' felt so peaceful and I found that my very being craved for nothing that I had left behind in the solid layer. However, just recounting old memories from my last incarnation was enough to bring all of the sensations back to me with everything as real as it was then. I could still taste the wine, smell the perfumes and see the colours. But here I had the choice to remember, and so re-live, as little or as much as I wanted. I could remember any period of my life as Jasper and it was as if I was there once more.

I became reacquainted with old friends, Ernest amongst them, and family. All around was the feeling of tranquillity and a full sense of belonging as I made myself comfortable with all that had happened to me during my recent time in the solid layer.

Then, because I am a Higher Being, I had returned to me all of the knowledge from all of my previous incarnations. The memories and knowledge of 'Jasper the Harlequin' have been added to them and I now *exist as the Higher Being that I truly am, the being who is the total sum of all of my solid and etheric existences.*

Ernest (as he is known in his current life) and I have been together for a very long time and for many solid and etheric lifetimes. We have been together since the first time we walked as solid people long, long ago. Our pathway is still long and we have much more to achieve. We will continue to work together for the betterment and enlightenment of all.

I am a Higher Being. I am not a god, I am not sent by a god and I am not associated with a god of any kind. I am a Higher Being simply because of the amount of knowledge I have gained in the very long time I have existed, and because some of my actions during my very long journey through time have made a difference to others in a positive way. There are different levels of Higher Being and we all continue to work hard towards moving to the next level. The levels are endless.

Sometimes Higher Beings walk as solid people for a purpose and so it was when I walked as Jasper. Ernest and I had a purpose then (with him at that time in the etheric layer) and we have a purpose now. This time he is the one in the solid layer with only his current memories. He does not have our great wealth of knowledge where he is now – he knows only that which I release to him and Lillie. They will both regain their full knowledge when they finish their work here and re-join me.

Where I am now, in the etheric layer I have as little or as much as I need to exist. I choose to use my last incarnation as a harlequin to bring you this information as this is how I feel you will be the most comfortable. I hope you think of me as Jasper.

I have all that I need and want for nothing. The knowledge that I have at my disposal is everything to me, I will never stop learning. I have a compassion for all living things and treat them all with equal respect. I meet old friends from the past and we are able to relive events that we encountered together. I can place myself in my theatre although its solid existence is long gone. I can walk in Ancient Greece with old friends. I can experience all of the senses that I had as a solid person. Even with all of this at my disposal I do not need any of it as my very existence with my friends is enough and my constant learning drives me on.

I mentioned that Ernest and I have a purpose now and you might ask what that purpose is.

You are reading it. [ENDS]

I am sorry that we do not have the time for you to get to know Jasper in the same way that I did.

First I got to know 'Jasper the Harlequin.' I got to know the Frenchman who lived in Paris in his theatre. He is naturally funny. He has superb timing and his delivery in certain situations is really unexpected and highly amusing. I laughed so much in those first few months and I had hoped to recount some of the amusing things which happened, but the serious nature of this work means it will not be possible. Maybe in the future I will be able to share those times with you.

Then I got to know Jasper the etheric being. This Jasper is compassionate and kind and warm. He has helped me and comforted me through some times of great personal trauma and distress. He has never once let me down and (of course along with Ernest) Jasper is the one I trust above all others.

Next I discovered Jasper the Higher Being. This Jasper gives me his gift of great knowledge and he gives it willingly and with such skill. He brings Elevated Beings and other Higher Beings to speak to me on such a diversity of subjects. They all speak with the wisdom of age, with truth and knowledge. Because of Jasper I get science and fact, not fantasies, conspiracy theories and fiction. Each new piece of this information I receive is more wonderful than the last and each new piece makes me yearn for the next.

As Jasper and I have got to know each other we have become more comfortable with each other. What started out as a rather strange situation has become natural for me now. I feel I live with both Jasper and Ernest and I'm happy with that. They have been friends for such a long time and it is a privilege to be included, even for this comparatively short time.

We laugh a lot, our work is so emotional that we cry a lot, and we are always talking to each other in one way or another. We share everything.

When I think of this Frenchman, this harlequin, this etheric being, this Higher Being - I think of him as just 'Jasper'. He is all of these things. But to me, above all, he is my friend.

YOUR QUESTIONS ANSWERED

When a friend or a loved one dies the sense of loss is terrible. Even knowing what we know Ernest and I still grieve when our own friends and family die. Although we know that they are safe and that they are where they should be, we still miss the physical presence of having that solid person in our lives.

When people die it is those left behind who need the most help and comfort. Whatever painful illness they watched their loved one suffer, or whatever accident or event took their loved one away, all of that has now ended and their loved one is recovered and well again. It is those left behind who are still suffering and in pain. If those left behind know the facts of where there loved ones are, then they can start to come to terms with what has happened.

What happens when we die has always been life's great mystery. But it shouldn't be a mystery. If you understand death, then in understanding that, you begin to understand more about life itself. Death is part of a natural cycle.

Nature has always had its cycles, think of the trees that 'live' and 'die' with the seasons. And so we should understand the cycle of our own life and death, it's just another part of the same science. It's the science of nature and it's a natural occurrence.

There are a number of questions which we have been asked often, and they all relate to the subject of life after death. I have asked Jasper to give us answers on the following questions, all of which, over time, have been asked of us by the grieving, the uninformed or the curious.

The Etheric Layer

Q: What does it look like there? Where is it? Do I go there in my dreams? If so many people have died over such a long time, how do they all fit in there?

Jasper replies ...

There are many questions that always trouble mankind but the most asked questions are always about death and the 'afterlife'. So what is death? To understand that you should first ask 'What is life?'

Everyone knows what life is - it is what you are experiencing now at this very moment as you are reading this book. Life is thinking, moving, loving, hating, breathing and so on and so on, I could go on to describe all of the things that make you alive. But although I am what you would call dead I still experience most of these things, these things that we have just described as being a sign of being alive.

I am dead, of that I have no doubt. When my body ceased to function and would no longer contain the spirit that is my true being, I walked away from that body, leaving behind all of the things that the body needed, along with all of the things that made it uncomfortable such as age, illness, hunger and pain, to name but a few. The body was dead and useless, but my spirit, the true me, has always been 'alive' and will continue to be so. Life does not end at the graveside. Life is eternal. So you see death is no more than a phase in our existence, our life. Death is a step on the pathway that leads on.

So, I am dead, but I still experience most of the things that I did when my body walked the earth. I still have all of the important things, all that I need, I want for nothing.

So where am I? Am I up in the clouds? Am I in some form of religious heaven looking down upon you? No, none of these. These lofty 'heavenly' places do not exist. I am where I have always been - right here in the same place as you, but with just a very thin curtain, a veil, between us. My etheric existence is such that only a very few gifted beings with the ability to communicate with both sides of the curtain can see and fully communicate with me and all of my companions here in the etheric layer.

How does it look? It looks much the same as where you are looks to you. I can see all that you see. I can hear what you hear. All of these experiences are still mine. Because I have elevated to a Higher Being, if I so desire I can put myself, using my consciousness, anywhere that I have been in any of my many past lives. I can relive experiences, I can still taste a glass of wine I once had. In fact all of my past experiences I can recall and experience. But I do not wish to. I have risen above the needs that where of the body. What I have cannot be compared to any such mediocre experiences. Even those in the etheric layer who currently have the memory of only their last material lifetime do not need to constantly relive their experiences as a solid being – there is too much anew here for them to experience.

I am familiar with this misconception that there would not be room here for all of those who have died. The etheric layer existed first - long before any solid being of any kind walked upon the earth or any other planet. We all need knowledge, it is this that makes us what we are and drives us on. We all began life in the etheric layer - there have been no more and no less, the number that exists has always been the same – it is just the number of solid beings in existence at any one time that fluctuates. So the etheric layer will never be overfilled, there will always be room for your return, but I am afraid you will have to wait until you have lived your current cycle.

There will be no sneak previews or little forays into the etheric layer to check up on your dear departed or to gain advice or anything else while your body sleeps. Dreams are dreams, nothing more, and you stay exactly where you are for the duration of your sleep. Anyone talking to you is talking using the words from your own imagination. Dreams come from you – not elsewhere.

People in the Etheric Layer

Q: What do they do all day? What do they look like if they've left their bodies behind? How do they recognise each other and will we recognise our loved ones when we get there? How do their needs change? Do they still need food, drugs, alcohol and sex? Do they miss us? Do they change when they die – are their characters, beliefs, temperaments different? What signs can I expect to receive from them? Can they make sounds, move objects and appear to me? Do they know when we think of them? Can they see us? Can they hear us? What about class, colour, wealth, status? What about relationships – what if I marry twice, who will I be with? What about homosexuals? The last words we spoke were harsh – will they remember?

Jasper replies ...

What do we do all day? Where I am we have no need to be controlled by time. A day, a week, a year, have no relevance. We are, however, aware of how much time passes for you because we watch you grow and age and we know when you will be making the journey to join us. My 'time' is taken up by my work. I like to seek out new knowledge and refresh my interest in old knowledge. I like to read ancient writings. Most of my 'time' at the moment is devoted to the work of bringing knowledge to the solid layer through my friend and relay, Ernest.

But what we do in the etheric layer is a matter of personal choice. Every being has that. We can choose to do as little or as much as we wish. But there is so much to learn and experience here that very few are idle. Those who have made the crossing recently like to stay close to the loved ones they have left behind on the other side of the curtain, some like to observe their old surroundings for a while. Most like to renew old acquaintances and seek out those who have arrived before them. Those who have committed serious crimes in the solid layer will have none of this freedom and do not join the others. They are held elsewhere and wait to face judgement before a decision is made as to where they go, or I should say where they are taken.

Everyone recognises each other. The body is just a vehicle, a container for the spirit. The physical appearance is not important here. We can recognise each other by the individual unique signature that each being emits. When a being enters the etheric layer those who are already here greet them with the appearance of what they looked like when they were last seen by the new arrival - so that for newcomers it is easy to identify their loved ones and friends from the physical appearance they expect to see.

Here our 'needs' are very different from those of the solid body. Of course we no longer need anything that just the body needed, but we do bring with us all of the things that the consciousness needed - memories, experiences, emotions and knowledge. Everyone here can still recall and relive experiences from their most recent solid incarnation and there are a small percentage of Elevated Beings who can also recall all of their previous ones too.

Many in the etheric layer have just the memories of their recent solid lifetime and they remain in characteristic and temperament the same here as they were in the solid layer. If they loved a certain person and disliked another that stays with them and they still feel the same. If they were grumpy or unemotional in their past life they will still be the same here.

Once judgement takes place and any crimes committed in the last life are faced and dealt with, then that person is given back all of their previous lives and becomes the sum total of what that being actually is – with all of their lifetimes of emotions and experiences. Then many of the characteristics remain but are diluted, and any anger or negative attitude which might have been caused by a certain set of recent material circumstances will be diluted by the happiness and the knowledge that they found in all of their other existences and the being becomes the sum total of all of their lives to date. That being, then, and only then, is the true being.

We have no bodily needs - we do not need food, drink, drugs, alcohol or any other stimulants here. Addiction to drugs or alcohol is of the body and once they are here they soon learn that they no longer need them. They are helped in this. The body, in solid form, experiences many sensations that cause pleasure. I refer to the intimacy that takes place between one being and another. The physical side of this intimacy does not exist here but the experiences to be gained in the etheric layer far exceed anything that can be experienced in solid form. True love stays with the being forever and is never lost. Lust is an animal instinct and not relevant to us here.

Of course, when people first cross the curtain they too miss the solid presence of those they have left behind but a being here soon becomes accustomed to their new existence and accepts where they are - and of course here we all know what you have to look forward to, whereas those in the solid layer still feel the loss and some who are not so well-informed still find death itself a mystery, which adds to their grief.

Ah, yes, the signs. There are many myths surrounding the so-called signs that those in the etheric layer use to communicate. I am sorry to inform you that there are no signs, just non-related coincidences. You can make anything you like into a sign. A small bird that flies into your house just after your father has died – that must be him letting you know that he is alright? Not so. This has probably happened many times before and you have just not noticed it. A rainbow in the sky just after your child has passed over – this must be her? Not so - just a rainbow caused by the play of light through moisture in the air. The noises in the house just after a death of a loved one are probably just pipes or the building creaking as it expands and contracts. Those flickering lights are probably a sign of a fault that should be attended to. And of course my own favourite the white feather - this must of course be from a guardian angel? Most definitely not. Just the result of something simple, like a conflict between two birds. What I am trying to say is that you can make a sign out of the most common of things - it is because you are low after a loss of a loved one you will clutch onto anything that will comfort.

Your loved ones in the etheric layer have just undergone a transition, but they have not gone from you. They can still see and hear you, they feel your emotions and yes they do know when you are thinking of them. It may be hard to accept but they are as close to you as they have ever been.

Class, colour, race, wealth and status - all of the things that are man-made and which cause such division, persecution and a lack of caring have no relevance here. We are all as equal as the next being.

Any relationships formed in the solid layer can continue and many beings do stay together but again this is the choice of the individual. If you have married twice on the solid side and a death of the first was not a factor then you have already made one choice - so it should be easy to choose again. But this is for you decide. When the first partner died and a second was taken then remember that those on this side understand the need for companionship and would not have wanted their loved one to be lonely. They understand and know everything you feel. All of the options are there for you, but remember marriage is made by man for the solid side. You do not need a piece of paper to show commitment on this side.

Love is love. It makes no difference if your love was for one of the same gender, it has no relevance. The feelings between beings are what are important, not the man made prejudices that have been built around what are (quite wrongly) considered unnatural relationships. If you truly love another being it does not matter about gender. It is for those without understanding to condemn and persecute - none of us here would do so.

Final words? It is often the case that you are too late to reach the bedside of your loved one and there are always endless words that you feel you would have liked to have said before that final moment. Or you may have said too much, maybe your last words were harsh ones said from behind your mask of tears and sadness. Maybe your loved one died in an unexpected and sudden way and you did not have the time for any 'last words'. Or maybe the harsh words were intended, it could have been your last chance to tell them just how much they had hurt or abused you. But it is not too late, even after the body has taken its last breath. Your departed do hear you, do not be afraid to say what you have to say – they hear, even although a long time may have passed since their departure. Tell them those words that mean so much or if they have hurt you then tell them how you feel about them. No one will stop you from saying what you feel. You do not have to forgive an abuser just because their body is dead. Religion teaches forgiveness but why should you *forgive? Judgement is not yours alone, but your words are unique to you so use them as you will. They hear.*

Children in the Etheric Layer

Q: Do they age? Do they grow up? Do they miss us? How will my child look when I get there? Will my child remember who I am? Will my child recognise me? Is my child happy? Is my child lonely?

Jasper replies ...

The spirit is without age, it is only the solid body that shows the signs of aging. If you have lost a child you must understand that the child has returned to what he/she really is – an etheric being. They are free from age and illness or whatever else may have taken them across the divide. But they will not ever be far from you, they will feel your love and your emotions. When it is your time to cross the curtain you will see your child as you last saw them. Sometimes, however, an individual may have envisaged what their child would have been like had they grown and then this is how they will be seen. Your child will appear in the form that most comforts you. Your child will of course recognise you because they have not been away from you. Many of your years may have passed before you meet again but your child has been in good company with those loved ones and friends who were there to meet them when they left you behind. They have known happiness but now they can share this again with you.

Not all however parted with their children in a loving way. The spirit enters the human body at the point of conception. From this point onwards it is alive, despite what 'experts' may tell you. The sexual act between two people brings pleasure but the primary result of this act of animal instinct is to produce offspring. The moral of the story is that if you do not wish to produce children then suitable precautions should be taken. This is the twenty first century - even the lowest of intellect should know that if you have sexual contact you will probably start the cycle of life and produce a child.

You have options, you can either prevent conception by artificial means (although some religions quite wrongly condemn this), or you can refrain from sexual contact if you are not able to accept the responsibility that goes with it. But once you have produced a life you can go either care for it or you can take the option of committing murder and taking the life of another living being.

The choice is yours. But, be warned, if you do take the second selfish option be prepared for what you will face when you arrive in the etheric layer. Not for you the love of a child that you have grieved for and longed to meet again, instead that 'child' will be there to meet you and ask you why you thought that you had the right to deny him or her the gift of life and a solid existence. You will be judged and you will face punishment, only then will your unwanted child be vindicated and ready to take the journey into the solid layer that you decided should be halted.

The Point of Death

Q: Does it hurt? Did they suffer? Were they afraid? Is the funeral important to them? Are ceremonies and rites and rituals important? Believer v non-believer, does it make a difference?

Jasper replies ...

Death is the great unknown and it would be a lie to say that when facing it the uninformed will not be afraid. Death manifests itself in many ways, some will die in their sleep and awake to their new existence without any pain, others will suffer greatly but at the very point of transition all pain, all suffering, all anxiety and fear, all doubt will be gone. It is the same for all. Pain is of the body and dies with it. When a person dies they will immediately have their answer – that death is not the end.

Funerals, remembrance services and ceremonies are only important for those left behind and the dead of body do not need this. It is an aid to grieving and shows respect and compassion for the loved ones left behind, but to the one now in the etheric layer the funeral is of no value.

Be you religious or a non-believer the curtain will be lifted for all to enter and embrace their continued existence. Once through all co-exist together in the peace and harmony which we experience in the etheric layer, which some man-made religions do not encourage in the solid layer.

Crime and Punishment

Q: Are we being punished in this life for something we did in a previous life? Will I be punished for something I did in this life when I get to the etheric layer? Someone I love was killed by someone who got away with it, is there such a thing as a perfect crime? People here lie and evade punishment for crimes they have committed, can that happen in the etheric layer? Should we forgive people on this side and are they forgiven on the other?

Jasper replies ...

Existence began in spirit, in the etheric layer, and will return and continue there. We are all given an allocated time to walk as a solid being in order to learn and gather knowledge and understanding. Some learn all that they have to learn in just one visit and others return to the solid layer time and time again until they have finally understood what it is that they need to enable that move to another level (which is the goal of all.) Each life is individual and we all have the responsibility to make of it what we will.

You are here to learn but you are not being punished for anything which took place in a previous life. Judgement takes place in the etheric layer after each visit to the solid layer. Then, after you have faced any punishment necessary (if needed) then you are ready to return once again to the solid layer - if it is found that you must do so. At the point of judgement you are shown all else that you have been and then you experience all of your total existence. But then, all of those memories stay behind as you, once more, make your journey to the solid layer. You take the first available place and you live a new solid lifetime without any of the knowledge you have amassed up to that point from other lives. You are free to try again. It is what you do during your time in the solid layer that you are judged upon.

Punishment in the solid layer is often unjust and does not fit the crime. A murderer or child abuser may feel that he has got away with a light sentence and the loved one of a victim may feel that justice has not been done. But justice and punishment on each side of the curtain is not the same. The murderer may have lied and had enough money or contacts to buy his way to freedom and relax thinking that he has got away with the crime - but I can tell you that we in the etheric layer see everything and that murderer, child abuser and all of their accomplices will be judged and punished. There is no escape for whatever crime is committed.

The taking of any life is wrong and anyone doing so will be punished. Even if the life is your own you still do not have the right to terminate it. We all have a predetermined time to walk in the solid layer, we have been given the gift of life, and a gift it is. Some would consider that to commit suicide is the final answer and the end to all problems, but this selfish act will have far reaching consequences for those left behind. Taking a life is the ultimate crime. Life is a gift that must be cherished and honoured - it is not ours to take away just because it was an easy option. Taking your own life will not speed you on to the next life, far from it, it will hold you in isolation away from the loved ones that you have not earned the right to join until the natural time of what would have been your passing occurs in solid layer time. You will have to answer for the committing of the crime the same as any other murderer. Euthanasia is not a 'kind option', it is often used to relieve the carers, not the sufferer, and whatever the motive - it is murder. The punishment is not for my comment.

Reincarnation

Q: What is it? Do we choose our lives and where we are born, and to whom? Are we affected (in the solid layer) by previous lives in any way? Do we decide on a pathway for this life before we come here?

Jasper replies ...

Reincarnation is embraced by some cultures and condemned by others. But it is true, it is a fact. We all have lessons to learn, we all gather knowledge and experiences, we must do this before we can move on to the next level of existence. Each life in the solid layer is individual. One solid life has no relationship to the others that a being has had. If we do not learn all that we need to in one visit to the solid layer we must return for as many times as it takes to fulfil all that we have to.

Life enters at the point of conception, we have no choice where we go or who we are born to. It is this randomness that gives us all of the chances we need to learn and progress. We do not decide before being born what life we will go to or how we will live, it is each individual's responsibility to live that life, once they are born into it. Only when you have completed your learning in the schoolhouse, which has its foundations placed firmly in the solid layer, will you be ready to join the teachers in the staff room with all of its privileges.

I hope this has answered many of your questions. If you are reading this book at a time when you have just lost someone then I hope these answers help you and give you some comfort at this time of loss. Although some of the answers, for example about the signs so many look for, seem harsh, they are the truth. And they should help to stop grieving people from paying so much money to charlatans.

We have been asked many other questions and some of those are answered elsewhere in these pages. Ernest is not a fortune-teller nor a medium and he and Jasper will not do 'readings' for people.

We made the mistake of allowing acquaintances of ours to speak to Jasper (and others from the etheric layer) early on in our work, and we were embarrassed by what our acquaintances spoke of and how rude and ignorant some were when they were introduced to etheric people. They were all given the opportunity to hold a full conversation with those from the etheric layer and how little they valued the great gift and privilege that it is to speak to these etheric people and beings. They have so much knowledge and they would have shared it willingly. Can you imagine my embarrassment when one particularly ignorant man, asked if he wished to ask an Elevated Being a question, said 'Will my business be successful?'

Different people will take away different things from our books. Some will just read them for the sensationalism of hearing from the dead. Others will read them because they have been told of some of the other controversial content. But some will genuinely seek to learn, and to those I say 'It is a pleasure to do this work.'

I have high hopes that people will learn from this book and yet as I write this I know that the man who asked the Elevated Being about the future of his business is at the moment facing the imminent death of his own mother – and Jasper tells me that what is on his mind right now is not the pain his mother might be suffering or any thoughts for where his mother will be going when she leaves the solid layer his only question is 'Where is the Will?'

I hope that everyone gets great comfort from this book and from the knowledge that we will once again be reunited with our loved ones. Life continues always and we do not need to have any doubts or fear when it is approaching our own time to part that curtain and join them.

HISTORY LESSONS

The history books and the world of fiction have romanticised many events and many periods in history. The following transcripts give evidence of just how much historians, books and films can change the truth. We hear now from some of those who felt it was necessary to set the record straight.

Although we continue to work in the usual way and you will again find transcripts of a two-way conversation between myself and those Jasper brings to speak through Ernest, there are also times when a piece of information is so significant that we have asked for more a lengthy insight into someone's life and this becomes then more of a narration.

South American Indian

[15th January 2007. I heard a very quiet voice]

Too Tow Tek said ...

How do I know I can trust white man's words? I am Too Tow Tek.

[I tried to convince this man he could trust me. He went on to tell me his story. It is obvious from his description of their 'hard skin' that he is describing armour and that he is describing the coming of the Spaniards to South America and I estimate he is speaking of a time anywhere between the 1500s and the 1600s. These are his exact words.]

Too Tow Tek continued ...

We were peace people and lived without any wars or fights. We speak and when we try to speak to them they laugh at as and they push us to the floor. They hurt people. Others come with those with the hard bodies. They wear long robe dress and they speak strange from book. They read words from book. They say because we do not understand words and read words we cannot be like them. They make us sit and they read us words. And they tell us stories we do not understand. We do not understand their words. They make children listen to words. They make children listen and when the children grow tired and want to hunt or fish or play they hit children to make them sit longer and listen.

They make a building, a lodge. A lodge that is different. They make from logs, not like ours. They make building where people sit to listen to these stories. They make us come to building. We not like inside of building but we have to listen to what these ones in the long dresses say because the hard bodies hurt and kill if we do not. They search everywhere, they take everything that they think is of value. They take our food freely and some of us go without.

Those that try to fight against these hard bodies are killed by firestick. We steal these firesticks but cannot make them work. They not work for us. We wait until some of them sleep. And we cut the throats of those that sleep without the hard body on. And then the next day they punish the first ones they come across, although they are not the ones who have done this thing, they punish them for it. So it is not good trying to kill and fight these people because they punish those that do not do this thing.

We do not want to listen to these stories, we do not understand the words of these people. We do not want these people here. We were happy before these people came. They take our children and they take our women and we never see them again. They do not come back. They take some of our young men as well and we not see them.

We have had enough of this and we must leave these lands that we have known for so many moons, for so long. And we must go where this man in the hard skin cannot take after us. But to do this we must go into lands where we have not seen, and we do not know those there. But other tribes are of our kind and they listen to us and we tell them that we must run from these hard skins because they will come after us and steal our people and take away what we have.

So we must leave our lands and move on. We move for many moons and they follow us but we are able to hide in the forests and we are better than them at this land because we know this land. We wait and we jump on these people and we beat them until they fall, but still they come but they come in less numbers.

We walk, we run and hide. We pick up others along the way until one day the hard body men do not come any more and we feel we are safe and we decide to make our lodges here. We stay here and we decide to stay here where the hard body man cannot get to us, he doesn't come any more. And we are safe now.

But we weep for the ones that will not come back to us and we dream of the lands we will not see again because we cannot go back in case these people are waiting there for us to take their revenge on what we have done.

We killed some of the ones in long dresses and we take their book and burn book. Some can speak our words and they tell us that if we do not listen to these words big fire will come from the sky and kill us. But it did not.

We still think they may come one day, but for the moment they are not coming and we can live together. We have joined with others who are very much like us and in so doing we hope that we can share and we can build strength against people when they come again.

They are very strange. We take some of the skins that we take off them and they are hard, such as we have not seen before. We put these on to see what they like. We feel that if we put on we will be like them. But we do not wish to be like them because we do not wish to be without heart like them. So we throw these useless hard skins away and not wish to see them again. We break the firesticks. We bend the firesticks so that they cannot be used and we hope we do not see them again.

For now we live in peace. We do not know if these people will come again, but for now we are safe and we are happy again. If they had lived with us they would have found peace. They would not have needed to steal from others. We would have given to them. But we do not own these things that we have, we just use them until the next man comes. None of these things that we use are ours to keep. What we take from the land we put back for the next man to use. I go now.

Jasper says ...

History tells again of how the savages of the Americas were discovered and 'educated' by the Spanish Conquistadors. These voyages have been recorded as great victories and the perpetrators of these crimes have been recorded as heroes. History records how these brave men brought civilisation to the tribes of South America. But read between the lines as much as you will, little is said of how these simple people were robbed of their riches, their dignity and their very existence

Had anyone stopped and considered that these 'savages' were already as civilised as they needed to be? Who are the true savages? Are you content to believe history books with their biased views or will you listen to those who lived through it?

As a Higher Being Jasper has the memories of all of his previous walking incarnations. Jasper knows all of his lives and can recall any of them. The last time Jasper walked here in Paris he was Jasper and died in 1853, but it is one of his earlier lives that he has recounted for us and which I include here. I cried throughout as I listened to this first hand account of Jasper's time as a Roman Gladiator. I was still horrified as I typed up his words and I warn you now that this makes for terrible reading. Ernest sees all of these events as Jasper speaks through him and so he and I were both devastated by what follows. But not as devastated as Jasper, who had to live through it and then, for us, relive it all again. Here are his words ....

The Gladiator

I was living in Cadiz, Spain when I was taken by the Romans and brutally thrown onto a slave ship. There were many others taken with me. On board the ship we were manacled, hands and feet, and chained to each other and also to a long tree trunk which ran the length of the hull. We were made to row, chained into our positions. There was a man seated at the front who was relentlessly pounding the rowing beat on a drum. We were whipped if we stopped or even slowed down to gain breath.

We did everything where we sat. Everything. We never left our seat. We ate in that seat and we did everything there. Everything.

The only time anyone was taken off was when one of us died, then they were just thrown over the side. If one of us became ill and could not keep up with the rowing, then he too was thrown over the side.

Finally, we had rowed this vast ship all the way to Rome, where we were offloaded. We then had to walk across land to the slave market. The young girls were 'lucky', they hadn't had to row or do anything during the arduous journey. The Slave Traders wanted them to look nice.

During the whole journey, both by boat and on foot, I had not been able to talk to anyone. The slaves were assorted nationalities, and even if I had found anyone who spoke Spanish I would have been severely whipped or beaten for talking. I was scared and alone. At this time I was twelve years old.

I, amongst others, was sold to the Gladiator School. I was too small to fight. So for six long years they used me to clean up, mend clothes and clean the armoury. I never moved outside that confinement. It was a Training Camp. There were many such places all over Italy. Many people think only of the Coliseum but there were many smaller 'Circuses' as they were called.

Every Governor had an allocated area of the land to govern, and he also had his own Circus. Lots of money and property changed hands, betting on the outcome of these Gladiator matches. Betting on whether their favourite Gladiator would live or die. The ultimate was to be able to take your circus to The Coliseum. That was big money.

When I was eighteen I was pulled away from the menial tasks, and fattened up for the arena. The school built the men up like prize bulls for bullfighting. I was given meat for the first time. I was given women. They did everything to build us up. Then they trained us to fight. We all received many wounds from training but we were taught in training not to inflict too much damage.

The Gladiator Master was a brutal, terrible man. If a man didn't fight he would whip and torture them. They would make the weak and badly injured men fight the stronger ones. This was when we learned to kill. We had to learn to kill and maim the people we had been living with for years. At first we didn't want to hurt the other, but it was kill or be killed. Then we became numb and some even began to like it. We were completely indoctrinated into having a murderous instinct, blood lust. Many began to like it more and more. They would talk about it and brag.

At first we fought in groups of five or six, against the more hardened ones. We were given only the most basic armour, we had to steal it from the dead ones as they dropped to the ground. We would fight until injured. If you were injured in the fight and it was what they called a 'good kill', then they asked for the thumbs up or thumbs down decision from the crowd or sometimes asked for the Governor's decision on life or death. If the injury was accidental they would drag you off and patch you up to fight again.

They kept us die-hard Gladiators away from the young lads so that we couldn't form any bonds. The young lads had nothing.

In time I went to the big arena, The Coliseum, and here it was no longer men against men. It was much worse now. There were the same Gladiators, mean fighting machines, but now there was the added interest for these many spectators. Here there were Christians and there were animals. Wild, savage animals.

The Romans kept the Christians and the Gladiators separate. They would bring Christian girls and women in from time to time for the men to use, but aside from that we were kept apart.

By now the crowds had started to tire of men versus men. They wanted more. More blood. More gore. So they started by letting the Christians into the arena with the animals. The crowd loved it. Men, women and children standing unarmed in the arena and they let the animals into them. A lot of animals.

The roar of the crowd grew loader. The bloodier and gorier it got, the more they roared. Then more horrific, the more they cheered.

They put women and children into the ring and sent in chariots to mow them down. They would ride them down with their horses, crush them under their wheels.

They made the Christians fight the Gladiators. The Gladiators would hack at the Christians. The more they hacked them about and made them suffer, the more the crowd loved it. They threw more money at the Gladiators the more they made the Christians suffer.

They let me and the other Gladiators watch what was happening in the arena. They also housed the Christians behind grills at the side of the arena. The Christians were forced to watch it all. The Romans wanted the fear heightened for when they in turn entered the ring. And the crowd in turn watched the Christians as they awaited their fate. The crowd watched with pure relish.

Some of the Christians would not fight when they did reach the arena. Some wouldn't run. They would just stand there and wait for the mortal blow to take them. They would just stand there and take it.

There were lions, tigers, bears, wolves. Anything vicious. Mad dogs. These were animals that the traders had collected from their travels around the world. The animals were worth more than the people. People could be replaced easily. The animals could not.

If a Gladiator damaged an animal and walked away, they killed the Gladiator. The Gladiator was expendable.

I didn't always watch. After the show the younger lads would be made to pick up the pieces from the ring and feed them to the animals. Arms, legs, heads, everything. I consider myself very lucky never to have done that.

I was injured a few times. As the crowd and the people became more crazed they needed more sensationalism. They started to match the Gladiators to the animals. But because of the value of the animals they would make sure the Gladiators were outnumbered. One man against six animals. It was a no win situation. When the men entered the ring they knew they were going to die there.

I have no idea how long I fought as a Gladiator in the Coliseum. It could have been days, or months or even years. I have no idea. I would fight and then crawl back to the cage, as they called our quarters.

The Christians were caged on the opposite side. There was a constant flow of them. They came from everywhere. Almost every day more would arrive and almost every day their cages would be full.

The crowd were addicted. They loved to watch the Christians being ripped to pieces. The Romans came to watch with their whole family, they brought their children to see it. They brought food too, made a day of it.

The Gladiators were part of a killing machine. We couldn't make friends, we couldn't get attached to anyone. You went into the arena, killed a few people and returned to the cage.

There were rumours of Gladiators being reprieved for good service and being freed. These were just rumours to motivate, to inspire but it was this which kept me going, this which trapped me into this awful cycle. I knew that my life was precious and that I must try and survive at all costs but there were no old Gladiators. We died young, all of us.

During our short lives we never once received any news of the outside world. We would only hear the crowd leaving the Coliseum talking about their fine day, talking excitedly about how people had died, how this was ripped off, did you see that arm, and of course how much money they had made on the betting.

For me days merged into night and the sounds of weeping and wailing went on all through the night. Mothers weeping for their lost children and babies, lost in special tournaments where they would just throw a pile of children in for the animals. The beautiful young women too, just piled them in there. A free for all.

And always the other Christians looking on, never knowing when it was their turn. Part of the torture. Fear made for better sport for the spectators to watch.

The Romans became even more crazed, if that were even possible. They became more bloodthirsty, nobody's life counted for anything. They stepped up the torture on their own Gladiators. They matched their own Gladiators with the animals, it was now all or nothing. Twenty men versus all the animals. Sheer carnage. Absolute hell on earth. This hell went on all day.

Then it was my turn to go in. I decided not to fight. I was put into the ring with all sorts of lions and tigers, fighting amongst themselves already. I was wearing a Gladiator's helmet at the outset, but that soon disappeared, stolen or lost. I had no face mask. No defence at all.

Then I saw the tiger, it attacked, head and neck. It was painful at first then the pain left. It wasn't there any more. And that is the last I remember. [ENDS]

Throughout, as he recounted this memory, Jasper had used a very controlled voice. I could tell he was fighting back the emotions to enable him to speak of it. When I looked at Ernest's face there were tears streaming down it. Remembering it must have been terrible for Jasper and knowing what had happened to his friend had badly affected Ernest. Jasper ended by saying 'And don't ever ask me to tell you this story again.' His final words on the subject of the Romans were that whenever people think of what the Romans did for other countries and Italy, whenever people talk of the Roman inventions, the Roman improvements and their technological advances, he would hope they remember this true life account. He said that the Romans were terrible, brutal people and you were either part of their fighting machine, or fodder for it.

I have included this piece here, in the chapter about how historians and film-makers distort the reality of events, because I shiver now when I hear them glorify the Romans. It saddens me how death on such a grand and terrible scale can be romanticised by those who run the Coliseum, and other places like it, as a tourist attraction. The same goes for the Tower of London and it's areas of execution, death and torture, and all the many torture dungeons and places of mass extinction all over the world that so many people like to take their children to.

It took Jasper a while to recover from reliving these memories and I have never spoken of it again to him. I have asked Jasper to comment throughout all of this book, which after all is his book, but in this instance I have not. It is word for word as he recounted it and I do not think we can ask for anything more.

***

We end this section on historical misrepresentations with the following piece of information which was given to me by one of the Higher Beings. There are many such Elevated Beings and Higher Beings who speak to me in this way.

One of the hardest things for me to understand at first was that so many of these beings came to me and they spoke of what we call ancient history as if it were recent. I have had to stretch my mind and my understanding in so many ways and 'time' is one that has been hard to adjust to. Jasper put this into perspective when he told me that I could not possibly imagine what the phrase 'the beginning of time' meant. One thing he said helps me when I think of anything connected to the time the Earth has been here. Jasper told me to imagine a ruler a meter long, and think of that as 'all time so far.' Then he asked me to consider how much time has passed on this earth since the dinosaurs walked here. And he told me that the time from the dinosaurs to now would only take up the thickness of the varnish on the end of the ruler.

Thus the time since dinosaurs is very recent history. I mention this now because the following speaker is talking of the time before dinosaurs. He came to speak to me, through Ernest, on 16th September, 2006 and his name is Barden. He is a Higher Being.

The Deserts

Barden said ....

Many millions of years ago on this earth there were people of great intelligence and intellect. Civilisations had risen to a great height with technology.

The areas of the world that are covered with desert are the areas which had the great technology. They were the sites of vast cities of advanced technology. These cities had risen from the ground over many millennia. They became sophisticated and technologically advanced. They were far in advance of anything which the Earth sees at the moment. There are those amongst you that feel that they have achieved and advanced scientifically but as yet you have still not reached the same level as was reached all that time ago.

The areas which are now desert were vast civilisations with great metropolises and areas around them spreading far and wide. It is the other areas of the world that were the wastelands.

You have deserts in Africa, North America and China. All of these were centres of vast populations and civilisations. The world then went through the same cycle as you have started now. They reached the height of energy and advancement in all things including their weapons of warfare. You have touched upon this in your recent history. The powers have risen to a state where they could have annihilated each other. They were pulled back from the brink by sensibility.

When you wage war and use weapons of such mass destruction it has far-reaching effects long into the future. These areas of desert mark areas where there was a large population and vast cities which rose from the ground. But there is nothing left.

The small particles that you see as sand are all that remains there. They are crystalline in structure and these are the vaporised grains of the civilisations that existed there. Nothing was left standing. The destruction was so great that everything was taken away.

It would be a lesson if anyone would listen. You see civilisations have risen and fallen many times. This should be a warning to all those that inhabit the Earth now that if you wage such war it has long-lasting consequences.

Does man ever learn? Or does he just change the questions on the paper? The energy they play with in this weaponry could sustain the world for eternity. [Ends]

I have learned much and I am still learning. Much of what I have been told makes much more sense than that which the archaeologists and so-called experts deduce. It seemed so logical to me when I was told that that those grotesque animals and birds who grew out of all proportion and who were such unlikely shapes, were also the results of that warfare. The dinosaurs were malformed due to the air-born side-effects of that terrible conflict.

Jasper says ...

Historians and archaeologists spend their lives making great discoveries. But you must ask the question, how can they really see the whole picture if a large part of it is missing? The answer must be that they make an 'educated' guess.

The earth is very old and has existed much longer than any scientist has guessed or could imagine. All recorded history is recent, it is beyond the comprehension of even the most eminent of scholars just what happened in the true past of long ago.

But there are those who do know the truth and will tell it gladly if you will listen.

History has its place, it is good to know where you have come from. But remember past is just that, it is past. It is the now and the future that carry the most importance.

You can learn from past mistakes and use them to mould the future, but first make sure that the past that you are looking at is really what it appears to be and not the fantasy of another .

Old Egypt

Jasper says ...

There is an area of history that would appear to inspire the imagination more than others, they call it Ancient Egypt. I will call it Old Egypt. Archaeologists and historians are transfixed with their obsession with this area and waste their time and resources trying to unravel its mysteries.

As I have stated elsewhere history contains a large percentage of educated guesswork. How can it be anything else given the limited access to what has been? The 'facts' are no more than the interpretations that scholars and those considered to be knowledgeable put forward as their theories. These theories have been accepted as 'fact' because of the lack of any other alternatives. Remember I have said that there are those who know and those who do not. Add to this those who pretend to know and they will influence those who will accept anything that fits, and between them all they will believe they have an answer.

The Egyptian hieroglyphics are recorded history. They were recorded by those who were there at the time and were part of it. Much has been lost in the sands that have scoured the face of Old Egypt and the scholars again can only guess at what the true meanings are. In some cases they have come very near to the truth (more by luck than knowledge) but in other cases they have been completely wrong.

To make such educated assumptions it is necessary to be absolutely sure that the examples that the theories are based on are reliable. For every work of fact published in the present day, there are many more works of fiction. Why should it have been any different in the past?

To read a text a book has to be read in the correct order and orientation. If you present someone with a book written in a text (or symbols) that they have never seen before they have no point of reference. Would it not be feasible that this book could be read in many ways; back to front, upside down, up the page, down the page, left to right, right to left - the options are endless. Even if you did manage to stumble upon the correct way of reading you still would not know if the book was complete or part of a larger collection.

So to put this simply - the scholars have read many of the inscriptions the wrong way around and have filled in the gaps for themselves, or guessed the rest. Who would question them? I would. And I could bring forward many more who would answer the questions if only they were asked to do so.

The discovery of Tutankhamen was a major find, but for who? The gold and riches found were like no others seen by recent mankind, but quite worthless in comparison to the true riches that were missed by the grave robbers. The gold and finery blinded the greedy. The true incalculable value contained in the ancient scrolls and parchments were trampled into dust in the scurry to grab a shiny trinket which they could turn into profit.

I do not use the term grave robbers lightly for I consider that anyone who enters the final resting place for the shell that is the body, can be no more than that. Fuelled by greed for wealth or notoriety - they are all the same.

Have respect for the remains, they are of no further use for the etheric beings that have long since vacated them, but they must be respected. How would you feel in the future when you look at the earth from a different perspective, as indeed you will, to find that someone is hacking the remains of your loved one to pieces in the name of science? When their true motive is to fill their own pockets.

There are many unsolved mysteries and Tutankhamen holds many of them. Scholars battle to be the first to solve them and publish the 'truth'. Let me steal your thunder:-

Tutankhamen was not an important figure in history. Had it not been for the riches found and stolen from his tomb, his name would probably never be spoken. He was a young ruler who did not want to be in the position that he was placed. He came to power at the age of eleven and by the age of fifteen he was dead. He was used by many to undo that which was left behind by Akhenaten. Yes, he was murdered by his uncle, by a blow to the back of the head. His successor was being installed even as his body lay cooling on the floor. He was entombed with great riches that were designed to cover the crime of his assassination and give the impression that he was loved and so respected by all. In fact he was no more than a means to an end for those who really wanted control of Egypt. But the mysteries did not stop with the exhumation of this unfortunate, insignificant boy. What of the curse that came after the ones who unearthed the tomb?

I am sorry to disappoint you but there was no curse, no revenge from the grave. Such curses were inscribed above tomb entrances to ward off grave robbers. Educated men and scholars should have known better than to have believed in them. *Archaeological digs by their nature and often remote locations, are not the most sanitary of places. Sickness and disease wait for an opportunity to pounce on the unsuspecting. A simple mosquito bite proved fatal to one. A tomb enclosed for centuries riddled with disease accounted for the others. The tomb had been enclosed for so long, it was not meant to be a meeting place for adventurers in the future, it had been sealed for eternity. Decaying matter and dampness became a breeding ground for bacteria. It was spores of bacteria ingested into the lungs of the unsuspecting explorers that caused the disease of their lungs and inevitable death, that in some cases took years to manifest itself.*

But these fine men who brought out the riches of Tutankhamen for the world to see have their bodies at rest, or have they? Do you think perhaps someone in the future might take their mortal remains away to a sterile room to discover the mysteries of their deaths in the name of science? Or would their true motive be no more than to gain fame and fortune? But they were not buried with the gold and trinkets wrapped within their shrouds, so perhaps they will escape that which they did to others.

Egypt does have entwined in its so-called mysteries certain characters that always come to the fore and fuel the most intense discussion. This book could be filled with messages from the visitors associated with Egypt alone, but that is not the purpose of this book. I consider that Nefertiti and Akhenaten are the most important figures in the history of Old Egypt, and the following recalling of their lives needs no explanation from me, but it will have far reaching effect on understanding the future that will come to the earth.

Nefertiti

[19 February 2008.]
I was a very young girl when they came to tell me that I was now Queen of my country. I remember sitting by the river watching the younger ones splashing around in the water as guards carried a golden throne towards us. We all stopped what we were doing and ran towards it. A woman alighted from the curtains and walked towards us. All the children were pleased to see her and she hugged some of us and touched the hands of all. We all shared a father, the King, but we had different mothers. This woman was my mother.

A priest came then and he had two scrolls and lifted them up as he read from them. Others gathered, more adults, and listened as he announced the death of my father, and that I would be Queen. My mother was alternating between crying for my father and smiling for my honour. She climbed back into the chair then and they carried it away. She didn't look back and this made me sad. The other children gathered around me, some were crying at the thought of me leaving them.

Then the veiled women of the court came to me and took my hand, leading me away to make me ready to take up my new position. A procession formed with the priest and his scrolls behind me, and many people following him as we approached the palace.

We climbed the big steps, walked through the two enormous columns and on into the palace. As we entered the large central area the women servants took me into a side room where they bathed me and dressed me in the most sumptuous robes of white silks. Everything was heavily embroidered with gold. They gently pushed gold bracelets onto my arms and hung a magnificent gold necklace around my neck. It felt very heavy against my skin. Then I felt the weight of the gold headdress as they lowered that onto my head. They placed my feet in delicate slippers and I was ready. They led me back into the large chamber.

I walked towards the throne in the centre, a large, carved stone throne, and climbed the steps up to it and seated myself. The women who had accompanied me there flung themselves to the floor, face down, and stayed like that for the whole proceedings.

Then the procession of well-wishers started towards me. There were so many. Many had black skin, like myself, many had the dark olive skins and some had lighter skins still. They came from a variety of lands to pay their respects to me, the new Queen of my lands. The lands you now call Ethiopia and the Sudan.

The procession seemed endless as the whole building started to fill with people. Each group brought a gift, many had brought gold or gemstones. As each group approached my throne they bowed to me, placed their gift before me and then dropped back to one side. Once in position everyone was kneeling. An aisle had formed in the centre allowing the newcomers through and a priest stood to one side reading from his endless scrolls to announce each delegation.

Then as the long procession stopped and the chamber was filled to capacity they all fell silent awaiting the new Queen. One of the advisors handed me a scroll and I stood to read these words which had been prepared for me to the assembly. As I stood, all of them bowed forward from their kneeling position, touching their heads to the floor in front of me. Once my address was over one of the priests dismissed all of the delegates, clapping his hands together loudly, and they all filed out.

Now I was to address my people, the people of my lands, as their new Queen. I walked slowly towards the doorway to see a tumultuous crowd outside. I was surrounded by guards, two either side of me and more behind me. All carried large shields and spears. As trumpets and drums sounded I walked forward to address the people. Once again my words had been prepared for me and were handed to me on parchment. I could feel the excitement of the people as I started to speak. I would have preferred to use words of my own, but knew this was not possible.

Then I was ushered back inside the palace and the guards closed the doors behind us. There were two guards at each door and as I looked up to the high windows which were cut into the stone walls I saw two guards at each window. Every direction I looked towards I saw guards. They were everywhere. Then the handmaidens took me into my bedchamber, bathed me and dressed me for sleep and I got into my bed with its many silk cushions. As I fell asleep I was aware of just how many guards were surrounding me and I felt uncomfortable.

I settled into my new life and a feeling of agitation started to come upon me. I did not enjoy the helpless feeling of everyone doing every little thing for me. I did not enjoy the attention and I did not like the lack of privacy. I did not feel confident enough at this stage to dismiss the many servants and guards. It was not the way and I was very conscious if my duties and obligation to my new position. But they did every small thing for me; they changed my clothes, they fed me, someone would bring me grapes and I was uneasy with all of this attention. Although I still carried the years of a child I was aging enough to know I wasn't really happy with my new role. And I was lonely.

Every time I left the building there were so many guards and as I walked along the people would stand aside and then fall before me, some would throw leaves in my pathway. No-one could ever come close to me, I was always flanked on all sides by guards. One day as I walked to inspect some new building work which was being undertaken I could see children playing in the distance at the side of the river. I would have loved to have joined them, but of course this would never again be possible for me.

As I walked back into the palace, that large temple-like mausoleum I felt like I was entering my prison. The palace was enormous, built of large square blocks of sandstone and although much light flooded into it from the large stone window-like openings in its stonework it felt dark to me. I had a feeling of being trapped and that I had lost all of my freedom. I would get the overwhelming urge to run outside but of course I could never do it. Every movement I made, someone would come with me.

As I grew a little older they started to carry me everywhere. I had lost all independence and I missed it. I came to dread the long sessions where I would take my position inside the palace, upon my throne, and I would have to pass a variety of judgements upon those brought before me. My subjects would be brought before me and they would tell me of their problems and of course I would listen. But then others would speak for me. I would just nod as these advisors and priests made their decision on my behalf.

Sometimes they were poor people who were very troubled and I would have liked to have helped them more and to do more for them, but of course I had to simply agree with the decisions of my advisors. There were endless streams of these people, some wanting me to bless their children, some needing a settlement of disputes about land or possessions, others needing help to feed their family.

I felt so helpless, as I sat on my throne. I felt the uncomfortable weight of my gold headdress, all of the gold and finery which was draped around me, the bracelets, the rings and necklaces, the heavy embroidery. But of it all I felt the weight of the helplessness the most, it was choking me. I felt I just wanted to scream and run away from it all. But of course this was not possible.

The years moved on as I left my youth behind. I was a young woman when the first talks of war and fighting came. It was necessary to inspect my armies and soldiers regularly, rows and rows of foot soldiers with spears. Hundreds of them, all black-skinned like me. It was also necessary to take an interest in what was happening in the lands which surrounded my own.

I spent all of my time inside the palace confines now, in the chambers or just outside in the courtyards, always heavily guarded. One day my soldiers brought prisoners to me who had been approaching our lands from the south. These men were strapped to wooden poles which were tethered behind their backs, their arms outstretched to either side of their torso. These had a lighter skin to ours and had headdresses of fabric wrapped many times around their heads.

Seated on my throne, now outside upon a plinth, I looked down at these prisoners. The leader of my armies took one of these prisoners, untied him and pushed him down in front of me onto his knees, then held his head up as he chopped his head off. He threw the head into a basket and laid the basket and head at my feet.

I felt sick. My General asked me what I wanted to do with the rest of the prisoners and those around me wanted them to be executed, but for once I made my own decision and had them set free and chased off from our lands. This was not a kindness really as they had no food and would surely perish anyway, but I hoped they would have more of a chance in that way. I had no head for war and violence.

One of my generals showed me a map drawn onto a large animal skin. I looked down at the lines of the river and the markings made to show the hills and they had drawn small stick men onto the map to show the positions of all of the tribes around us. They were very worried.

[5 March 2008.]
One day I received word of a large force of people coming towards us from the North West. The news was carried by a delegation of warriors, eight men with shields and spears who had marked a map onto a skin to show the direction these unknown men were coming from. They said that they were coming from this direction but that they did not know what lay beyond them, what lay in the direction they were coming from. They had marked many lines onto stone to indicate the large number of men approaching our lands.

The army wanted me to lead them into war, to go with them into battle. My General pleaded with me to go with them and said that the people needed a figurehead. My own advisors told me it is was not possible for me to go and left me no choice. My General picked up his maps, looked up at me, bowed his head and left. As I took my place on my throne and my many servants were tending to me, anointing my feet, feeding me grapes and tending to my every need, I felt a terrible sense of frustration. I knew I should have been leading my people.

When I next spoke to the people from the steps of the palace it was the usual way of a spokesman reading from a scroll as I stood with my eyes fixed on my people. Once again I had not been allowed to use my own words, or even speak to them, even in this time of trouble. I looked into the faces of my subjects and I saw fear there and I felt their sense of unease.

Once back in the palace I watched as barricades were put up and our defences strengthened, the number of guards increased and I felt more of a prisoner than ever. Everyone was scurrying around and there was almost a sense of panic.

Then my General made his way into the chamber and told me that our first wave had been defeated and pleaded with me to go out with him and lead the army. This time I would not listen to the priests and advisors and agreed.

I had a great sense of anxiety as they dressed me for battle. The shoulder plates were cold against my skin and as they placed the metal helmet over my head the nose piece felt most strange. They wrapped my body in long strips of copper metal, each strip tied with ropes to the next until it formed a circular skirt. At my chest was one plate of metal. Then they brought me a heavy sword with a broad blade, a staff with spikes and a shield faced with thick animal skin and fur which they strapped to my arm. Finally I was supplied with a spear which was lighter than the sword.

As I walked I felt heavy, clumsy and awkward but I felt lifted by the great cheer which rang out as I walked out to my people who were waiting outside. I was shown to a wooden chariot with two wooden wheels, and I stood in the chariot as someone beside me used the reigns to make the two oxen we were using move away from the palace. As we moved away my army formed up around me, thousands of soldiers, and then thousands more of my ordinary subjects fell in behind us. The army was well-equipped but the ordinary people had just makeshift spears to fight with.

Slowly we moved forward, leaving the city behind us. We left our own beautiful green lands behind and moved off into parched lands where there were just a few bushes along the way, and the terrain became harsher as we travelled further from the city.

Then we saw them. Hoards of men coming towards us on horseback, moving faster than us, charging at us. As they came nearer I could see they were lighter skinned than us, bare-chested men with leather headdresses and long pikes and spears. They had no shields. But they were coming at great speed and in such numbers that we were instantly overrun. There was some bloodshed but we soon realised we had no chance against such numbers and such an organised force.

I was terrified and I watched as these men moved through my own ranks and approached my chariot, ignoring me completely. There was fierce fighting around me as my own men sought to protect their Queen against we knew not what. But within a very short space of time I was left standing, alone, in my chariot which was still tethered to the now fallen, dead oxen, in the midst of my fallen protectors.

Then men came forward from these lighter skinned warriors and turned my chariot around, pulling it into position by hand. My men were roped together in lines, one behind the other, and the invaders escorted us all back to our city. No-one had spoken to me, or tethered me in any way. They simply took me back to my own palace, led me back inside it and shut the doors behind me, closing me in.

All of my guards had gone. The priests were still there and the servants who helped me to remove my armour. There was a terrible fear coming from us all. We did not know what was happening. My servants tended to the many cuts on my arms and legs. All we could do was wait.

After a time the outer doors were flung open and a young man walked in, flanked by his soldiers. He had a tight-fitting gold headdress which fell down and coated his ears at either side of his head, a skin across one shoulder, leather skirted tunic and laced sandals up his legs. As I watched him walk towards me a great anger swelled up inside me and I went as if to lunge towards him. At that point all of his soldiers drew their swords and my own priests calmed me down. I could do no more than sit down upon my throne.

When I once more looked towards this man I found that he had approached the throne and was kneeling before me, head bowed. Behind him, his vast army of men were all doing the same. The man was Akhenaten.

Many days later we were seated side by side in my palace and the number of priests around us had been swelled by the priests Akhenaten had brought with him from his own lands, the lands you now call Egypt. The guards around us were now a mix of both Akhenaten's and my own.

We were to take part in a ceremony symbolising the joining of our two lands against all others in the region. One of the Egyptian priests placed a golden headdress upon my head whilst one of my own priest's placed an identical headdress upon the head of Akhenaten. We were each given a small golden jewel encrusted staff and both priests read from scrolls as we sat aloft, side by side, and looked down upon the assembled dignitaries of both lands. All were before us, bowing down to us.

Akhenaten and I were of similar ages. He was tall, broad across the shoulders, with angular features and a long elegant face. He was very beautiful, almost feminine in his beauty and his pale smooth skin. He had a great presence and grace in his movement. And I was fascinated by him. We had talked for many days and it was the first time anyone had spoken to me as an equal since I had become Queen.

I found Akhenaten to be a just man and my admiration for him had grown very quickly. He had a sense of right and a manner of judgement older than his years. He was very fair and extremely honourable. He discussed with me the possibility of joining our two lands and I readily agreed. It was good to finally rule without the advisors and priests making all of the important decisions. And I no longer felt alone.

The ceremony over, we walked together out of my palace and there were thousands and thousands of our soldiers waiting for us outside, now a mix of our two skin colours, standing with their backs towards us, waiting to escort us away from what was now the southern region of 'our' lands. We had left a force in charge of this region, some of my own people and some of Akhenaten's, all carefully selected, and we were going to our other region, Akhenaten's Egypt.

They set us into throne chairs and carried us, side by side, down to the river, close to where I had played as a child. There waiting for us was a long ship which had come from Egypt, made of wood and curled up at its front and square at the back, I was amazed by it size. Oars were poking through its sides where rowers were seated below its deck and on the deck itself there was a covered area, a canopy on poles, for Akhenaten and I. They carried our thrones and placed us, side by side, under the canopy. A force of guards and soldiers, all carrying shields, joined us.

There were three more large ships in the river and our priest and some of our soldiers marched onto these and took their positions for the long journey. The rest of the very large mass of soldiers marched alongside us along the banks of the river as we glided along. I could feel the movement of the oars as we glided. The sun was very hot and beating down upon us.

[7 March 2008.]

After a long journey we saw the river starting to widen and the banks were further apart now. We kept going, night followed day which followed night which followed day. At night we could see lights flickering along the shoreline as we moved on and on. In the daytime we could see small clusters of village huts along the banks. We followed the left bank and the right bank seemed a very long way away.

It was in daylight that we approached the city. In the distance I could see tall sandstone buildings with columns rising up from the ground. By now there was a mass of smaller boats around us and I could see the sunlight glistening off of things on the shoreline ahead. As we drew closer I could see that it was coming from the shields and spear of soldiers. They were made from a polished copper. Rows and rows of soldiers were lining the side of the river as we moved in towards the bank.

Our boat came in close and a large gangplank was put in place. This took us onto a sandy shoreline. There were no buildings there, just two wooden landing stages. There were a couple of ships here too, both had masts and one had a sail. There were so many people waiting there that I became a little overwhelmed. Thousands and thousands of Akhenaten's subjects had congregated there to welcome us.

I had to alight first, alone. I walked down the gangplank, and there were twelve of my handmaidens behind me, in long robes. Each one carried a small box or casket. Waiting at the shoreline were four soldiers, bare-chested and bronze. They wore headdresses flapped over their ears and carried staffs which were curled over at the top.

Then a bald-headed man, with a long beard which was cut very straight and formed a rectangle came towards me. This was the High Priest. He had long ornate gold pieces clamped over his ears also forming rectangles and a chain of office which ended in a bejewelled, bright gold sun, the chains which hung from his neck were made up of another series of flat plates of gold rectangles. His robes were long and white. He too carried a staff and in his left hand was a folded square of leather, inside were sheets of parchment which he read aloud from as he greeted me.

He turned around and I followed him as he lead me away from the bank of the river. The four soldiers took up positions around me, a discreet distance away and the procession of my handmaidens followed us. We were taken up a slope to a large throne chair, with carrying poles at its corners and a canopy on four more poles suspended above it. Inside was a sumptuous padded seat. The priest gestured me to sit there. The four soldiers took up their positions at the four corners of the throne, one hand on their staff, one ready to lift the chair. Seated now, I looked back towards the ship. In my elevated position I could see past the crowd who had moved towards the ship. I could see the gangplank and the canopy which we had been seated under.

Akhenaten was approaching the top of the gangplank, with guards in front of him. He had been careful to select a mix of colours of the guards, some black, like me, some of his own skin type. This sent a clear message to his people that they must accept the newcomers. There were six guards in front of him and four behind him. As he stepped onto the gangplank the waiting musicians started to play. They had strange trumpet-like metal instruments which curled into a strange shape above their heads.

Akhenaten looked magnificent in his full gold Pharaoh headdress with gold down the sides and longer down his back, a solid piece of gold and jewels with only his face showing. His robes were a dark orange colour, heavily embroidered in gold. He wore a belt with a dagger pushed into it at one side and carried a highly ornate and bejewelled staff in his left hand. As he walked slowly and sedately down the gangplank his subjects began throwing long leaves and rushes in his path until eventually he was walking along a bed of leaves.

He stopped at his own throne chair, heavily decorated in gold and jewels, as was mine. He took his seat and the soldiers raised him up. At the same time the soldiers around my own chair raised me aloft and we formed up into a procession. A double line of soldiers with their assorted skin colours, then Akhenaten, many more mixed skin colours of soldiers, me, then a mass of soldiers, all mixed together at the rear.

The people lining the route were waving pieces of cloth now, coloured cloths, some were throwing flowers as we continued along. The crowd moved back then as we arrived at a large flat area where they set down our chairs. Akhenaten was slightly ahead of me and to my left. We both stepped out of our chairs at the same time and I walked up to join him. My hand was outstretched, palm down and he covered my hand with his and held it there. Holding our joined hands in front of him and with his staff in his other hand we walked ahead and slowly climbed the stairs to an enormous building fronted by columns which supported the roof of this impressive entrance. Looking off to the sides I could see stone pyramid shapes of buildings inter-dispersed with square stone buildings and many palm trees dotted about within the confines of the city.

We were seated now at the top of the steps, side by side on two stone thrones, and we looked down onto a great mass of people, there were people as far as the eye could see, just a mass of heads. I was not afraid, not even apprehensive, but I was finding this a little overwhelming. Soldiers and guards were holding back the crowds and they had made a wide pathway around where we were sitting and a wide pathway on either side. The soldiers who had been part of our procession from my lands were still coming towards us and they took up their position along one side of the route, backs to the crowd, lining the route. Then the Egyptian soldiers who had journeyed with Akhenaten came then, lining the other side of the route. Ranks and ranks of soldiers coming now, taking their sides and lining this route as the crowd had to move back again and again to make way for them.

Then came a long line of prisoners, all taken during Akhenaten's journey from a variety of lands, all enemies of us both, and these were tied together in chains and ropes and they were paraded along the route and off to the left of us and away.

Now more people came along, black-skinned like me. These were the people who had chosen to join us in Egypt. Women in robes, men with turbans and they filed past us and off to the right.

Now animals were led along the route. Oxen, elephants, horses (from my lands, so they were large clumsy animals, not the sleek swift horses of Akhenaten's lands), ranks and ranks of a variety of animals. Some of the elephants had decorations fixed to them and the oxen had decorations hung around their necks. My people were herding the animals, and leading the larger animals along.

Now platforms were carried along on poles, laden with boxes. More soldiers, an endless, endless procession of people, soldiers, on and on and on.

Then standard bearers came carrying long poles with material symbolising who they represented, they took up their position in a half circle in front of us, standards all around us.

Then it was the turn of the priests. All bare-headed and without hair, all in long white robes, they walked towards us, two abreast, fifty or sixty of them and they stopped at the bottom of the steps. Now one priest approached the steps. He had a headdress like a close-fitting cap made from leather, with flaps at either side over his ears and dropping down behind his head. He wore a light brown leather yoke of a necklace which draped across his chest. The leather was decorated and had holes punched into it in an intricacy of design. Coming out from beneath this chest plate of leather were his coloured robes which hung down and reached his feet. He wore sandals laced up his legs. A blue belt, plaited like a rope, was tied around his waist and hung down in front of him. He carried a box before him.

He walked up the stairs, bowed first of all to Akhenaten and then to me and then laid his box on the ground. Opening it he took from it a large scroll with each end fixed to delicate poles and opening it with a pole in either hand he stretched the paper out to his sides (narrow at the sides and wider, not lengthways) and started to read to both of us. Then he addressed the Pharaoh and Akhenaten repeated his words, then the Queen and I repeated them. Then he turned towards the crowd and addressed them, still reading from his scroll. The priest then turned back to us and Akhenaten once again took my hands in his, his on top of mine, palms down and wrapped a fine piece of cloth around us both, binding us together. The crowd cheered excitedly. Akhenaten and I were married.

Now the soldiers who had been lining different sides of the route, black to one side, lighter skinned to the other, came into the middle of the pathway and mixed, all mingling until they were one mixed mass in front of us. The crowd, too, had pulled forward and were throwing flowers and cheering. There was a lot of excitement and activity.

Akhenaten and I were still seated as they carried food past us and on into the large building behind us. Whole cooked animals on skewers which men carried on their shoulders, big jugs of drinks, trays of fruits, breads, more meats, roasted birds on large platters. There were endless trays of food and finely decorated plates, flagons and bowls. Processions and processions of food went past us, and when all had entered we stood to go inside.

Still bound together we entered the enormous hall. In front of us were low stone tables and all the food had been placed upon them ready for the banquet. Akhenaten and I took our place at the head of the tables and seated ourselves on cushions. The hall was already filled with dignitaries seated on the floor alongside the tables beneath us. Servants were running backwards and forwards with more food and drink.

When they closed the big doors to the crowd outside the celebration banquet could begin and I had time to look around at the beautifully painted, decorated walls which were so colourful against the sandstone. Sunlight flooded in through the openings and I could wonder at the sheer beauty and elegance of it all.

I do not know, in truth, if the joining of Akhenaten and myself which I agreed to back in those early days as we talked at length in my own palace, was undertaken solely because of the duty I felt I had for the safety and future prosperity of my own subjects (as that is what I had always been brought up to think of), but I can tell you that the Queen of Egypt who sat beside her Pharaoh on the day of that joining had no doubts about her personal feelings. By now the deep admiration and respect I had for Akhenaten the King, and the happiness I felt at being at the side of Akhenaten the man, had progressed to much more. I was in love.

Akhenaten

[12 March 2008.]

The marriage was a marriage of the two of us, but it was also a joining of the two civilisations. Two civilisations who stood together and would have stood for all eternity if we had not been turned upon. Both of us tried to introduce new ways but the old ways were very slow to come through again and strangle the roots which we hoped would start afresh.

We tried to start a new belief. We knew that the stories of the ancient ones had been misinterpreted over time and the claims that they had been 'gods' were false. I wished to have one focal point for all to use for inspiration and to stop this worshipping of gods. At that time a Pharaoh was worshipped as a god himself and I knew that this also was wrong. I did not wish to be worshipped in such a way, so therefore it was appropriate that I should find a new centre for our people to use to take their inspiration.

I honoured the ancient ones and I did not wish, in any way, to discredit them, or belittle them, for I knew the truth of them and that they would be very uncomfortable at being a target for worship. They were not gods. So I felt it was time for a newness, a new beginning. We needed a seat of power for our now combined civilisations to rule from, so this seemed the ideal time to build the new centre and change everything.

But I did not know that many of the old regimes had not been suppressed, the many religions who profited in many ways from peddling their stories were still around and I was not one to suppress them with violence, I preferred diplomacy and I am afraid that we were betrayed, my Queen and I, and those that I thought would help me, did not. I did not realise that when my Queen and I no longer walked upon the earth that all that we had achieved would be defaced and returned to the old ways. The old lies.

This should have been a way forward for Egypt, for us all, we could have united and my Queen and I could have ruled the world together but by returning to the old ways I am afraid that Egypt eventually crumbled and never took its place where it should have been, among the leaders of the world.

I will let the historians play with their writings and let them think that they have the answers, but of course they do not. My Queen was a very popular Queen, even now I know they look for her remains, but I can tell you that they will not find them, nor should they desecrate that which we have left behind, it is very disrespectful.

Egypt was wonderful, far more wondrous than the historians have depicted, they show it as a sandy landscape with stone structures but it was green in our time. We walked among the trees and the meadows together, not sand beneath our feet, but grass.

Nefertiti.

[27 March 2008. She continued her narration] There was a feeling of uneasiness everywhere, mistrust. You could feel it in the atmosphere. There were so many holy men, religious men who kept advising Akhenaten and I on religious matters. Some would say this way was good, others would say another was the path to follow and that way was bad.

Akhenaten and I decided it was time to put this whole matter into an order. We set out to see these places of worship. Walking together and escorted by the various priests and holy men we went to many, at every corner there was a different temple or shrine, each worshipping a different god. There were so many, one god had the head of a bull, one had the bird head of Ra, some were worshipping a snake, so many different temples in so many areas – we looked at large opulent temples, simple temples on simple streets and even small shrines in individual homes, all serving a variety of masters.

One large temple had all of these gods. This would be suitable for someone who wanted to please all of these gods and offend none. Here we found columns, twenty or thirty feet high, and bright decorative paintings on the walls of all of the gods. We watched as people brought offerings of fruit, even jewels and gold to place before their gods. There was total confusion. This was a time of peace, of prosperity. There was no warfare but the conflict was within our own people. There was no real religion, no real belief, just confusion.

Akhenaten and I were always seated side by side in all meetings of matters of state, and constantly we were being asked what was our allegiance, which god did we favour. Some would come to us with their problems – should they worship this god or that god? And there was such violence between them. They would smash each others shrines, such conflict, bands of people persecuting each other in the names of their chosen god. Walking through the streets one day we came across a man being stoned because of his beliefs and of course we stopped it.

Akhenaten called a meeting of all the priests and religious leaders. Side by side we sat upon our thrones and Akhenaten spoke to the assembled men – priests in long robes with their shaven heads, some of them dressed in simple manner and some in great finery.

He told them that our marriage had taken place to unify the lands of this great Egypt but there could be no unification all the while everyone was fighting amongst themselves over their beliefs. In order to unify they must recognise that there was only one source of inspiration for all. One power for goodness that was there for all nations and all peoples. If our people were divided, how could they expect to become strong? If we were to grow in strength together we must come together as one.

He told them that they must cast aside all of these false gods and recognise the one power source of inspiration for us all – and to represent this power we would, from now, use the symbol of the sun, that tangible giver of life-force and energy, given freely to all within its rays. It was not to be worshipped, but it was to be respected. This was not a replacement religion, it was a complete new way of thinking for them. There had come a time for a new beginning and we must rise to the heights where we could become stronger.

The people dispersed, some welcomed it, but there were many who voiced their discontent, particularly those in the finery who could possibly lose the lifestyle their allegiance to these false gods brought them.

One night Akhenaten and I were in our bedchamber, beneath the many veils coming down from the ceiling and we lay, side by side on the many cushions upon our bed. I was awake and Akhenaten was asleep beside me. Through the opaqueness of the veils I saw a flicker of a torch and a great feeling of fear and apprehension swept over me. I shook Akhenaten awake just as a man lunged at him with a big blade. I pushed the man away as they started fighting. The man was dressed all in black. I started to scream for help and hardly felt the knife cut into my arm, but I was aware of there being a lot of blood. Then there was a burst of light as the chamber doors were flung open and our guards ran in, there was a scuffle and I heard the noise of many blades hacking down upon this man.

They brought in torches and there was much blood over the floor and in its centre was a priest in black robes. Our bed was soaked in blood from my arm and the many cuts on Akhenaten's hands. They draped robes around us and escorted us into the brightly-lit ante room and the comfort of the many flames of the torches.

The guards brought in two more men. We had guards from my lands and from Akhenaten's and we kept those we thought we could trust most close to us at all times. First they dragged in another priest. This one had a shaved head, heavy earrings and lots of chains around his neck, his jewellery flashed at us in the light of the torches. He wore the white robes of many priests. He stood there looking nervous. Then they dragged in the second man who was in the same black robes as the dead man in our bedchamber had been wearing and threw him down at our feet. The priest in white fell to his needs begging for mercy, for forgiveness, but the man in black lay upon the floor, saying nothing.

Then one of our Army Generals came into the room. All the guards straightened at the sight of him as he strode towards us all. He was dressed in a long tunic which finished below his knees and his copper breast plate and shoulder plates gleamed in the light from the flames. He had a large curved blade at his side.

He approached the two men and spoke to them. We heard the priest in white pleading for his life, kneeling upright at the feet of the General, hands clasped together begging for mercy. The General raised his blade and with one blow to the side of the neck of this priest felled him, dead. Then the General gave a command to the other soldiers and they all set upon the priest in the black robes and in a very short time they dragged both bodies away.

I was left feeling an unease and I know Akhenaten felt the same. It was time to take control of these religions and it was time to leave this city.

The Pharaoh and I were in a chariot being pulled by horses. We had left the city behind us. We were flanked on all sides by guards and soldiers on foot. Our chariot had a canopy above us and we were out in open grasslands. Now there were some drier parts and we could see the river in the far distance. We stayed at nights inside a cloth canopy and moved on again the next day. Back on the road again, we continued until we came to a very flat area of land.

Akhenaten took me by the hand and lead me into this clearing and stopped. He picked up a piece of sandstone and placed it upon the ground. He took a second piece and laid it on top and then a third and laid it on top yet again, he motioned all around with his outstretched hands and said 'This will be our future. This is where we will grow from. This will be a new beginning. You are looking upon the face of the new Egypt. From here we will build our new empire and respect the forces of nature and (as he looked up at the sky) take our inspiration from the energy of the sun. Here is where our life begins.' I felt such pride. Looking at the ground, just sandy soil and rocks, I could feel an excitement. And more than that I could feel the great energy that emanated from this man I had married.

Time moved on and the area was filled with masses and masses of people. Soldiers, stone-masons and many workers. Akhenaten and I were seated under a canopy in our makeshift camp which would be our home for the long time it would take to build our new city, and from there we made all of our decisions and ruled Egypt itself.

Men would come in with large parchments stretched on frames, drawings of the many buildings and Akhenaten and I looked and approved each one in turn. Each building had a plan, a drawing of each one, drawings of blocks of buildings, and a large drawing of the overall plan of the city itself. At the heart of the city was a large building with columns which were so tall they would look as if they could touch the very sky itself, and at the summit was the symbol of the sun.

Akhenaten and I looked at this large city plan with pride, and as we stared down at it he took my left hand and smiled at me.

[6 April 2008.]
I would like to be humble and say that I was happy living in such temporary accommodation but I am sorry to say that the luxury I had become accustomed to in my fortunate life had not prepared me well for such surroundings.

Akhenaten and I lived beneath a large canopied structure on poles with only layers of curtains between ourselves and the many guards around us. The inside was finished comfortably with many cushions and a comfortable bed, but however happy I was to be with Akhenaten I did miss the comforts of a solid palace, especially when the whole thing was rocking and swaying in the wind of a sandstorm.

Standing in the doorway of our 'tent' I could see the silhouettes of the buildings rising up in the moonlight, many buildings covered in a scaffold. There were so many men working on it all, and it became more obvious at night as you could see the thousands of torches moving around as they worked night and day to build our new city.

It was in this temporary accommodation that I gave birth to our first child. The handmaidens attended me and bathed me from a large pot of water. I lay back upon the cushions with our very contented baby girl alongside me and Akhenaten looking down at us both very proudly. I however was very weak and very tired. It had been a difficult birth in our home which, whilst comfortable, was after all, a tent.

The buildings were becoming quite magnificent in the daylight and I soon regained my strength to be able to walk around them. Quite magnificent stone buildings with towering columns. Lots and lots of labour, hundreds, no thousands of men, all pushing and pulling stones into place. There was a large area alongside the buildings where the masons would fashion the large stones. I watched as they delicately chipped away at the rough stones with their stone chisels and hammers.

Then they would take the large stones to the site and I would watch in awe as they used their big wooden blocks and a series of ropes and pulleys to raise everything upright and into place – even the long, towering, perfectly smooth, round pillars which fronted the large centrepiece building. The enormous number of men working at the hauling up on the ropes – pulling, pulling, pulling these massive stones into place was what made it possible.

The numbers of men was quite astonishing to see. Men standing on the sturdy scaffolding platforms, slices of wood held up by what were not poles – but the very trunks of trees themselves, so enormous was the work they were undertaking. The noise was tumultuous – men shouting to have stones moved the very smallest measure so that the stone they were lifting over a hole was in place before they lowered it, slowly, slowly into place before dropping it soundly into position. Then the masons would move in and tap, tap the joints, chipping off the most minute of blemishes to finish it.

Then, having dropped each stone into place the master masons moved in to put the finishing to it - facing it. In one particular building there were four round columns across the front. Four large square blocks of stone were put in place and again I watched the men use their blocks and pulleys to haul these stones into position.

They dragged the stones on rollers to get them to the buildings, rolling them along on logs, big strong ropes tied around the stones as they moved each log from the back of the row and moved it to the front, thus the stone was transported along.

The masons were constantly working, constantly chipping the stones in place, looking at their drawings and parchments and some would draw on the ground to show others what they wanted, scratching into the rock.

The workers, the labourers were all bare-chested men, wearing only loin cloths and the overseers wore long white robes. These overseers would check for the precision of the buildings with their instruments – a square piece of wood with a triangle set onto it. They also had a staff with a right-angled piece attached to it, at the end, and they would hold it in front of them, resting the base upon the ground and with the right angled piece in front of them look at the building through it to line up various parts of the building with the top of their staff.

In some of the areas men had stone dishes of water and they splashed the water onto the walls, flicking it with a long piece of spliced twig which resembled a brush, over and over. Once the wall was wet they used small stones to grind against the wall to polish it, using a circular motion. They would really polish and then add more water, then grind, grind at length until it became like a paste polishing the walls of the buildings.

I loved to walk around and watch the progress. In another building there were two bases at either side, two plinths made of massive stones which would hold two statues and the plinths were shaped like animals feet.

All around there were big temples and buildings, enormous towers, enormous columns, growing up above me. Some of the building walls had half sculptures, friezes built into them, lions and big animals, Egyptian figures carved into the walls with the large headdresses, standing 40 ft high in their magnificence, carved into the walls. At the finishing stages the men on the scaffolding rubbed pigment into them to give them colour. They did not use paint and brushes, they worked the pigment in from the palm of their hand and slowly rubbed it into the very stone itself.

They used the same method to colour the giant columns with their blue bands around them, using a blue pigment, very, very colourful with a beautiful intenseness. One particular building had a square top built upon it, like a stone roof which the columns were holding up. The massive lengths of stones, single pieces of stone, which made the columns were once again pulled up by the massive manpower as they used their ropes to haul these stones into place before coaxing them the last measure and dropping them into their final resting place.

There were no slaves used in the building of the city. These were craftsmen. There was no enforcement used, these were working men. The overseers would tell them what to do but no force was used to control the men of many skin colours who built our city.

The buildings were taking shape and then they started to put down the big stone slabs to make the walkways between the buildings. All led to the centrepiece of the temple building rising up to the sky with its wall of friezes.

Akhenaten and I walked between the colossal buildings and the shadows that they cast gave a cool place to walk in the hot sun, a coolness in the shade. I felt excited and proud and I loved every minute of this as we looked at everything. We walked together and looked up at the massive buildings, everywhere was so beautiful, the stonework and the vibrant colours of the friezes in them. There was a half sun looking down at us from the top of the building and as we entered the building side by side we could see the chambers and rooms carved within the building, built into the sides.

Some of our buildings had been cut into the very sides of the rock formations so where there was an outcrop of rock we had built into the rock. The buildings went on and on. There were some wooden buildings, like barns, which leaned against the outside of the walls. These were the stores and were full of bales and containers. Oxen were used to move everything around the city.

And the city continued to grow and grow in the same way as our daughter did. It didn't seem long before she could walk around the city with us, and sometimes Akhenaten would stoop and pick her up to carry her as she tried her hardest to keep up with us. She was beautiful with a bronze skin that was a mix of the two of us and jet black hair. She joined us whenever it was possible and we were happy for her to do so.

The buildings were nearly finished now and the temple in particular was very elegant and beautiful on the outside. It was carved in a light coloured stone and it had been faced in something like a marble which was almost white. Inside there were friezes, one of Akhenaten and one of me, and we stood together looking at them. They had captured my black face and long black hair correctly, and as I looked I saw that they had been quite kind to me as what I was looking at was much more pleasing than when I looked in a mirror. They had slimmed my face and it was most flattering but I could see that they had done the opposite to Akhenaten – they had rounded his elongated face.

This was 40 or 50 feet high and our figures were surrounded by everyday objects in the frieze. There was no representation of any of the gods. Rather we had animals, soldiers, the priests and the people. It also showed the buildings as this was a portrayal of how we had built the city. This was the temple, a place for contemplation and to take inspiration. It had a flat polished area, a cleared area at its heart with a table for burning incense, and shafts of light flowed into this beautiful, tranquil place. It was very beautiful. A beautiful place of peace.

And we had our palace here too. It too had been completed. Through slits of openings in the walls we could look out onto the city. Everywhere was clean and tidy in our home, cushions and carved furniture and a bed on the floor with sumptuous cushions and covers. It was the comfort and privacy I had been craving. And as we looked out of our palace we looked upon a near-finished place which was alive and bustling now with people.

Akhenaten left by ship to return to the old city. He was going to tell the people that their new city was ready for them, and bring them back with him. I watched him leave. When he returned, quite a time later, many did come and join us, but some did not want to come and so they stayed behind in the old city.

We showed the priests around the new buildings, in their long robes and some with their great finery and jewellery around their necks. I watched them as Akhenaten was talking to them – some were smiling and looking approvingly, but there were those who showed they were not interested, even to the point of rudeness. When we took them to see the walls of the temple some actually left, a lot stayed but there were some who left.

The new city was a community now. People were living there, there was a market place selling bread and fruit and life was thriving there. Soldiers walked around it, people pulled carts through it carrying provisions. It was very colourful, very vibrant. It was thriving. If you stood on the outskirts you looked out onto fields where people were farming now and there were ships, too, in the river, with small buildings there, also.

The buildings in the centre of the city were large and they had smaller, square stone buildings set around them. Some had rounded rooftops and some had flat roofs, some had lean-to timber buildings built onto them and some had canvases attached to them. The place was full of women and children as well as the men, and the women walked around carrying their vases on their shoulders. The whole place was thriving.

Our daughter was in her forth year when I gave birth again, this time in the comfort of our palace. This time I became very ill with a fever during the first stages of the birth – first hot, then cold, and when the child finally arrived it was dead. They brought the child to me and put it in my arms but it was dead.

I never recovered from that fever. I did not again get out of bed and I could no longer walk around our beloved city. My strength was diminishing by the day and I knew I was dying. I worsened quickly. My daughter would come to me in the bed and lie alongside me, cuddling into me as if she knew.

Akhenaten and I discussed what was to be and we both knew that it would be expected of him to take another wife and although he did not wish to do so, his loyalty to his people meant that this would have to be so. It was also important that he have more children. I knew this did not in any way diminish what we had or belittle our love. It was his duty and his position, This was not a decision made by the man, it was a decision made by the Pharaoh.

He brought the chosen woman to me, for my approval, and I was still strong enough then to talk to her and I have to say I found her very kind. I explained, as best I could to my daughter that this lady would be taking care of her and watched with some relief as they spent time together. I watched as she brushed my daughters hair in a most gentle fashion, Akhenaten sitting beside me and looking very sad, very sad. At times his future wife would also reach over and hold my hand in kindness.

I was growing very weak now and Akhenaten held our daughter to me one last time and then sent everyone away from us. It was just him and I now. He sat down beside me, holding my hand. There was a terrible sadness as the flames of the torches went down and I became weaker and weaker. As I lay there my line of vision started to close in, it was getting darker and closing, smaller and smaller, until it had gone.

Then I was looking down at my body on the bed, Akhenaten still holding onto my hand and I watched as he knelt beside me and brushed his hand gently onto my face. I was surprised to see my skin so very thin and that I was almost grey. My limbs were so very thin and I only then realised how very ill I had become and how I had looked. Then I moved to stand beside Akhenaten as he and I looked down at my body and I watched as he cried.

After a while he called the people back into the room and they changed the clothes on my body. Then they washed the body and tidied it. Akhenaten looked down at my body and then went outside to tell everyone. Some of the women were crying and the men looked very sad. I watched the preparation of my body and as they placed it into a sarcophagus I watched as they closed the lid.

I followed it on the funeral procession, many were crying and I went with them as the whole procession moved out of the city. They took my body a long way out of the city and journeyed on and on and on for what seemed a very long time, off into the wasteland. The numbers of the procession had been getting less and less until the time when there was only Akhenaten and ten men who stayed with the sarcophagus.

They came to a slope with a hole in the ground and as we entered there was a large chamber and all watched as they put the sarcophagus into place. One of the men was a priest and he read some words over me. The other men brought in some containers and chests which they placed around me. They exited the chamber and dropped a big stone into the front, then pushed an even larger stone down the slope and filled it all in with sand.

Then, as I still watched, they brought animals with rakes on their backs and they began to plough up the land to remove traces of their tracks, and they cut down trees and burned them to change the landmarks. As night fell they continued, cutting down the bushes, burning everything and even smashing up any larger rocks which could have been landmarks.

In a solemn procession now they left in the opposite direction, away from the city and every time they came to a tree they chopped it down and destroyed it. The same with bushes, they moved rocks, walking, walking, walking. Then they found another hole in the ground and filled it in, doing the same as before. They dug a few more holes too on the way so that no-one would know which they had used. Akhenaten watched carefully the whole time.

Now they headed off down to the edge of the river where a ship was waiting and each of the ten men joined their families who were waiting aboard the ship. Soldiers arrived now and handed over large chests full of riches and coins for each man, to pay for his silence. Akhenaten watched as they sailed away.

I stood alongside Akhenaten as he watched their ship leave and then turned back and looked towards the wasteland where he had left my body. Just wasteland now and he had been so thorough that I doubted even he truly knew where my body was. The soldiers accompanied Akhenaten then back to the city.

I stayed around Akhenaten for some time and I watched as our daughter and he consoled each other. At the time of my death she had been in her sixth year. I hated leaving them but of course I knew I had to do so, and I walked away towards a tremendous brightness.

I returned often to be around Akhenaten. Although he carried out his work as a Pharaoh and re-married as was his duty, he did so in sadness. He did not join his new family other then when it was absolutely necessary, preferring to stay in our bedchamber alone for the rest of his life. I watched once as a handmaiden brought a newborn baby to show him and at the news that his child was a boy Akhenaten managed a small smile, but then he sent the woman and child away and stayed alone, thoughtful and sad in our large bedchamber. He thought of me constantly.

I returned often and watched my daughter grow and watched as Akhenaten spent all of his free time with her. I stayed around them both and it pleased me, although I did not like to see that he was always so sad. He never recovered.

There were other children in the palace as well by that time, and when Akhenaten's son had reached the age of his tenth year, by which time my daughter was of course much older, the son died and I once more stood beside Akhenaten as he grieved all over again, this time for his son.

Ours was, and in my heart still is, a wonderful love story which is etched into my memory and feels as wonderful and powerful today as it did all of those years ago. I am pleased to have shared this with you and hope that it has set straight much of what has wrongly been written about us by historians and those who choose to call themselves experts.

Akhenaten

[Later that day.]

When my queen died no-one could give comfort or consolation. It was the end of an era, because we were destined to rule together. Together we were powerful, we were wonderful. Separated we were diminished. It was better that she went before me because I would not have liked what they would have done to her if she had been on her own. I feel they would have seen it as a time to close in around her. I know what they did when we had both left the earth and I know they did return to the old ways, and I would not have liked my queen to be there to have seen that.

But it was a time of greatness and our new city will always be within our memories and within our hearts and I can look upon it now in all its splendour. The memory of it is still vivid in my very self.

There are many so-called scholars who would like to speak to me and to ask me so many questions, but of course they will never gain this opportunity. I will let them play with their hieroglyphs and let them make their guesswork but they will not have this chance. There were many mysteries surrounding the both of us and I hope now we have been able to answer some of them.

Nefertiti and I being together was not by chance. We had met before and there was no chance involved in our meeting, it was engineered to be so. I knew that she would come to me and I knew that I would have to meet her part of the way. Together we were wonderful, but I wonder if the world was not ready for us. Are they ready now?

Nefertiti

[The same day.]
When Akhenaten and I walked here we knew that the beings the priests worshipped were not gods and that they had never been gods. We knew the truth of them. We knew that the very ancient hieroglyphs which these people had come across, and used as their own, showed portrayals of humanoid forms with a variety of head shapes, but they did not show gods. They were not pictorial representations of the attributes each god possessed – they were simply a true account, a true record of how these beings had actually looked. These visitors were made of flesh and blood as you are now. They were not from the Earth but they were civilisations who had come to here from afar, from planets far distant.

They came not as gods, but in craft, as alive and as solid as the people who walked here. They first walked here before the time of your dinosaurs. So it was over a very great period of time that false stories of them as gods emerged, as each generation handed down story after story and each generation made it something more fantastic than the one before. Eventually it had changed out of all recognition from its truth and had become folklore.

The later generations who lived upon the soils and sands of Egypt emulated these very ancient beings in many ways. One of the ways was by building structures in the shape of a pyramid. Here they were emulating the very craft which some of those who visited this Earth had used to bring them here. The craft these visitors used were built in the shape of a pyramid and Akhenaten and I knew that they, like others, had come from the stars. [ENDS]

KNOWING JASPER
PART TWO

SPACE

Jasper says ....

I would hope that having read through the first section of this volume you have begun to open you minds to many possibilities that you may never have considered before. Or maybe you have considered them, but you had found them to be beyond your understanding or beyond your naturally inquisitive nature to look any further.

The first section now completed, you should begin to be more open to accept new knowledge. As I have always said knowledge is all, it is knowledge and our thirst for new knowledge that drives us on and makes us what we are.

By now you have been introduced to many who have spoken across the barrier between the etheric layer and solid existence. You have heard from people from many backgrounds and lives. I would hope that you have found something in each and every one, all whose words have been reproduced here. If you can accept even the smallest part of what you have read, and having accepted it, understand it, then your journey of knowledge is ready for the next door to be prised open for you.

I hope that by now you accept that life continues after the material body stops functioning and that the ones that you have known and loved are still close by you and not gone forever. Having accepted that life exists in the etheric layer you must by now ask yourselves how much further you can go on your journey of knowledge.

Anyone that has stood on the Earth and looked up to the stars and tried to understand just how many points of light there are in the night sky, must have also wondered about the possibility of life existing around those distant points of light.

Space is vast and the area occupied by mankind on Earth is microscopic when compared to the whole of even the visible area of space. Take what you can see with the naked eye or even the most advanced piece of viewing technology and none of this will begin to give you any idea of the sheer vastness of existence.

By now 'modern' mankind accepts that even the remotest parts of the Earth have been explored. Even the sea has given up some of its mysteries but holds some back for later discovery.

Just look around at all you can see, then look again out into space. The human mind by now must have grasped that there must be life on other planets. But as always with the minds of man, what he cannot see for real he fills in, filling in the missing pieces from his imagination. Fiction writers have made good income from their imagined monsters and imaginary vile civilisations coming to the Earth to take away what we have, coming here simply to invade and destroy.

But let us put everything into perspective. Keep the fiction and the monsters for frightening children into sleep at bed time. Let us consider the truth not fiction, let us consider the beauty not manmade horror.

Before moving on. I will pose the questions again for you that you must have asked before picking up this volume.

Is there life after death? Yes there is. I hope that the examples from the first section of this book have opened your minds to this.

Is there life on other planets? Yes. Endless varieties of life exists in space and although they may be of many different shapes and sizes they are just like you.

Read on now and I will introduce you to just a small selection of those who have spoken to Lillie and myself. I hope you enjoy what you find and wish to prise that door open wider and absorb the knowledge that is there for you if you just reach out and accept it.

***

Lillie says ... On 27 August, 2005 I was shocked. Because that was the first time that I spoke to someone who wasn't from this planet. I spoke to a member of a civilisation called Randah, and it was as if that opened the floodgates for many more to speak.

There are thousands of inhabited planetary systems in our universes and I have since spoken to many of the truly inspiring people who inhabit them and travel the universes from them. I will gladly share these experiences with you, but before we embark on our journey through these universes (and further still) we should spend some time to discover how our own planet has been badly damaged and manipulated by others. Before we can move into the future we need to understand the past.

EARLY HISTORY OF PLANET EARTH

Earth's current historians (and their predecessors) have always had a problem in dating events in very ancient history. I feel that when you are looking so very far back it doesn't even help to put dates upon it – nor in many cases is it possible to do so. I am starting this section so far back that the best we can do is to put it into an order, using a timeline.

The Great Meeting

I would like to start this section of the timeline at a time before dinosaurs walked the Earth. And at this point in Earth's history the Earth had already developed into being a meeting place for many other civilisations who came here from other planets near and far.

Those on the Earth and on other planets in these universes had developed to a highly advanced state of evolution. Most civilisations in the universes had already conquered space travel a long time before and were travelling between each other's worlds and mixing freely. They had planned, long before, to meet when the time was right and discuss the unification of all of their worlds. The host civilisation of that meeting was situated on the Earth and the Earth was the place designated for what was called The Great Meeting. It was a highly significant step in the evolution and advancement of all delegate civilisations.

At that time the people of the Earth lived in highly advanced cities which would put our current science fiction writers to shame, so technologically advanced were they in all their towering beauty. There were a number of extremely large cities scattered across the planet, each of these cities was situated within a vast glass-like dome structure which covered the whole city.

I am taking you to a point in time when most of the representatives from a large percentage of those civilisation who were to attend the meeting had already arrived (by craft and other means) and were scattered over the planet. Most of them were already in the domed cities and a very small few were transporting between the cities and thus outside of the domes. Without any warning a co-ordinated attack from off world destroyed every domed city, all of the buildings and infrastructure within it and all of the people. The destruction was instantaneous and terrible in its totality. In a split second each city went from a thriving, bustling city filled with expectation and hope for the future, to nothing but tiny particles of dust. It is this dust which forms Earth's current deserts and the deserts of North America, South America, China and North Africa still bear the scars of that terrible day. The sands of the deserts are the vaporised remains of what was once there.

Those who survived because they were between cities when this took place could only look on in horror. Any civilisations on their way to The

Great Meeting turned back, fearing for themselves, and they beat a hasty retreat to their own planets, where they put up defence systems and waited. The alliance of civilisations which would mean the peaceful advancement of the universes had been halted by that one action and it was to take all civilisations a very long time to recover.

The Making Of The Dinosaurs

Back on the Earth the radiation from the weaponry used became far reaching and in time the animals and the birds, all wildlife started to show signs of malignancy. In time the new births became more and more contorted in shape and so malformed that eventually they evolved into what our own history books have labelled 'dinosaurs' and what little number of man that still roamed the Earth soon died out.

Only an Ice Age halted the terrible malformation as man and beast waited in the etheric layer for a natural 'cleansing' of this planet to be complete. Then solid life (animal and mankind) was ready to be re-born afresh on a planet which had re-grown its vegetation everywhere except on the site of the dome destructions. The deserts could not grow anything and were to remain as a terrible reminder of what warfare can do.

Populating The Earth

And those who had perpetrated the act of aggression which had destroyed the domes had not finished with this planet. Once everything was ready for life they brought a very large selection of solid people here from a variety of other worlds. By fair means or foul these aggressors and manipulators, a large group under the authority of three individuals (Avandna, Hilas and Unksal – who will re-appear later in this, and other Jasper publications) 'delivered' large groups of solid people from many other planets to this Earth. These are your ancestors.

Life evolves naturally on all worlds and these new people had already evolved into their own shapes and skin colours, as they stepped foot here for the first time it was very obvious that they were all from different beginnings. They had been 'collected' from far and wide and many of them had been promised a new life with a variety of false promises made to them.

Once they arrived here they were kept in their groups and all technology (for they were all highly evolved and advanced people) and anything which could identify their origins was removed from them and they were handed simple clothing. Then a land mass was allocated for each group and they were 'delivered' to their new homelands.

And those who had played that terrible trick upon them left them here and went on their own way, back out into space. The advanced people found themselves in an underdeveloped world where natural life was just restarting. The were highly advanced members of mankind forced into becoming cavemen. Over time they devolved from their advanced selves and Avadna, Hilas and Unksal put a system in place which warned future space travellers not to come near the Earth. In the main all the advanced civilisations kept well away from here.

Avadna, Hilas and Unksal

After a very long time Avadna, Hilas and Unksal and those who banded with them and committed these atrocities were caught, judged and removed from where they could influence others. We are no longer in any danger from them, but we bear the scars of what they did to us here on the Earth. Their involvement was long and involved. They kept a hold over this place for a very long time and manipulated it and its people in many ways – none of them good. Now they are gone.

But they left a terrible legacy. So that other space travellers would stay away from here Hilas had made sure that any who came within close proximity of the Earth thought that this was a prison housing those who had committed heinous crimes against on other worlds. The falsified 'records' showed that they had been brought to the Earth to serve lifetimes of sentences. This was a very clever defence to stop others seeing how this world had evolved and to prevent them from suspecting foul play. There is now so much greed, anger and uncaring in this world that the falsehood of it housing prisoners would not seem unreasonable.

The people of this planet have been manipulated in many ways and over a very long period of time to become the way we are today. It is only recently that Avadna, Hilas and Unksal were forced to release their terrible hold on the people of this planet. And when I say 'recently' I mean very recently, the last fingers of their terrible hold were prised away as recently as August 2009. They are gone and we are free to think and act for ourselves for the first time in millennia.

CLUES THAT ANCIENT VISITORS LEFT BEHIND

Although this Earth had an exclusion area around it and most stayed away, but there were those who had no choice but to venture here. They sometimes had no alternative but to land on the Earth to repair craft and some simply crashed here. Others accidentally strayed here by other means.

So, we did have visitors from other worlds. They arrived at a variety of points throughout our history, they stayed for a brief time in various locations and in many cases there are clues still here, which if you can read them properly, are very obvious.

Many historians and other 'academic experts' have tried to answer the mysteries of various relics and ruins which are on our planet. They use supposition and theory. Here are the facts. Here are the answers ....

The Sphinx

[19 January 2009. From Gaynor, a Higher Being]

Gaynor said ....

I observe your written works. There are areas that you need answers for, and I suppose I am the one who must supply it. There is one particular area where you speak of this structure called the Sphinx. It is over 10,000 of your earth years old. It was originally constructed in the image of something else than you see today. It was fashioned by a race of beings who came to your earth as visitors.

It quite often happened that visitors came and settled for a short while, to carry out repairs to craft or to await a rescue which could take a long time in coming. Thus they would need to settle, to build colonies. And this area of Egypt had always been one of attraction, because of its location I suppose. It was warm, it was verdant, it was quite fertile. When the visitors came it was good farming land. It was good, green land, not dry and barren as you see it now. They were great builders these people. They fashioned many things in stone. They built them in all shapes and sizes but then after a short time, as they were only every supposed to be temporary settlers on your Earth, they moved on once rescued, as quite often happens.

What you see there is the carving of one of their animals I suppose you could say. The base, as you see it now, is as it was originally constructed but the head was carved in later times to be more stylised around the Egyptian way of life. What was seen there originally was an animal-type head. An animal head which was more like a dog in construction. It was more like a ferocious animal. The beings themselves were not quadrupeds, they were bipeds, and this resembled one of their animals.

The original structure was to scare people. It was constructed to be a fierce animal. You must remember that at the time the earth was very primitive. This carved head was illuminated at night and from a distance it would be enough to frighten the people away.

When the visitors moved away the primitives moved in and destroyed where they could. They destroyed or re-used the other structures but they did not touch the sphinx for a long time. They disfigured the face on the animal, so for a long period of time the animal-like creature sat there, with a figureless face, with its features destroyed and beaten away.

It was when civilisation again returned to Egypt that the face was restructured. At first it was considered to destroy that and take it away completely, but I suppose along the same lines as before, this time not to scare but to give a feeling of superiority, the face would be carved to look out over those and survey all that it sees.

So the actual original structure is over 10,000 years old and it was modified in later years. Your scholars and scientists can try as they will and they can put their theories upon it, but of course the original stone work that formed the head has been long since carved away and there are no records.

You only have to look to see how out of proportion the whole thing is. These people were great builders. They were great technical builders. They would not have fashioned such a thing with disproportionate features.

I like to help where I can. What the civilisation built was long since destroyed, nothing was left. As with many visitors they take everything with them and anything which is left behind in the way of debris has long since decayed or disappeared. I am pleased your written work is going so well. I needed to assist in some way.

Easter Island

The statues on Easter Island had been fashioned to resemble visitors who were here also over 10,000 years ago. The visitors, whose heads did resemble those of the statues, had settled here awaiting rescue and when they were finally rescued and left the primitive people who lived on the island fabricated the statues to try and attract them back. Centuries later (coincidentally) the islanders themselves died out because they had destroyed their eco system. They used all of their trees and other vegetation and being an island could not replenish it from elsewhere.

Pueblo Bonito - New Mexico

The ruins of the large once-circular 'city' hewn down far into the ground was once the long-term base of a group of visitors. Their circular craft crashed and they built a city beneath it to house them as they too awaited rescue. There are later editions on and around what was original, as many from Earth inhabited it long after the visitors had left, but what was deep beneath the craft was fashioned by visitors from space.

The Nazca Lines - Peru

[14 September 2006 – A Higher Being came to speak]

He said ...
You have an interest in the South Americas. The Nazca Lines were decorations, they served no purpose whatsoever. The original visitors left before these decorations were produced by those from the Earth. The visitors had interacted with the earth primitives and had left knowledge with them – they had been mapping the terrain to send co-ordinates and mapping details to those from their home world who were coming to rescue them and had used some of the earth inhabitants to help. Thus these Earth people had gained knowledge of how to plot vast distances of straight lines, using the coordinates from the sun and the stars. In places they also drew pictures. They could never hope to see what they had drawn but they knew that if they kept faithfully to the map references they drew upon, they knew the pictures would be true. They thought the bigger the picture the more chance they had of being seen. They thought it would please the visitors from other worlds and they wanted them to return. They had no other way of communicating with the visitors who had left – they had no telepathy, no technology, the only way they could communicate was pictorial and they knew that the people who had left had gone to the sky. [Ends]

South American Pyramids

There is a very ancient civilisation who came here despite the warnings of it being a prison, and left behind pyramid structures in South America. They used these structures as a form of transportation. Thus the primitives, long, long before the Mayans and the Aztecs, would see them enter these structures and disappear. It is not hard to see how generations of primitives, passing down this information, long after the civilisation had left, changed the facts. The visitors were a highly evolved civilisation and were very peaceable. When they left they removed all technology from these structures but the empty carcass of the stone structures stayed.

The visitors would not have wanted their structures, a very few of which are originals (others are much later replicas) to have become places of sacrifice. They were not gods and once again we have the situation of information being passed down through generation upon generation until it changed into complete nonsense and folklore. The Mayans and Aztecs are not descendants of these beings and simply invented their own religion, as has so often happened.

This ancient civilisation of Higher Beings were very advanced, even then, and extremely kind and compassionate. Other space travellers tell me that there is evidence of them having been on many other planets. Many speak of ancient ruins similar to those in South America, and those who have better recorded history than us speak very highly of the builders who left them behind.

That ancient civilisation exists still. They are called Randah. They long ago elevated away from any solid presence and are all now completely etheric. They are extremely elevated (not gods still) and they now exist in a place far distant from here. Being so elevated, however, they can keep a watchful eye on us here, and all of the universes, and they do so constantly.

Communication through space is far faster and less cumbersome than space travel itself and the very long distances that Randah and others can speak from are too vast to comprehend. You will hear of Randah again before the end of this book. They hold a position of great importance in the hierarchy of the beings who exist in the universes. You may remember that it was Randah that I first spoke to on 27 August 2005, when I was so shocked to have my 'First Contact' with beings from space.

Mesa Verde Ruins - Colorado

The city, hewn out of rock, was built by descendants of another civilisation of highly elevated, intelligent and very spiritual visitors from elsewhere. They had strayed here and could not return.

Egyptian Hieroglyphs

Nefertiti mentioned the hieroglyphs and the head shapes portrayed in them. There are hieroglyphs which were painted inside the various tombs and rooms which have been opened, and there are also hieroglyphs which were cleanly etched deep into the outer stone of many old stone structures. The 'experts' have long wondered how these deep straight carvings and straight lines were etched or carved into the stone – this was simply done by a chemical formula – or as a particular Pharaoh told me – by 'use of alchemy.'

But it is not how they did it that is important. That is not the mystery. It is the knowledge contained within the hieroglyphs which is important. And it is the knowledge of what is within the depths of the tomb of Seti I which is the most important of them all.

These are the drawings which give genuine historical information and if they could be read properly what a tale they would tell. Even when they were written they were written to confuse (to protect the valuable information from those who do not deserve it) and so who is to blame today's 'Egyptologists' and their predecessors for what they have got so very wrong. But those who wrote it know well what is written there.

These walls and ceiling show a variety of beings of a variety of shapes and sizes. All bipeds, walking upright but with an assortment of head shapes. If you could see it you would see bird heads, baboon heads, jackal heads and many more. They were all real. They are just drawings of what they actually looked like. The wall itself is a record of all of the beings who were here to attend the Great Meeting. They came from the far reaches of the universes to attend that meeting. That tomb wall is a record of all who were there. Modern day solid beings with similar head shapes to those represented upon that wall exist still – alive and well and living on their own planets.

I have spoken many times to the Higher Being who walked here as Seti I – elevated now back to his true form of a Higher Being. He exists far from here now and yet returns and speaks to me often. Seti's mummified body is well-known and his carcass is paraded as one of Egypt's best preserved mummies. I had been looking at a picture of it on the internet earlier as he came to speak on 11 August 2007 ....

> **Seti said ...** I looked on when you found images of my body. Now it is nothing. The driving force, the spirit ... it is the spirit which gives the body its beauty, and in some cases its ugliness. The body is nothing without the spirit. The shell is nothing. I feel it is wrong to place the body on view, it should be cast to the four winds. It was not something to be worshipped and looked upon.
>
> It is a shame that your Earth history does not show the true side of our existence. They know only of the building of the great structures, of the so-called 'gods'. There were no gods. Let them see us as builders and collectors of gold trinkets – they are blinded by the gold. It is the test of the true measure of a being to put him in a room with a scroll and a bar of gold. The fool will go for the gold. The true mind will be mindful of the scroll for the knowledge. The conquistadors did such terrible things in the name of their 'god'. Had they looked upon the images which were depicted in the gold which they melted – this was the true value, not the melted-down liquid they clamoured for. There were many places on your Earth which contained great knowledge. [Ends]

Crystal Skulls

A few of them around today are genuine and they were left here by visitors. They used them for health care. Advanced civilisations can perform surgery without invading the body at all. This particular civilisation used light refraction to show the area to operate on if there was repair needed to the head of one of their kind. These are replicas of the actual heads of the patient who needed treatment.

Cup And Ring Marks

There are many copies but some genuine ancient marks in stone do exist. The genuine marks are very old. It is easy to recognise the originals – they are concentric circles, not a spiral, and they have one straight line from the centre to the outer rim, like a radius line. These marks are the universal symbol of rescue. If a craft had to land because of problems, or crashed, then the occupants would be stranded. Although at first they would use their own technology to send messages they would eventually lose the power source which powered their technology and yet would still need to identify where they had crashed for later rescue parties.

This symbol identifies that visitors were stranded in that area and the number of rings identifies how far away they were from their home planet when they became stranded - the more rings, the further they are from home. They etched it into rock because they knew that this was the only way to guarantee the longevity of the message.

UFO Reports

This from an Elevated Being, Eshe, is interesting, as she speaks of the reality of many 'sightings' ...

Eshe said ... Your earth has been isolated from other worlds for a long time. In the last 10,000 years I can tell you that although there have been a very few genuine sightings of stray craft from a variety of other worlds there have been no planned landings and most of your 'sightings' of what you call UFO can be explained by real events coming from your own world such as military and non-military tests of aircraft, the lights from recreational planes in anomalies of weather which cause a 'trick of the eye', fakes mocked-up for fame and notoriety and many, many instances of individuals who have simply lied about what they have seen, or rather not seen.

There have been a very small number of incidents where craft not of your Earth have accidentally crash landed, for the most part these have been disguised or destroyed by the originators of the craft so that they would not confuse, but an even smaller percentage have fallen into the hands of earth governments – these were either secreted away or dissected and used for their technology. [Ends]

Earth's 'stay-away' status' was lifted in 2008 and there are now many more genuine sightings than before. There is still a type of 'universal code of conduct' for travellers who are aware that they should not interact and interfere with other worlds (unless it is to assist in some emergency) but there are those who do draw near enough to monitor this sector of space – they are explorers and knowledge-gatherers and they come from a variety of sectors of this and other universes. They are not a threat and not aggressors – that scenario is the domain of Science Fiction writers. In reality there is nothing here these travellers could possibly want.

Ernest and I see them in the night skies and wonder why the people of the Earth do not see them for what they are – but in reality it is because people expect the exciting coloured lights of rapidly darting-about flying saucers and the other weird and wonderful craft of the science fiction writers - they do not see these real craft for what they are – they presume they are just stars or Chinese lanterns, and the authorities are happy for us to think that way.

Why No Intercepted Transmissions?

If those from other worlds speak to each other with such frequency then why has our Earth scientific equipment never intercepted these communications? Is it possible that I am able to speak at such length to other worlds and that not one piece of equipment here on the Earth has ever picked it up? The answer to both is 'yes' and the reason is telepathy. Advanced civilisations all use this method of communication. They transmit and receive information with the power of the mind and they do not use vocal chords or sound. They find our way of communicating extremely primitive, which it is (and we are) by comparison. We understand that 'stealth technology' cannot be detected, so it should be easy to understand that off world communication cannot either.

Telepathy can travel much further than any other form of communication and it can transmit a larger amount of complex information at much greater speeds. There is one set of telepathic messages which was sent by a civilisation so advanced, whose telepathic signal was so strong, that their messages were inadvertently received here by many people. This civilisation from a far distant planetary system in our universe were transmitting a friendly 'hello' message to anyone in the universe who might hear it and respond. None were capable here at that time of responding and certainly none here were capable of interpreting correctly what they were 'seeing' subliminally. But there is evidence that many here saw it. And this will come clear later in this volume.

So now that we have explored the history of our own planet and how space has interacted with it, let's move off world and look at the rest of our solar system and its history.

OUR SOLAR SYSTEM

There are ten planets within our system. Yes, I said *ten*, and I have some basic information on each one.

Mercury

Mercury is closest to the sun of all the planets and so it is completely uninhabitable. It always has been, nothing has ever lived there or ever will live there – it's just too hot. The temperatures are so extreme and there are so many stresses and strains on the surface of the planet. The extremes of heat and cold cause structural faults like earthquakes all the time, the surface is constantly cracking and reforming. It's volcanic, like a barren desert with craters. The atmosphere is acrid and un-breathable, it always will be.

Venus

Venus was once populated by colonies of visitors, before the Earth was inhabited. It's warmer than the Earth and has extremes of temperature, but the extremes are liveable and the colonies were sited in the most environmentally beneficial areas. The environment is made up of gasses which are not breathable by Earth people and the gravitational pull is different, so we could live there, but we would have to live inside structures with an artificial atmosphere. The people who lived there in the past lived in domes. They were visitors. They were humanoid. They left.

Mars

Mars was once the most populated of all of the system planets and people lived there before the Earth was populated. They lived in domes. On Mars there is a Memorial Garden dedicated to all of those who lost their lives at the time of The Great Meeting, that terrible conflict on the Earth which destroyed the areas which have now become our deserts. There is a partially buried dome remaining on Mars but no-one is there. Mars has water beneath the surface. It has an area of permafrost beneath the surface of the planet and whole areas of the planet are covered by a frost layer which has soil on top of it. It has extremes of temperature and it has ice caps at certain times of the year. It currently lacks the right constituents to support life on its surface. It could be colonised, but only in dome structures. It could, eventually be possible to change the atmosphere to make it almost liveable, but it is more than likely in the very far future that people will live there who have adapted to survive in a slightly altered atmosphere rather than altering the atmosphere to suit the people.

Jupiter

Jupiter is the largest planet, a massive planet and it had small colonies on it (before the Earth was populated) again in domes as it is very heavy in poisonous gasses, with a surface devoid of any kind of growth, any kind of life. It is a totally hostile environment. Those that lived there (long ago you must remember) were only scientists and data gatherers. There were no civilian populations – it's just not habitable.

Saturn

Saturn is very hostile in its environment and has never been occupied. There have been short-term visitors there in the past, but just data gatherers who stayed there for a short while. It's very hostile and also very difficult to navigate because of the amount of debris circling around it. The rings are rock particles circling around it, they are of a magnetic nature and have stayed there because of the magnetic attraction around the 'equator.' They stay outside Saturn's atmosphere.

Uranus

Uranus is mainly a cold surface with lots of hostile gasses. Life has never been there. It's rings are within the upper atmosphere and formed in the same way as those of Saturn but differ in that these are inside Uranus's atmosphere. They are held by the gravitational pull of the planet.

Neptune

Neptune moves from extreme to extreme and doesn't get very warm. It changes from a liquid structure (like a sea) to being frozen overnight in large areas. It's too cold and the atmosphere is not breathable.

Pluto

Pluto is too cold. An ice planet, it never gets warm and it's too small to retain any kind of heat. Any heat that it does pick up from the reflection of the sun is lost almost instantly once it is in the shadow of another planet. Too cold and extreme.

Omea

Omea [pronounced oh-may-uh] is the 'unknown planet' which no-one on Earth will ever see unless they go around the other side of the sun. A planet that is almost equal in orbit to the Earth but on the other side of the sun. It follows a pathway which always keeps the sun between it and us. It's on an equal rotation to the Earth, and paces the Earth, so as the Earth moves around, Omea moves around at the same time. It would not even be fully visible from the other planets because it's on the opposite side. The outer planets may glimpse it, like an eclipse, but it would be very rare and also it wouldn't give any indication of it being there because of the sun's radiation and the corona. You would never be able to see it from Earth and you would never be able to detect it from Earth and we certainly would not be able to get there from here using currently available methods.

Omea has had its visitors in the past. It has been inhabited in the past. It has an environment very similar to the Earth but its constituent is more water than land mass. There is life on it currently, water-inhabiting creatures, some amphibians, but they are very low on the evolutionary ladder – not yet intelligent life as we would know it. It has not been heavily explored or populated because it is a solitary planet now. There were others near it but they were unstable and broke up long ago. They are what formed part of the asteroid belts.

And there you have it, whereas 'experts' pontificate long over such matters and use many long scientific words and phrases to impress - that, I believe, is all you currently need to know about our solar system. It's much more exciting to move on again, and out into our universe.

THE UNIVERSES AND DIMENSIONS OF SPACE

As with much of the knowledge contained in this book it is necessary to keep expanding your mind (always keeping an open mind) and as you journey through the universes in this section here I hope you will experience your mind expanding along with that which you are learning about. Much of what follows is extremely complicated and I have tried to simplify it as much as possible using un-scientific terms and avoiding jargon where I can. We will start by looking at how your own system (and all others) were formed.

How Planetary Systems Are Formed

Jasper says ...

Have you ever watched two little dust clouds meet each other as they play along the ground? Sometimes they pass within inches of each other and eventually lose all of their momentum and collapse and deposit their dust on the ground to wait for the next air current to come along and pick up what's left. Or if by chance these two singular insignificant wisps of dust should touch each other who knows what the outcome will be. Even the most powerful and destructive hurricanes and whirlwinds began in this way.

Whether you like it or not if you are a solid walking being you are just a mixture of particles of 'dust' put together in a certain way. Add to this the true you, the spirit, and this is what you are. Space is full of dust in the mixing bowl that is the vastness of space. It just needs for these particles to meet and start off the whole cycle that eventually makes the ground that you stand upon now.

If you had time to do so (and it was possible to stop and wait in space for such a 'beginning') I can tell you what you would see. But first you would have to find an empty area of space. No stars, no planets nothing - just an empty area with other systems way off in the distance. The universes have it all, every particle to build anything imaginable (and much more that you couldn't imagine) are there.

Eternity comes and goes and nothing happens but just by chance one day two 'dust clouds' deal each other a glancing blow. Now it's a different story. Then another and another join the mixture, endless dust clouds, endless particles twist and contort, combining what they have with each other. It will be a long time before you can see the effect of this combining. At first just a dimly illuminated swirl in the black emptiness. But it grows bigger and bigger and brighter and it spins at a speed that is incalculable and too fast to comprehend. Meanwhile, far away in other universes entire solar systems have burned themselves out and been reduced back to the dust that they came from.

But where you are the show has not yet started. Bigger, brighter, faster, and hotter. The mix goes on endlessly until the exact moment when all of the components that have amassed together can no longer contain themselves - the gravity that this spectacle has generated has pulled and compressed the particles into solid masses and others have formed together into gasses. But the particles are all still there. They have formed into groups, some weak, some strong.

Then the inevitable happens. This mass can no longer defend itself from the massive stresses - and the ensuing explosion lights up the blackness. Again endlessly, the explosion goes on, until everything begins to slow down. The centre of the 'explosion' has now become a ball of burning gas.

A new star has staked its claim and settled down for a brief stay in this once dark corner of space.

The solid masses, formed now long ago, have tried to escape the energy that is the gravity produced by the new star but they have slowed and stopped to begin their gentle orbit around their sun. Smaller masses, unable to escape on their own, have attached to the masses, the planets, and become moons. The leftover particles, too big to take their place back with the dust, have settled themselves down in a gentle orbiting ring pacing the planets as they track around the sun. Some of the dust has escaped this mixing bowl and will drift on waiting for the next 'gathering'.

The forces have settled down and the new 'solar system' waits for life to begin. But not all ends well during the confusion that ensued around the forming of this new phenomenon. Some of the masses formed have escaped and embarked on a journey that will take them who knows where, but the path that they take will be a circular one and one day they may just return to the point of their conception and hopefully pass by to make the circuit again.

As it all began - so it one day it will end. But if an end means returning to dust, then that is were we started this journey and so it goes on. Let the dust particles play their games. Life was, is, and will always be. That will never change. We are all made of much, much more.
[ENDS]

And perhaps now you know why I asked Jasper to write it. My no-nonsense, blunt way of telling you facts is all very well, but in the way in which Jasper writes it you get to experience the beauty of the whole thing. I would have said something along the lines of ...

> Empty space has dust particles everywhere and at a certain point in time stray dust clouds form together and spin, gathering momentum until they form a mass, which explodes and forms a sun (a ball of burning gases.) The explosion which formed the sun spat out solid masses, planets, which

169

begin to orbit the sun and their very rotation formed them into spheres as they cooled, some ready to evolve life, if it is a suitable environment for it. Stray particles from each planet are sometimes thrown out on a wider circular trajectory at the formation, and these take a long arced journey and head back towards the planet they span off from, hopefully missing it and continuing on their own orbit. Other big chunks of particles did not leave the area and formed asteroid belts.'

You would have received the same information, but not the same experience as that which I hope you had when you read Jasper's version.

All planets have the same components – they all have the things we on the Earth call 'precious' – they all have gold, silver, platinum, diamonds, emeralds and rubies. But unlike here, most are more advanced - they know that these are worthless things. Only in our material Earth society has man's greed developed a method of finding a scarcity, claiming it as his own and then selling it to others to make the largest profit. No other civilisation would come here to take away what is ours. They have no interest in what is here – other than thankfully a humane interest in the people. We must stop thinking we are the more advanced. We must stop thinking that we are superior. Far from it. Anyone who comes here can learn nothing from us – except possibly how not to do things.

The Universes

Each planet is part of a solar system. There are endless solar systems – it is a number which changes 'daily' and so it is impossible to calculate how many, new systems are forming all the time. The collective term for a number of planetary systems is a universe.

If you are lucky enough to live somewhere without urban pollution, and especially if you live in open countryside, then stand on the next cloudless night and look up. As you keep looking your eyes will become accustomed to what you are seeing and more and more stars will become visible. About half of the stars you are looking at have intelligent life walking on the planets which are rotating around them. And you are looking at a very small part of this universe. I know that the time light takes to travel to us means that the star are no longer where you see them – but despite that you are starting to get an idea of the enormity of it all. And I hope you are also getting an idea of how very small we are. Our planet is like a grain of sand in a desert, and there are many deserts.

Time to expand your mind once again when I tell you that there are many universes. The universes are separated by vast areas of emptiness. Think of a world map where you see areas of landmasses separated by sea – space is the same, there are areas of a collection of planetary systems (universes) and these universes are separated by empty space. Just as Earth's early seafaring explorers set out into vast seas without knowing if they would ever reach any land beyond, so early space explorers set out over vast areas of black, empty space without knowing if they would eventually (generations later in many cases) reach the next universe.

Now, in your mind think of that World map wrapped around a globe. Picture a spherical globe and then picture the landmasses scattered over it, divided by the seas. The collection of universes are also situated in spherical form. And the spherical form which they take is known as a dimension. So a dimension is spherical in shape and consists of 'masses' of universes separated by areas of empty space. And, of course, by now you are getting used to expanding your mind ... there are many dimensions.

The Dimensions

Are you beginning to realise just how small we are? Looking up into that clear night sky try and think of the size of the planet on which you are standing. Look up at the stars and start to try and feel this universe which you are a part of. Then imagine the neighbouring universes. Then those beyond those, and those beyond those, and beyond again.

The dimensions are spherical, like larger versions of the planets. Like the planets have land masses, the dimensions each have collections of universes. The easiest way to imagine a dimension is to think of an onion, layer upon layer. The dimension is a spherical layer, with another layer outside it, and another inside, like Russian dolls if it easier to think of it that way.

The different dimensions are different ages. The youngest ones are nearer the centre and the oldest ones are on the outer layers. They are formed near the very heart of it all and move out, away from that which made them, as other fresh dimensions are formed. There was no 'Big Bang' which started the whole thing, it is a progression. Our dimension is not at the centre – but it is nowhere near the outer reaches. The dimensions are separated by an area of emptiness called The Void. The Void is a series of routes and pathways which access the whole of existence, with rapid access to all planetary systems, universes and dimensions. The Void is accessible only to very elevated and advanced Higher Beings.

Movement and communication between dimensions is restricted. All in a dimensions can communicate with one dimension above and all below. Each dimension is guided by beings from the next dimension outwards, and guides the dimension below. Randah are the civilisation from the next dimension who guide this one. The Higher Beings who are 'of The Void' have unrestricted movement and communication skills to travel to and speak to all dimensions.

There are many misconceptions about Dimensions and many works of Science Fiction use the word quite wrongly. For now, the subject is very complicated and perhaps the most we can hope for is that you understand that you don't understand them.

Time

We have already discussed that time is experienced in a different way by those in the Earth's etheric layer and those of us in the solid layer. So it should not be too difficult to comprehend that time moves differently for those on each planet. I am ignoring the fraction of time which necessitates our Leap Year adjustment in the following examples.

Our Earth revolves around the sun every 365 days (making our year) and spins on its own axis once in every 24 hours. A larger planet would take longer to travel around its sun, and of course longer to spin out its day.

Those who use aircraft to fly around our own planet from land mass to land mass know that they take off in local time for the departure and land in local time for the arrival. There is often a time difference. There are more complications to inter-planetary time differences, one of which is the lifespan of the solid bodies of its inhabitants. Imagine if your body lived for thousands of years, instead of under a hundred – then imagine what percentage a year would be of your total life. Time would have a really different meaning to you. There are many more differences but I hope that you take from this that 'time' moves in different ways on different planets. But imagine this example. You could travel to another planet, a great distance away, even in the next universe using a transport system to be explained later in this book (which take 'no time') and once there you could experience many months of the other planet's normal life, then travel back via this same mode of transport and arrive back on the Earth the day after you left.

It's very, very complicated, and perhaps the most I can hope for is that you understand that you don't understand time.

The Colours Of Space

The problem with my matter-of-fact way of explaining all of this is that sometimes you miss out on the great beauty and wonder of it all. Here I am including a transcript of a space traveller who gave me the following information when I asked him what were the most memorable memories from a very long journey traversing the universes. He was on a space craft 'close' to our Earth as he spoke to me in 2008.

Tovan 375 said ...

I have tried to recall some of the things that are uppermost in my memory really and I think that the things that I remember most from my journeys are the colours. It's strange, the light plays strange tricks on you and planets change colour and they look quite beautiful. From a distance you see warm planets appear to be a warm, orangey red, a warm glow, and cold planets are a bluey green in colour. But as you move closer to them they move and shimmer, and sometimes they go through the whole colour spectrum. And it's like a light show, just for us really. And you feel very privileged to see these things that not many beings have ever seen before, especially when you pass these planets where they have never ventured into space and you think that their planet looks so beautiful and they don't see it.

This one that you are on now, this one you inhabit now, it's been ravaged by time and warfare, but it still looks very beautiful The blues are very deep, the greens and the browns are very vivid and the colour is quite wonderful. From a distance now, from where we are, it looks very blue. It's very blue.

It's quite wonderful, as I said, how the colour spectrum changes and you have this wonderful light show just for us, the travellers. And then there are the particles in space that the light from the various stars play upon. You can't see them from where you are, because the atmosphere you are in filters them. And there are all of the strange constructions as well. You look at the various planets and they have asteroid belts around them, like your planet Saturn, it appears to be striped and it's very strange, but when you get closer it changes completely.

These are wonderful images that I will never forget, we will never forget. But they are always so welcoming. We spent a long time in the black emptiness of space between the universes with no ... not even a pin-point of light for such a long time, then suddenly it's all upon you. First one star, then another and suddenly, before you realise it, the whole horizon, all of the field of vision, is full of stars. And then when you get closer to these stars you see the planets that are around them, the different colours, the shapes, the sizes, the moons that orbit around them, the dust clouds, the coloured gas clouds that orbit them. Quite wonderful.

When you are in an area of space that has so much to see, you cannot count the stars there are so many, especially if you are moving, because they change all of the time and when you think that every one of those stars has the potential of having a whole collection of planets around it, and you think that each one of those planets could have life upon it, and each one of those planets has continents where different types of people live, and different plant forms and life forms, and you realise really how small you really are. [Ends]

SPACE TRAVEL

Science Fiction writers have conjured up some very impressive space ship designs and write of many ways that people move around space. The reality of space travel is more than even the most inventive writers of fiction could conjure up. How those with different advancement and elevation travel in space, and how Higher Beings travel vast distances at a speed so great that it takes no time at all to get anywhere, is almost impossible for us to comprehend.

Space Craft

Put aside your images of silver metal flying saucers ringed with flashing pulsing lights of all colours as they dart around the skies avoiding the cameras of UFO chasers. Put aside all of the weird and wonderful shapes of the many craft (with their advanced technology) which have adorned our screens, as the special effects of the film makers become more advanced.

The reality of the flight decks of most of the current craft traversing the universes might well disappoint by comparison if it is shiny panels, switches, dials and buttons you are looking for. Most space craft now are controlled by the power of the mind. Do not expect cavernous engine rooms. Most are powered by solar collectors or the use of the magnetic pull present in all planets.

Current craft do vary in shape, and vary again in size depending on how far they are travelling and how many solid people need to travel in it. There are spherical craft, flat saucer-shaped craft and a variety of almost misshapen craft - space travel does not need the aerodynamics needed for flight within an atmosphere. One shape which we have already referred to is the pyramid shape – still used today by the ancestors who brought that same shaped craft to Earth not knowing that long after they had gone their shape would be copied and always surrounded by mystery – the pyramid. The pyramid shape makes for an extremely stable structure and can be added to, or reduced in size, with ease without compromising its stability.

Here we have a transcript from someone who remembers the original pyramid craft similar to those that came to the Earth. She travelled in them, and she gave us this information on 6 August 2007.

Eshe says ...

We are standing in front of a pyramid craft. It looks like smooth black glass on the outside, highly polished. We can hear a humming noise and feel that the whole atmosphere around the craft is charged with a type of energy, it almost makes your hair stand on end. As we stand outside it and look up it is like looking up at an enormous building – maybe 80 feet high. The tip is glowing now and it has changed into a luminous green colour.

We stand back, well away now, as the craft is about to take off. The humming noise is more intense now and the craft lifts, levitates and appears to hang there in the air, a few feet off the ground. Then it accelerates and very quickly it has risen and gone. There are no marks upon the ground where was.

Now we walk towards another craft which is humming and this time we will board. We walk through the side of the ship and feel no sensation of having passed through anything. Inside is black glass with a lot of polished white metal fittings. It is not dark inside, it seems like daylight. This is the largest space, remembering its pyramid shape and there are accommodation areas, recreational areas, eating areas and cargo areas on this floor. There is also a lecture theatre with screens. Everyone is speaking telepathically to each other.

Looking to the centre of this level and we see a shaft of light, a beam which streams from top to bottom. We step into the shaft of light and it takes us to other levels. We step out at other levels. Each floor becomes smaller as we move up the pyramid shape. There are many levels. These are all levels for the crew and storage. As we get nearer to the top the appearance changes. As we step out onto this particular floor it seems that the walls of the craft have disappeared, this is not so but to the eye it appears completely open at the sides. We see the floor below and the ceiling above but the sides seem to be open to the outside. There is a 360 degree view of what is surrounding the craft. There are about thirty large comfortable seats facing outwards around the perimeter. This is the control room. Each seat has a console which comes up from the side, out of the armrest, and a panel with controls and a small screen.

Continuing the tour of the craft we go up one more floor in the beam. The beam stops here, you can travel no higher. This floor is smaller and has a metal hand-rail all the way around its centre. As we stand behind the rail, and look to the centre, in the middle is a big ball of light floating in the air. Green luminous light. As we look over the rail now we see ducts in the walls surrounding the energy and these open ducts transmit the energy to the different sections of the ship. As we watch, the energy pulses and grows brighter and darker. It is the source of the humming sound. Looking carefully we can see small particles moving in trails around the energy and shooting off in different directions. We can feel the energy vibrating through our bodies in this room.

We return to the room below and take one of the seats. The arms immediately clamp themselves into place and lock, the same with the leg and foot rests. The sides of the chair move around and forward, and the torso and head is wrapped and cushioned with padded supports which mould to the body. On the armrest, beneath the fingers are the buttons which control the seat. If you press the middle button all of the harness restraints fall away again. They are there purely for safety and comfort. Now we are free to work on the screen and we have buttons which change the chair's seating position and relax or tighten the pressure on the body. One buttons rotates the chair 360 degrees and as we look out now we can see everything to the sides, but also now we can see below and above us also. It is as if the floor and ceiling have disappeared now too. We have perfect spherical vision. Looking down it is as if there is nothing between us and the ground and above we have open sky. It is as if we are sitting on chairs in mid air.

Others are now taking their seats and the humming has become more intense. We look up and although there is no ceiling we can see a glow. There is no sensation on the body but we can see by looking out that we are lifting. We rise slowly ... slowly .. hover ... and now we accelerate and can see the ground disappearing yet there are no feelings of movement. The ground has gone and we see it beneath us now, as a planet. We go even faster now until light sources we pass are just a blur. [Ends.]

Pyramid craft are also used today by the ancestors of those who came here all of that time ago. Although now their power source is solar, most of the description Eshe gave of the craft they used so long ago still stands, so well-designed was that original craft.

The Tubes

There are a series of fabricated tubes which run throughout most sectors of the universes. They are fabricated by Elevated Beings. Historically they have never been close to this planet, Earth. Solid visitors who travelled here in the past did so by craft (which could use these tubes and travel at high, almost instantaneous speed) to take them to the nearest point to here, and then they would take the craft on at normal speed. Even if the tube networks had been here our instruments would not have detected them. The tubes themselves are constructed by Elevated Beings who are part of advanced civilisations.

The tubes make use of the difference between the two layers – solid and etheric. Each tube starts from the solid side, travels through (but does not have exit points en route) an etheric layer and exits once again into the solid layer. This form of tube travel takes a matter of the equivalent of seconds. It is hard to comprehend but let us just say that vast distances can be covered in a very short space of time through these tubes. Solid people use craft which travel through the tubes whereas etheric beings can travel within the tubes without the need for craft.

The Circles

I have already said that the reality of what is here is much more sensational than that which fiction writers imagine. And if the idea of a network of tubes criss-crossing the universes with their infrastructure uniting a whole dimension is hard to grasp, then 'the circles' will stretch your comprehension even more. The circles cannot be seen with the naked eye of a solid being and they could never be detected by any instruments in the solid layer. They can only be 'seen' by extremely Elevated Beings and Higher Beings and the way they work is even harder to explain. Perhaps it would just be easier to let a Higher Being who has used them explain how it feels to travel in this way.

Teelagh says ...
As you stand and look ahead of you can make out a hazy disturbance ahead. As you look more closely you can see a change in density ahead which makes the air in front of you seem slightly distorted, out of focus almost. The disturbance is a large upright circle, as though it is the circular entrance to a large tunnel. Through the circle you can still make out the continuation of the land you are standing upon, as if you are looking through a giant ring covered in a very fine gauze, but still able to see through it to the other part of your current location.

So to give you an example: If I was standing in a field filled with sheep I would be surrounded by sheep and looking through the gauze-like quality of the circle I would be able to see the remainder of the flock standing on the far side of the circle.

To complicate matters further, and I apologise for the intricacy of this explanation but I know just how difficult this must be to grasp, if I was standing with other people who were not as elevated as I it is likely that I would be the only one who could actually see that the circle was there. And if I stepped forward to walk into that circle to those around me I would simply have disappeared. Any others who walked beside me and also entered the circle would walk on and join the sheep behind it. I, however, would exit the circle in the equivalent of one stride and no time at all, and be standing on a completely different planet, in a completely different solar system, sometimes in another universe.

I know it does not sound believable and I cannot even begin to explain to you how this is possible A good lesson for you to learn is that when something is impossible to understand the missing factor in the equation which makes it possible is either 'time' or 'dimensional'. Often the missing element to full comprehension is because time moves differently on all worlds, but here the answer is that this type of travel is dimensional and the use of the circles is restricted to Elevated and Higher Beings who can be trusted with what could be highly dangerous if misused. [Ends]

Sometimes it is just not possible to comprehend such things, and the best we can hope for is that you understand what is possible without knowing how. Perhaps the best we can hope for is that you understand that you do not understand dimensional travel.

The Pathways of Space
There is another form of travel which, once again, Teelagh, describes. [Teelagh - 16 January 2009]

Teelagh says ...
You cannot imagine what it is like to be completely etheric and to be alone, in the vastness of space, surveying the enormity of what 'space' is

and knowing that you can travel it all, visit it all, explore it all. To 'stand' alone and know that you can do this is an indescribable experience. You see how big space is and yet you feel at one with it. You do not need solid ground to stand upon and so it is possible to stay suspended in space, nothing close by and survey the enormity of space itself. All around you, far distant in all directions, are stars.

The first time you see a pathway it is a shock. Ahead of you, like a straight but shadowy light is a pathway. Have you ever been in a darkened room when it is bright daylight outside, there is a chink in the door and a stray ray of light comes in from the brightness outside and in that ray you can see the dust particles from the room. The pathway is like that, vague, not solid. You look again, not sure if you can really see it. Then it seems clearer to you. It stretches out ahead of you and you know you could follow it. You stand and look for longer and as you do so you see other pathways – rather like if you, where you are, stare into the night sky for long enough you start to see more stars than you thought were first there. It is similar when you are staring into the vastness of space peering to focus on the pathway - then you see more and more pathways, a network of them, criss-crossing each other. Some are straight and some roll along like a country lane ahead of you.

Not everyone can see these pathways. Once you reach a certain level of Higher Being then, and only then, can you see the pathways. And once you start to use them you realise how fast they are. You traverse the universes using the pathways, turning off at where they cross and taking another direction and all at a speed which is so fast that it becomes incomprehensible that you are travelling at all. After a while of using these pathways it becomes such second nature that it seems as though you only have to think of a destination to actually be there. But you have travelled a great distance and you have used the pathways. The pathways are not manufactured by solid beings and they have always been there. [Ends]

THE ALLIANCE

There are 5,192 members of The Alliance. Each member is a civilisation and each civilisation exists in its own solar system. So, to put it another way - there are 5,192 inhabited solar systems in this dimension and all of the individual beings who live in the solid layers or exist in the etheric layers of the planets of these systems are members of The Alliance, including the Earth, we are associate members.

By now you are becoming used to existence being in layers. You are in the solid layer and there are others in the etheric layer. Those in the etheric layer are more knowledgeable than those in the solid layer. They know more, comprehend more and understand much more than you do. They are not tied by the bigotry, narrow-mindedness and misunderstandings of the solid layer and so accept truth more readily than you. Those who exist upon other planets are already talking to the etheric layer here and have been for a long time.

Membership of The Alliance is on two levels. Full Membership is given when a civilisation has advanced sufficiently in ways which I will discuss later in this section, but part of the criteria is that both etheric and solid layers have to communicate freely with each other and mix freely.

The secondary level of membership is Associate Membership and this means that although the Associate Member civilisation has been included the in The Alliance they have not yet advanced sufficiently to be capable of taking a full or active part in many areas of the operational work of The Alliance.

Many Associate Members of The Alliance only have communication with The Alliance from their etheric layer and this is the case currently with the Earth – we are Associate Members and currently members of The Alliance communicate freely with our etheric layer. Jasper is in the etheric layer and Ernest and I are able to communicate with that – and so those who inhabit other planets communicate freely with us and have done so for some time. They have never communicated with psychics and mediums in the solid layer and any here who say that they have heard from 'aliens' are lying or confused.

In the following sections I would like to give you more information on some of the Alliance Members: the people, their civilisations, their craft and their home worlds. You will find represented within the following pages a very small selection of people from other planets.

First Contact

Works of Science Fiction make much of First Contact, a time when one civilisation speaks to another for the very first time. I was privileged to be able to experience First Contact for myself recently. There are many who travel in space. All solid beings travel in some form of craft, usually in a group and in one or more craft. They travel for many reasons – but they are all explorers in a way. It is one such group of explorers that I inadvertently sent a message to on 29 July 2008.

That evening I was standing at a first floor window and I was gazing out into the darkening night sky. There had been a series of very bright white lights out in the sky for some time. They were so obviously not stars and as I sat there looking out there was one in my line of sight. Jasper had told me a few days earlier that they were craft and that the people inside the craft did not pose any threat, they were just explorers, and they were a very long way away from the Earth. Ernest and I had watched them on and off for some days.

I looked at the craft and said aloud 'I wish I could speak to you' and thought no more of it. All communication from off world had come to me, I had never tried to make contact with anyone. Then, about half an hour later I found that I was seeing an almost blinding bright white light – not, of course with my eyes – such visions are the work of fiction writers – but I could 'see' an almost blinding white light. Then images of the inside of a space craft – some equipment and an interior that was not from my own memory.

Jasper told me that what I was seeing was the power source of the craft I had been looking at, and their interior. They were sending me information they thought I might find interesting! I was shocked – then pleased – then shocked again. And then more images started to come and I asked Jasper if he could speak to them on my behalf and ask them to speak to me through Ernest so that I could speak to them and record what was said. Here is a transcript of our First Contact. I am speaking to a being I later knew as Tovan 375.

First Contact with Tovan 375

T: [Hesitant and very slow at first] You ... you ... listen ... for ... me.

L: You are welcome, my name is Lillie.

T: Welcome ... Lillie.

L: I apologise for this primitive method of communication. [via Ernest]

T: Yes, we have monitored your Earth's technological communication output and ... and have understanding of your communication patterns. The ... the more that we use this way of communication we will become faster. Why ... did you contact us?

L: We saw you there. The people of this sphere ...

T: Sphere?

L: Planet, sphere.

T: Yes.

L: They do not understand that they are looking at a craft. They think that they are looking at a star ... a sun. We have been watching you and thought we would like to communicate with you.

T: We do not have contact in this way, we just visualize I think is your word.

L: Telepathy.

T: Yes, to speak without speaking.

L: This is ...

T: Old way, I understand. We do not venture very close to any planets. We look on from a distance. We do not want to alarm any beings who exist on the spheres that we pass by, we are travellers and cartographers. We are many in other craft and we travel together most of the time. It is our task to travel. We have in each of our craft an artificial atmosphere. We grow substances to eat and drink. We have complicated recycling that constantly keeps us alive. We have organic matter that grows and filters. We are self-sufficient. Among the craft that travel with us there are similar sized craft that carry only these supplies that we can use as reserve.

L: Supply craft.

T: Yes, and that way we are never depleted. And the technology of the craft which we travel in is self-perpetuating.

L: So your craft is organic?

T: In some instances, yes.

L: Thank you for sending us the images of your power source.

T: We use the light emissions from the sources to power the craft. At the moment we are using the reflection of your sun and we use the rays of light and heat that come from it to transfer into energy that we can use. There are no bi-products of this energy, it is clean.
We have been here for some time and we observe the rotation of your sphere many times and we look on with interest. You are not unlike us in form but we do not have the exposure to the elements like you do. We have made no attempt to contact anyone because we did not think there would be any interest. I understand you are different from the others. We listen and monitor and although we do not wish to be eavesdroppers we

do receive the thought patterns of those who inadvertently transmit them, and they do not wish to contact us. We can tell by the way they use their knowledge.

L: This is a very violent and aggressive sphere in parts. Parts have no food and no water and other parts have excess. It is unbalanced.

T: As I speak to you now all of my people are listening, so when one of us speaks we are able to speak as one. There is no jealousy between us, we all share what we have. There is no envy, or greed as you call it, we would not have been able to survive our long journeys had we not been able to practise in this way. It is strange how on your earth, as you call it, there are those who reach out to travel to the stars and they leave their own home world in such turmoil. We cannot understand why you wish to reach out when you have not cured all the ills on your own world. It is very sad. We passed this way before and we have long avoided this area because we were warned not to come here. Now we find it is more welcoming. What made you suspicious that we were here?

L: We saw your craft.

T: Yes, we use the power of light and heat but in doing so we emit a very high reflective signature. We absorb the light from your sun but the instruments on our craft amplify the intensity so therefore I can understand why those observing from your surface would think that we were ...

L: A star.

T: Yes, this is acceptable because it keeps our anonymity. We do not use any method of artificial transmission so if anyone was listening they would pick up nothing. We use the power of the mind to transmit. This is how we communicate with our home. There is a delay in time transmission between us but it is much faster than any artificial means and we are able to keep in regular communication. I do not mean to be in any way disrespectful to your people but our interest is not in your sphere or the people upon it, we map the routes which go past it. But I would be interested in continuing the communication with you, now that we have made this link together I feel that we must make maximum use of this short time that we have together. Is there anything that you wish to know of us?

L: No, not for the moment, thank you.

T: How very strange because that is not the answer that I expected. I rather thought that you would want to know many things. We are very similar to you in form but we do not have the varieties that you have. We are all the same in many ways. We have a build that is slightly taller than yours and we have not so much capacity on our bodies because we have evolved to be much leaner. We only use that which we need to function adequately.

L: You said that you had been this way before?

T: Yes, much a longer time before, when life such as yours did not walk here. Your planet was not inhabited at that time. But we do follow the same pathway sometimes, especially if we find an area is un-passable to us, we return. It is our task to chart all areas – we do not wish to leave any areas uncharted. This communication is unexpected, we thought we would pass unnoticed.

L: I think you have, to most.

T: We can speak again at this time if you wish. It is interesting how we are able to use this translator. [Ernest]

L: We are a good team.

T: We will speak next time. In the meantime we will analyse and be able to speak with command of your language. I will communicate my label existence when I think of something to translate. If you have a need for a name I will find one. You have given us much to speak of. Goodbye. [Ends.]

I spoke to Tovan 375 again many times and it was Tovan 375 who gave me the description of 'The Colours of Space' featured earlier. Since then I have spoken to others of his civilisation. Here are some more transcripts of conversations which will introduce to you Tovan's people, who are one of the leading civilisations in The Alliance ....

The Thirteen

The Thirteen are so called because they inhabit a system of thirteen planets situated in our neighbouring universe, which makes them a very long way away from here. There is a vast area of black empty nothingness between this universe and that which The Thirteen inhabits. Once through the emptiness there is another vast distance of occupied space, in either direction, before you come to the Thirteen or the Earth.

The physical appearance of The Thirteen is very similar to ours. They are taller, almost 7 ft tall, and slimmer than most of us but their facial features are very similar. They have very long blond hair and blue eyes set in kind faces. They do not suffer the stress and strain that we do, living in our complicated over-material society, and so their faces look more relaxed and I suppose you would say that they all look quite similar. They do not smoke tobacco or take drugs and so once again they do not have the craggy appearances we might have – nor do they have that stretched look that the present day trend here for cosmetic surgery can give. They look natural and relaxed. They are a very tolerant and kind race. They have great patience and a thirst for knowledge shared by all space travellers.

As my relationship with Tovan 375 continued I found Tovan was genuine in his want to know more about me and my kind. Like all travellers passing by the Earth he was able to monitor all of our output of signals of all kinds – including radio, television and the internet and so he already knew much about our ways. He found how we behave very hard to comprehend, and did not understand our cruelty to animals, and each other. He struggled to understand that we can have so much wealth in some areas and yet there are people starving and suffering in others. He did not understand the obsession we have with material things of no consequence and struggled to reason why we abuse our environment so. Wars, violence, crime and neglect of others do not occur on his home worlds and it was hard to try and explain why they exist here. As I spoke to him I found that I am not very proud of my kind.

The Thirteen are highly advanced and elevated in their ways. There are many difference between them and us. The first of these is that they think as one collective consciousness. They progressed (as we all must do) from the starting point of thinking as a selfish individual to thinking as a family unit, then as a town, a country, a continent and then to thinking as a planet. This took a very long time and they didn't stop there, over a very long period of time they amalgamated with their other twelve planets until now, when you speak to one, you are speaking to all of the population (both solid and etheric) of their thirteen planets. All thirteen planets are populated and all are bigger than our own planet. Speaking to all of those beings at once is a little daunting at first. Can you imagine how much knowledge and experience they have – they all know everything. What one experiences they all do. This works in a very beneficial way in that if one is hurting they can all feel it – this is why it would never happen in their civilisation that even one of them could die in the terrible pain of starvation.

They have their privacy if they want it but they are used to their ways and would not even consider that a problem. But of course all are not interested in everything and so it works more that they can tap into any part of the collective that they are interested in, and also they can access all of their archive material of knowledge and experiences. This works in this way – as I was speaking to Tovan 375 he would hold all of the communication until it ended and then telepathically add to the collective what he felt was of interest to others. Major events are automatically telepathically streamed to all. All of the time Tovan and his associates were on his craft they had kept up to date with what changes had taken place back on their planet and received news regularly from home.

All highly advanced civilisations have the ability to deeply analyse and The Thirteen are no exception. They can analyse anything, and do. They instantly know when someone is lying, bending the truth or even thinking of lying. They instantly know the motives you have for something and not only do they know when you are lying, they know when you are withholding something. Jasper has already said that you cannot hide anything you do from the etheric layer and we are always judged on our actions – but this goes much deeper than that. The Thirteen know what you have done, yes, but they know also what you were thinking of doing, and why. This is more than mind-reading, this is 'being-reading' in a very deep way. You could never, ever, try and fool them, betray them or harm them. It would be impossible.

Their knowledge, their collective consciousness and their ability to look deep within me and know me (probably better than I know myself) was an unusual feeling at first. But as I grew to understand them, and of course trust them, I realised how special it is to be associated with them. Of course going through their 'vetting process' is deeper than any university examination you could sit here, but, once through then it is a testament to your own honour and truthfulness to be accepted by them.

They could almost sound unfeeling to you at this point, I realise that, but let me share with you some facts which Tovan told me about their life on their own planets. They dearly love animals and birds and all life is precious to them and they have many different creatures who share their worlds with them.

They have a large animal a little similar to our horse and they befriend these and ride them, much as we do here with our horses. The difference is that just as they speak to each other telepathically so they can hold conversations with their animals and Tovan asked me to imagine how wonderful it is to be riding a horse, looking at the beautiful green countryside you are riding through, whilst discussing just how beautiful the place is with your friend, the horse.

Some of their people choose to live on land, some in cities, some in the countryside and farming areas but some choose to live underneath the sea in domes. Their seas are crystal clear and the wildlife within the seas co-exist happily with them. Imagine standing at the glass walls of your underwater city, looking out into this beautifully clear water where a large underwater mammal, about the size of our dolphins, (but resembling what I can only describe as our cartoon ideas of a cute dragon) is playing around in the water with his own kind, and occasionally he swims to his side of the glass of the dome to talk to you. Do these people sound unfeeling?

[21 December 2008. Here is a transcript of another conversation I had with Tovan. I had asked him to tell me about the organisation of his society on his home planets and had cut short our previous conversation as I had a bad cold.]

The Thirteen's Society

T: Hello my friend I hope you are feeling well. I understand you were feeling quite ill.

L: We are susceptible to a variety of air-born viruses. It is an inconvenience more than anything, but I am fine now thank you.

T: It is hard for us to try and comprehend this. You wished to know more of the structure of our society?

L: Yes, the reason for my question is that just as you cannot comprehend, from where you are, the way our society is based on money, so I find it hard, from where I am now, to understand a world where it is not used.

T: Money is just a means of transferring your wealth from one source to another, isn't it?

L: Yes, but here we have to buy water, we have to buy everything but air, and if we lived inside domes, as some of you do, they would find a way of charging for that. So I cannot imagine what it is like to live in a world without it.

T: We have, I suppose you could say a kind of credit system. It is something that goes back long into our history. It was adopted long ago and it was necessary because our society was growing and advancing, and we all became very much equal and dependant upon each other and we needed to equalise our society. So long ago we decided to appoint governing systems where the allocation of resources would be equalised, so everybody would be allocated, I suppose you could say a unit of income. But also everybody was allocated a unit of workload. So it doesn't matter, we are all multi-tasking, we can all function in all areas, so we have doctors, we have people who farm, we have people who build, we have engineers, we have all walks of life. But we all have the same allocation of resources, how we choose to use these resources are entirely our own choice.

So, our food situation and our clothing situation and our own comfort situation – we are allocated a number of credits for each part of our life, so for instance if we work we are given a credit system where we are given a quota, a figure, and we all earn the same in that way. We all have a credit system, there is no change of money, no change of hands of any kind of currency, it is a system that is of course within our memory. As you know we have a vast memory capacity it is all common access to all, so we don't need to keep records in what you call computers.

L: Because you are the computer.

T: Yes. So we have a central memory core that we can all access, and although no actual tangible credits change hands we all have an allocation within the system. Say for instance we did a job of work in the field we would be allocated a number of credits, and we could spend those credits however we wish. There is no difference between the engineer and the farmer – we all consider that all jobs, all tasks, are equally as important as the next. There is no class system, there is no superiority or inferiority, the engineer cannot feel superior to the farmer and the doctor cannot feel superior to the labourer. They all have the same status. We all learned long ago that we all depend upon each other, so the only difference is how we spend these credits.

We have the same amount of allocation of food units for each person so we cannot over-indulge, but there is a very strict control to ensure that we all receive enough to sustain us, so you could not have a situation where somebody is not eating enough to sustain them. There would be no starvation, there would be no poverty, so if somebody is not spending their right amount of credits on food it would be noticed. And there would be, I suppose you could say it's like your welfare system, there is a system where they would be checked upon to find out why they weren't eating. This could be the sign of an illness, it could be the sign of some kind of disorder, so we keep checks on how much people consume. They can consume anything they wish to, within the number of units, so they may choose to eat a great deal of fruit, they may choose to eat a great deal of roots, and each thing is given a nutritional value so no matter what you eat you always achieve the desired nutritional value, so there would be nobody who was eating something that would not sustain them. They would not be eating, I think you would call it 'Junk Food'.

L: [Laughing now and delighted at his command of the language] Oh yes.

T: They would not be eating food just for convenience, I know it may seem a very ordered society but they would eat what is required for them.

L: But that is for their health, it is not a matter of control. I'm laughing because your ability with this language amazes me sometimes. This expression 'Junk Food' is so modern!

T: Well we analyse all speech. We have of course stored it in our databanks.

L: Of course, yes.

T: So, the society, nobody is under-nourished and nobody is over-nourished, we don't have problems with obesity and we don't have any problems with people starving. Nobody can actually eat more than their fair share. The same applies to clothing, they have an allowance within their credits for clothing and they can buy whatever they wish. They have an allocation for recreation and pleasure. They have an allocation for what they can spend on their dwellings. The whole of their income is broken into allocations. They can, of course, save their allocations over periods with such things as clothing and furnishing and entertainment to eventually buy something more. And then owning this thing would not make you any more superior to someone who spent all their credits regularly on smaller items. So, they cannot buy something they don't have the means for unless they save for it.

The work is allocated a number of credits. And the same credits are for everybody, but because we have a collective intelligence we rotate the work that we do, so everyone works at something, they do not spend their whole lives in the fields, they do not spend their whole lives as an engineer, we rotate and everybody, in turn, does every job.

L: What about things like doctors? Can everyone be a doctor?

T: No, it's a specialisation and what would happen with such specialists is that they would train at greater length then the others. They would have an aptitude towards caring, so we have a system where there would be carers, there would be people who would nurse the old and the sick, although we have a lower percentage of illness than you do. So they would progress from that to become doctors. With, I understand, your situation here, a doctor trains to become a doctor, with our society you would be a carer first of all and then you would be a nurse, and then you would be a doctor, and then you would be a specialist. So you would have gone all of the way through the whole of the areas that associate with it. And that way it gives you more knowledge in what you are doing.

L: And also I think sometimes, I suspect, here that there are those that become a doctor because they enjoy the power and the science or the control and the money it brings, but they are not necessarily of a caring nature.

T: Yes, well there isn't that with us. But they don't gain any more credits for what they do, so unlike in your society where somebody can earn vast wealth by whatever they do as a profession, this cannot happen in our society, so no man is richer than the next, or poorer than the next. And it works very well because we learned long ago that we all depend upon each other. Of course we have a form of government in the form of Elders who earn their position over a long period of time and have a trusted and respected position and bear the overall responsibility for us all. It is they who make all of the decisions which affect the total. They are also accessible by all. We never need more than we have. I suppose you could say our choices are much more limited than you but we believe that by having less choices we don't have the complacency, the over-expectation of what is there.

L: But you have the arts?

T: Yes, and if you wish you can spend your credits on going to see an art exhibition, or listening to music and this in turn goes to pay the credits of the entertainers. So, it all works quite well really. We don't own any of the structures, the buildings. The structures belong to all of us. The structures are very much the same, there are no ... I think you call them .. luxury ... there are no luxury apartments, there are no workers apartments, they all have the same basic dwellings. We all participate in the upkeep and the wellbeing of all of the structures and the areas around us.

We learned long ago that in order to function as one we would all need to be equal, we could not allow some to be elevated above others and others to be lowly, we all had to be on an equal status, as we are. So we all have to take our turns in doing all of the work, because we were mindful long ago that the society could have been such that, as I believe is in yours, where you could have those that did not wish to work. Well, I'm afraid we have long since dispensed with this – if you didn't work, you didn't eat basically and we have learned over the period of time and now we are all happy in what we do.

No-one is ever over-indulgent. They can't be greedy and they can't be selfish in their ways. If we travel from one region to another for any period of time, we take the resources with us, so we do not deplete the resources of the areas we are visiting. We take food and sustenance with us and do not deplete their supply. The same if we go to another sphere, we take our own sustenance with us in adequate quantity. We do of course accept hospitality we do eat and partake in sustenance with the other people but we would make sure we take enough with us to replace that we have accepted. On expeditions such as the one we are on it doesn't apply.

L: Because you are growing your own.

T: Yes, we are, in fact, our own sphere. Each one of us, each craft, is self-sufficient. When we first set out on this expedition we did share between us because we needed to make sure that everybody had the same. Some production systems were under-producing and some were over-producing but they have all been long since equalised.

But this society works. There is no greed. No poverty. No starvation. We are all self-sufficient, but if one of us is ill or incapable we will all know. The credit system is such that when people grow old, as they do, before their transition to the next life, their next body, when they become old and feeble, the credit system is such to sustain them in the same way as they were sustained when they were fully working. And this applies to everybody so nobody objects to this because we all have the same opportunity, when we grow old we have the same opportunities. So the same credits are paid to everyone, even when they are too old to work.

We no longer have young. We don't have children any more so this also dispenses with a generation, an age that does not have any input. I know some societies may find it hard but we don't need young offspring, we have long since dispensed with that.

In the early stages we did exchange between all of The Thirteen planets to equalise resources, there was a period of equalisation until we all came to a level of the same. So those that were overproducing added to those that were under-producing and so on and so on, until there was an equalisation.

There is no wealth here. You cannot grow rich, but you cannot be poor. You cannot be over-fed, but you cannot starve. And everybody is happy. Because we all have the capability to do the same work there is no class system.

It will take a long time for your society to evolve because from what I have learned they are all very much dependent on wealth. And there is too much of an extreme between those who are wealthy and those who have nothing.

I know when you first met us you felt we were devoid of emotions but we have learned to filter out many of the emotions within us, we are able to control our anger. There is no greed, there is no admiration or jealousy. Some would say that we are a boring society but we are happy society. We have everything we need, we need no more. The only thing we need is knowledge and that is why we have all been on these expeditions, to gain this knowledge, and then when we have it we wish to share it with all we come across, we do not wish for anything to further our own civilisation in any way. We don't wish to find wealth. We are not looking for hidden gold and resources. We are indeed happy. [Ends]

At the time of telling me about his society Tovan was in his craft (the one I had seen from my window when we first made contact with each other) heading homeward to his planet. Tovan's buildings on his home world, and his craft (and the other craft travelling with him) are all organic. They are not built, they are grown. These particular craft were grown in space and the crew, including Tovan and his partner Tana 283, boarded them and left their planet to travel an ovoid route away from and back to their planet, mapping the routes through space on both sides of the craft as they went. Many craft left at the same time, in Tovan's fleet there were forty craft and there were many such fleets – each group following a route the shape of a petal moving from the 'centre', the location of their planet. They are all back on their planet now.

Tovan's group of craft passed this planet on their way outward. When they passed this planet (the first time) our Earth was just cooling and there was life on Venus, Mars and Jupiter. I know this gives us no idea of the time he was travelling - except to know that we cannot possibly imagine or understand just how long that was.

The Thirteen are so evolved that they do not need a basic cycle of reincarnation such as ours, their bodies have a lifespan and become old and unserviceable after a time, but their same spirit is re-born into a new adult body. Each 'body' is numbered as part of their name, so that you can tell from their number system how many 'body lifetimes' that same spirit has had. The new bodies retain all of the memories all of the 'bodies' had, and so for all intents and purposes there is very little change. When Tovan got into that craft and left his home world he was Tovan 5, when he passed our Earth for the first time he was Tovan 13 and the one I spoke to in 2008 was Tovan 375.

I am not the only one who spoke to Tovan from the Earth – Jasper also spoke to him. Jasper has no need to sleep and whilst Ernest and I are sleeping Jasper takes that time to speak to many. Whilst The Thirteen were 'nearby' Jasper was speaking to Tovan every night. Jasper is etheric and so can travel much more easily than you or I and he was invited by Tovan to visit their craft. This particular craft is one that The Thirteen used for their mapping expeditions, they have other craft for other mission work. Jasper went to Tovan's craft twice before The Thirteen moved away from the vicinity of our system and describes here for us the first time he visited their craft. It was on 5 and 6 August 2008 ...

Jasper Visits Tovan's Craft

Jasper says ....

I have met many beings and observed so many things that very little surprises me any more. But I will admit that meeting Tovan for the first time was like nothing or no-one I had ever encountered before. We had spoken many times and I had become very comfortable with both Tovan and his people. When Ernest sleeps I am able to move away from him. So I made the journey to Tovan knowing that all was safe behind me. The journey was over quickly for me but if anyone reading this would like to attempt the round trip you would have to set aside several light years.

Seeing Tovan's craft for the first time is a shock in itself if you would believe all that the Earth has written in the way of science fiction. This was not the gleaming piece of machinery with all of the high-tech attributes that you would expect from a race of people as advanced as Tovan's. If it were not for its sheer size you would be forgiven for paying it very little attention at all, no more than you would any other piece of 'driftwood' floating in space, because that is what it looked like. But as I drew nearer to the craft I became aware of its size - I would estimate that at its longest dimension it would be in excess of six thousand feet from end to end. Its appearance looked very much like a discarded peach stone, rough and craggy with many indentations over its surface. The overall colour was a dark green to brown. I knew from its appearance and from my own perception that it was very, very old.

Any doubt that I had about arriving at the right place was quickly dismissed by a telepathic greeting from Tovan. He and his people had been awaiting my arrival. Once inside the craft I was immediately overwhelmed by the feeling of complete peace. I sensed no tension or apprehension in Tovan's greeting. There was very little sound from inside the craft and as Tovan and his people speak entirely by telepathy the silence is not broken even by speech.

We spoke at great length (telepathically) about many things. We were constantly investigating each others thoughts until we were

191

completely at ease with each other. As you know by now it is not possible to tell anything other than the complete truth to Tovan's people. We now trusted each other and Tovan began to tell of his mission and his contact with Lillie and myself, of his journey and many other things. I met many of Tovan's people directly, but of course talking to Tovan was enough to communicate with his entire race due to their collective consciousness.

The inside of the craft is lit by a very soft green light and as I watched the members of the crew going about their tasks I was still aware of this complete feeling of peace. There was no urgency about any of their actions - just a calm methodical approach to whatever each individual was doing. Tovan guided me around the craft and I observed many areas devoted to their mission, charts and screens showing endless numbers of white dots. At first the significance is not clear until you understand that each dot is a star which in turn is a sun to a complete solar system. The craft is almost devoid of any conventional technology - no vast machines to store the information that Tovan and his people have gathered in their journey. A journey that has taken them an eternity to complete. Instead all information is stored in their collective consciousness and immediately available to all.

I passed through recreational areas where people were sitting quietly. Some eating some of the various fruits and food types available to them, some drinking juices, others just sitting quietly. But of course what was not obvious was that they were probably having complete conversations with each other. Then Tovan paused for a moment and told me that we were about to enter the area that made their entire existence on their endless trip possible. We stepped through a doorway and I was shocked (although this is something that rarely, if ever, happens to me.) I was shocked to find myself entering a forest.

Tall trees towered above me plants and growth of many types stretched as far as I could see. Fruit trees were laden down with their loads, and berries of many types sprouted from uniformly-planted rows of bushes. Other areas were planted out with root crops. As we moved further into the thicker part of the forest where there were only trees, no crops, Tovan stopped and asked me to say what I could hear. My senses told me that I could hear nothing at all, absolute and complete silence. The other parts of the craft had been noisy when compared with this complete silence. Tovan said that this is where his people came to completely relax and be at one with their own thoughts.

The forest has many uses, as well as providing fresh food and rest for the crew members, it performs its primary function of providing the breathable air, the atmosphere for the inside of the craft. It is perfect, it needs to be. The craft, and in particular the forest, was grown to be completely sterile and free from any chance of disease and ultimate failure that would have catastrophic consequences for Tovan and his people. Being sterile the forest was grown completely devoid of any living organism that could affect its well-being and that of the people. This meant that there were no parasites, no wild life, but most noticeably

- no birds. It is this complete sterility that gives the forest its unique silence. I have never experienced such peace that exists there.

But of course even my time is limited and soon I had to make my apologies and start my return journey back to Ernest. But before leaving Tovan did briefly show me the source that powered the craft. I am sorry to disappoint, but to me it was no more that a chamber containing a ball of energy that was almost too bright for even me to look upon - I didn't really have much interest here - I had already seen the most wonderful part of the craft. [Ends]

***

A Familiar Face

Earlier I said 'Telepathy can travel much further than any other form of communication ... there is one set of telepathic messages which was sent by a civilisation so advanced, whose telepathic signal was so strong, that their messages were inadvertently received here by many people. This civilisation ... were transmitting a friendly Hello message to anyone in the universe ... and there is evidence that many here saw it ....

If I were to describe an 'alien' with a small body and a larger hairless head, pear shaped face with a small mouth, pointed chin and gigantic eyes, would you be able to picture them? Yes, I know you would. Because that face is in many Science Fiction films and books. It is our classic 'alien'.

They are known as I.V.O [pronounced eye-voh] and when the Higher Beings of their civilisation sent that friendly greeting out into the universes years ago they did not know that they would cause such a spark to the imaginations here. The face certainly imprinted itself into the minds of many, although the stories of alien abductions and alien sightings are simply the work of overactive minds as none from IVO have ever been to our Earth. My own First Contact with them in 2009 was their first interactive communication with here. IVO are the most advanced civilisation in this dimension and so their signal was so strong it had somehow 'got through' as a visual sign. What followed over the next years was pure fiction.

On 12 May 2009 I had a very vivid image in my 'mind.' I was aware that there was a transmitted message and that I could 'see' the being that was sending it. And it was the classic 'alien' face that so many have described here on Earth. I had seen this face on toy dolls and in endless science fiction films and illustrations.

Whenever I receive anything which is 'odd' or 'unbelievable' (and by now it takes a lot to shock me) I ask Jasper to check it for me. He agreed that this was a being with that description who was sending a message.

The message was a transmission, it was him, this being, trying to send the message in a variety of ways – the usual way of things in space, telepathy, and then hand signals and also just a set of images. The message was being repeated over and over. They were saying hello, and this time they were trying to speak to the Earth, and surprisingly, to me. I sent a message back (telepathically) to say I had received it. On 27 May 2009 I received another message back saying that they had received my acknowledgement. I knew from this delay that they must be a very long way away. They sent a few more messages over the next few days and then once again I asked Jasper to arrange for them to speak to me through Ernest and here is the transcript of Earth's genuine First Contact with this classic 'alien-faced' people.

I.V.O

[2 June 2009]
K: I am Kra.

L: I am Lillie. I am very pleased to speak to you.

K: Yes, you have spoken to others of ours.

L: With messages, yes, I received your message.

K: We have constant quest to speak to others. We are explorers, we like to meet with people. We have listened to your speaking, your messages, those your Earth transmits with technology – that is how we know how to speak to you. But you are aware that we speak with mind.

L: Telepathy, yes.

K: We were told of you by a visitor. We have many visitors. There is such a distance between us.

L: Yes, I believe now that you are also speaking to some other friends of mine, to The Thirteen.

K: Yes, when we speak to them they all listen, but we cannot speak to all from your Earth, because they do not hear us.

L: I think in solid form there is only me.

K: We have been trying to communicate with your Earth for a long time. We wanted to make contact in the past, we tried in varying ways and we could not make contact. We used signals that we believe were too weak – and some were far too strong and we believe that these communications may have implanted images within people's minds.

L: Of your ......ah! [Realising] ... because, yes, there are images of your face.

194

K: It would be possible that if we sent too strong a signal a lower intellect would receive this and not know what it was they were receiving. So I am afraid we may have caused some confusion. [Ends]

I heard from them again and now they speak regularly to me. They are a small race (well under 5ft tall) and easily recognised by their appearance which we know so well. They are so highly advanced civilisation that their elders already travel by the pathways of space. They use a form of dimensional travel to transport their solid members in craft. So now we can all put a name to a very familiar face.

I have spoken to many different people from IVO of many ages and advancements. I spend a lot of time speaking to one of their most elevated elders Angd and his partner Atax. The more I speak to them the more I like them. I find them very friendly and sociable and extremely kind and compassionate. I was also pleasantly surprised to find that they have a really good sense of humour.

I would like to share with you a most remarkable experience, as in February 2010 I met the children of IVO for the first time. My friend Angd had asked me if I would speak to the children of their worlds and I happily agreed. Here is a transcript of our first conversation...

IVO's Children

Angd and I had arranged that I would speak to the children during the evening of Saturday 20 February 2010 but they came through early that morning. Angd spoke to me briefly before he allowed the children to speak for themselves ...

Angd: I think I am early but the children would not wait. What we have done is we have taken a representation of regions – like your Earth, you have countries – we have taken representations from different regions because we realised [laughing] you wouldn't be able to speak to all of them, so we have taken representation from all areas. So, what will happen, they will ask whatever questions they have ... I think they are being quite polite because they do know the answers to lots of them ...

L: [Laughing] I am sure. I did realise that despite their 'age' I would be speaking to people who are more intelligent than me ...

Angd: [Laughing] Don't underestimate yourself. Yes, they are very intelligent and we are very proud of them. We did think at first that you would like to be introduced to the names but there will be so many of them, but by way of explanation I will tell you first of all that the young generations of our people, the names really depict their age. So the younger people have just two letters in their name – so you will find names like Al and On and At and Il – just two letters. And then you find that as they become older they have the third letter added – that is why you have Arl [another member of IVO I had spoken to] and when you become old like me ...

L: You get four.

Angd: Yes. And they are added on at the end of the name. We just add on a letter and the letter that is on the end of the name depicts the group that they belong to – like your own surnames. It is like a family name. So that is by way of explanation so all these children who come to you have just two letters in their names and that is why we find your language so amusing because they have names like On and At and It and Is, all of these names that are ...

L: That we use all the time.

Angd: Yes, I'm sure they found that amusing. And so when they studied your language (as they have done) they found their names appearing in the sentences, which would have been something of an amusement to them. So, before I let them speak, I cannot say how it will go ... I think they will be ordered as they can be, but I think they will become excited.

L: Well I am too.

Angd: Now I will let the children speak to you, but I will come back to you at the end, just by way of really bringing the conversation back to some kind of normality and order. I will let them speak for themselves ...I will warn you that you may have to cut it short ... they will speak for eternity so you will have to stop them ...

Al: Hello. [a childlike voice]

L: I'm excited.

Al: Are you? [sounding surprised] So am I. So are we all. I am Al. I am one of the Al's anyway. There are many Al's. I could count them? I could let you know how many Al's there are on this planet of ours.

L: You could tell me how many letters you have?

Al: Two.

L: No ... oh, yes, in Al ... I meant in your vocabulary.

Al: Letters? Oh, you mean what structures your language.

L: Yes. We have twenty six.

Al: Oh! [sounding very surprised] How do you manage with that? We have four hundred and ... sixty ... two. Four hundred and sixty two, yes.

L: Gosh, so when you give me your name do you get the nearest that you can get, using my letters?

Al: Yes. Yes ... you know so much about us.

L: H'm. A bit.

Al: Your name is Lillie. Are you old?

L: No ... it doesn't work like that.

Al: Because you have so many letters. I mean no disrespect to you.

L: I understand. Your name means that you are two letters old.

Al: Yes.

L: No, there is no connection here with age.

Al: You would be many centuries old.

L: But you know we don't live very long in our lives here, compared to you.

Al: How long is long?

L: H'm. On average around seventy years.

Al: Seventy years ... that is ... seventy revolutions of your earth around your sun. Ah [upset] that is sad!

L: Not really because we keep coming back. But I am already fifty seven.

Al: So you have seen fifty seven revolutions of the sun. I see. Yes ... yes ... I see that, thank you. There are others who wish ... thank you for that ... there are others who wish to speak to you.

L: Oh, I'm sorry I feel I took your time, was there something you wanted to ask me?

Al: No, no that ... it was that really. Thank you.

De: Hello, I am De [pronounced dee]

L: Hello De. I am Lillie.

De: A long name.

L: Yes, but not my age.

De: No. I understand that. Do you ... do you ... travel elsewhere?

L: Other planets?

De: Yes.

L: No, sadly, not from here. We have, our people once went [laughing] to our moon, just the rock ...

De: Why would you go there?

L: I know. Ridiculous. Because [laughing] it's the only place they could get to. And do you know what they did when they got there?

De: No.

L: They put a flag in it and they came home.

De: That sounds like a complete waste of resources.

L: Correct. And the resources they used to do that would have fed all of the poor people on the planet many times over.

De: Well that sounds quite silly.

L: It is silly. It is completely silly. And, no ... there is no-one here with the capability to travel to other planets.

De: We travel far.

L: I know ... do you travel as children?

De: Yes, we learned from a very early age to travel with our elders. Numbers of us are taken when they travel. Its is a great privilege to travel ...

L: Oh, how wonderful!

De: And we all, all of us experience travel from early.

L: Oh, you are so lucky!

De: We travel with our units ... our families. Yes. Thank you.

L: No, thank you.

In: Hello. I am In.

L: Hello In. I'm Lillie.

In: I'm a girl.

L: Are you? Oh, the last one was a boy, sorry I didn't realise.

In: Yes. We have one of each here. Boys and girls.

L: Oh, well I'm a girl. Good.

In: Why are you so tall? Your people.

L: Is it connected to gravity, your size?

In: Yes.

L: Well then that's why, because of gravity.

In: Ah.

L: But are you all the same size as each other, because we are not.

In: There is some difference slightly. But those of us who are small are all small together ... and then we grow ...

L: Taller. Well we here are many different sizes, that is a big difference.

In: Well there is ... we are not all exactly the same size ... some are .... Er ... slightly bigger than others and some are slightly smaller.

L: But in our case it can be as much as ten, twelve, sometimes fifteen per cent taller, at the same age.

In: Oh, no, no. And also, I do not wish to be ...

L: The width?

In: Yes. I notice that you have much more ...

L: Fat.

In: Is that what it's called ... flesh. We have very little ... on ... we are more, what do you say, the structure ... skeleton is closer to the surface.

L: Yes, you Have evolved to be able to utilise what you take into your body in the correct way. We here are not as advanced and we eat too much. We eat more than our body uses and so the body converts it to fat which is a layer underneath the skin, and it would be ... in animals it would be a storage to use later, but we never use it because we eat more than we need.

In: Why do you have hair on your head? Does it feel better when the heat from the star comes down to you?

L: I am so used to having hair that I don't know how it would feel without it.

In: Thank you.

Is: I am Is. I am a girl. Yes ... I have no hair.

L: Oh, OK. You don't need it though do you?

Is: I do not know what it is to have it, so I do not know.

L: Well, it's a bit of a nuisance really.

Is: Oh, yes. You have animals.

L: Yes.

Is: We have animals. Yes. I like animals.

L: I love animals.

Is: When I become older I will look after animals.

L: Oh, is that what you will do with your ... time.

Is: Yes ... yes. You eat your animals.

L: [wincing] I know. It's so bad.

Is: Ours, we recognise that they are lesser of intelligence than us and we look after them.

L: I wish we did.

Is: So when I become older I will be one who looks after the animals for children to come and see.

L: Oh, how marvellous. You're lucky. What a lovely thing.

Is: Yes.

L: I hope in time we will stop eating the animals here, but for now our bodies have developed to need them, sadly. Very sad I don't like it.

Is: Yes, I know. I've had this explained. I thought that it was not very nice ...

L: It isn't very nice, but unfortunately now our bodies need it.

Is: Yes, I understand that. But I like animals.

L: But you know I have an animal who lives with me. [Telepathically showing her a picture of our dog, Arthur]

Is: Do you speak to him?

L: Yes, but not in the way that you can, sadly, we have a very small amount of communication. Just that he can tell me when he needs to drink or when he needs to eat.

Is: He can tell you that?

L: Well ... only by, you would find it amusing I'm trying to show you the picture [showing her Arthur scratching away furiously at an empty water bowl] ...

Is: Oh, by his actions. I see. Ah, that is good.

L: So we have a very small amount of communication.

Is: I see, thank you.

Ag: I am Ag.

L: Hello Ag. I'm Lillie.

Ag: Yes. Thank you for speaking.

L: Oh, it's a pleasure. I love this.

Ag: I am boy. I thought I would tell you.

L: You have a slightly different sound, the boys and girls.

Ag: Why do you all travel so slowly?

L: Because we do not have the capability, or the intelligence, or the advancement, to travel any other way.

Ag: I am very interested in all things that are, you say ... machines, mechanical. And I study machines at my classes and when I become older I will make these machines. But I thought that I would try to learn from the Earth ... but I find it a mystery, because your machines that fly – they should not.

L: No, I know,. They are so heavy and slow and really ... it defies your knowledge of physics.

Ag: They need so much energy to lift them into the sky but if they were not so heavy to start with they would not take so much. And I am very interested in these machines that travel on the surface. By touching the surface it makes them slow. They have wheels that rotate – if they did not touch they would be faster. I would like to see some of these, one day. Because they are – all of your machines are so complicated, but they do so little. Our ... you say craft, space craft have so little in them but they can so much. But your machinery is so wasteful. That is all.

L: Well I hope one day you get to see them – because I think they will just amuse you.

Ag: Yes I would like to look at them. Yes. It is intriguing to know that such complication can do such a funny thing.

L: Yes, and I hope sometimes that you think of this – and I hope it makes you smile to realise – those who invent and work at this machinery think they are so clever and so advanced ...

Ag: H'm.

L: I hope that makes you smile sometimes.

Ag: It does make me smile to think of this. Thank you for your time.

To: Hello. I am To.

L: To. I'm Lillie.

To: I am also a boy.

L: OK. I love your names.

To: Yes, thank you. Your name is old – sorry I do not mean disrespect.

L: No, I understand, because it has a lot of letters, but it doesn't mean that. My name is the name of a flower. [not complicating it with the different spelling]

To: A flower that grows?

L: Lily, yes. [showing him a picture of a lily]

To: We like all things that live. We are told from very young that all things that live are important. No matter how small or whatever they look like, they are important.

L: I wish people here would learn that. I hope they will one day when you all come.

To: But you see you must look. When you look at anything you must look at the structure and when we look at the flower, like you have shown me, we look at the beauty in the structure and it has its right to be there.

L: Yes.

To: I have a question about your water. We have water around our lands and we swim in them. Do you swim in your water?

L: Well, some do, some do not, but your know that the big problem with our water is that some parts are very polluted and dirty. Your water, I imagine, is beautifully clear and imagine you could drink it or swim in it, the same.

To: We can see for a long way down.

L: In some places we can.

To: It is only the refractive index that makes it darker it is not the content,. It is because of the depth. As we look deeper into the water it becomes darker because of its distance.

L: Some of our water is very polluted and dirty.

To: Can you breathe in the water?

L: No. Can you?

To: Yes.

L: Oh, aren't you lucky! No, we cannot. I know there are many civilisations that can. Oh, you're so lucky!

To: You cannot?

L: No.

To: That must be very difficult for you.

L: So when you go into the water you can breathe under the water and speak to your sea creatures?

To: Yes.

L: Oh, gosh you are so lucky!

To: And you cannot ...

L: No.

To: That is sad.

L: Yes, it is sad. We have to wear apparatus which is very heavy and very complicated.

To: Because you cannot breathe. We cannot breathe in space.

L: Some of us cannot even swim on top of the water.

To: On top ... oh, I see yes. We cannot breathe in space. We have to have artificial means to help us. But also if we came one day to your Earth, if we were ever allowed, our elders said we are not at the moment, but if we were ever allowed to walk upon your Earth, we would breathe your atmosphere but it is different to ours.

L: Oh, but you could exist in it without apparatus?

To: Yes, our bodies adapt to breathe different ... providing the makeup is not poisonous we can breathe it.

L: But would it be uncomfortable for you, at first?

To: At first it would be ... yes, because I believe that the ... I have been told that the chemical content of your atmosphere is different than ours, so at first our breathing, lungs as you call them, would labour with the situation. I speak of all these things because when I grow older I will be a ... you say physician, doctor. Yes, doctor. So I am beginning to understand all of the things that make the body work, and the lungs is one of them ... you say lungs?

L: Lungs, yes.

To: Our bodies are very advanced. I do not wish disrespect to you but your bodies of the Earth are very un-evolved. Ours have evolved to breathe as we do. But yes, I will become a doctor. We do not have ...

L: Do you make your decision of where you will ... which area you will move into, very early? I know we cannot compare our ages but how long have you known you wanted to be a doctor?

To: Always.

L: Oh, really. So, is it dependent upon your group? Are others within your group doctors?

To: No, we decide from what ....we ... how can I say this ... we decide from the information given to us, what we want to do. Options! That's the word, options. So we decide early. But there are all kinds in my group. We are free to do what we wish.

L: Oh, OK. So it is not because your elders were doctors that you become a doctor. I understand, yes.

To: No, it is what I want to do.

L: How very interesting. Well I'm sure you'll be very good at it.

To: Thank you. Thank you for speaking to me.

Go: I am Go. I am a girl.

L: Hello, Go. I'm Lillie. A girl too.

Go: Lillie. That's nice.

L: Thank you.

Go: Yes. Er ... I can't think of what I wanted to say ...

L: Do you know what it was in connection with ...

Go: Flowers.

L: Oh, flowers. How interesting, is that what you will do when you are older?

Go: Smell flowers?

L: No, not the smell, I thought maybe you were going to be an agriculturalist or ...

Go: No, I am going to be ... the word is ... artist.

L: Oh, really.

Go: I will make pleasant images for people. Artists ... that's the word.

L: Do you know, that is something that I do not have within me and I really admire that in others, the ability to do that.

Go: Yes, well, we can go anywhere, but there are ... we move from place to place and some people, like I understand your people, will live in an area but they were not born in that area, they move there because they work, but they like to take images of what they remember ...

L: Yes, I understand, yes.

Go: So, we make images for people to take with them. So, if they live on one side of our planet and they miss something that was on the other side of their planet they would take an image of what they left behind them.

L: I see, yes, we do something similar.

Go: And it is that that I will do.

L: I understand.

Go: So I would make images of flowers, which is a particular interest of mine, and make them into pictures, images, and people would take them with them.

L: How lovely. How very beautiful.

Go: Yes.

L: You are very lucky to have that talent.

Go: So, I was going to ask you if you have time to look at your flowers.

L: Do you mean now?

Go: Any time.

L: Well let me show you some now. We have a very complicated flower with many petals, [picturing a rose] this is called a rose.

Go: Yes, but that has spikes.

L: Yes, indeed it does.

Go: That is a design of the flower to stop you from picking it.

L: Oh, really, how clever. Try this – this is a very pretty flower – that's a daffodil.

Go: Yes, that's very complicated. It looks almost as if it should make some sound from the top.

L: Yes, and in the spring … we have four seasons here … and after the cold winter has gone … I'm trying to show you a field with many of these spring flowers growing …

Go: Tiny.

L: Yes, beautiful. And that's a sign to us of the world awakening again after the cold winter.

Go: Well now perhaps I will make images of what you have shown me.

L: I wish I had time to send you more.

Go: Well … you can send them to us.

L: OK, if I think of you … your name is Go … so if I think of you, there is a link, can I send you pictures?

Go: Yes, but if you send them to Angd, he will give them to us.

L: OK I will send you pictures of flowers. I will send you many pictures of flowers.

Go: Thank you.

L: And for the others I will send some pictures of the animals. I will send a selection of pictures.

Go: Thank you.

Do: Hello. I am Do.

L: Hello Do.

Do: I like your words.

L: [Laughing] I like the way your names are used all the time in our language, its very beautiful. It makes me smile.

Do: Yes, when we first looked at your words we thought you already knew us.

L: [Laughing] Ah, yes, I can see why you did.

Do: We learn all about you. We learn about many. We learn very early that there are many others outside of our world, our planet, and we try to learn as much as we can and I am particularly interested in languages and all methods of communication and I think that you learn to communicate with all people, it helps you to understand them more.

L: Yes I agree.

Do: So, when I grow old I want to be able to speak to everybody. I do not want to be ... you say ignorant ... of people I want to be able to meet everyone and speak to them all.

L: Do you know that there are people on my planet I cannot speak to. On my planet.

Do: I know, I have been told that there are different languages. But you see we speak like this [telepathically] all of the time.

L: Yes, which is easier.

Do: It is easier but it is not so exciting.

L: No, and it is a little more restricted isn't it.

Do: Yes, so I share, as do some others of our elders, the interest in languages and I find it fascinating and that is what I will do.

L: I like languages, but I am not as intelligent as you ... so I cannot speak many.

Do: You say that without knowing, but you are intelligent. You write. This is something we do not do.

L: Only because you do not need to read to get your information.

Do: Yes, but it would be nice to look upon these. We have ... we have books ... old, really old books that we have to make special arrangements to go and look at. But ... does it take a long time ... when you write words, does it frustrate you that it takes you so long to put the words onto the paper?

L: No, because I enjoy the actual action. I have a love of writing in whatever form, even handwriting – I'm showing you now writing by hand with a pen. I love it.

Do: It is this that I was interested in. I know you have machines that you use to put your words, but it was this more primitive, but I feel more beautiful way of writing ...

L: Well I have ... I'm just showing you now, look, can you see these [transmitting the image as I flick through hand-written journals which were close to hand as we spoke] I have these books and everything that Angd has said to me I write by hand, look, can you see this?

Do: Yes, yes. It takes you a long to do this ...

L: But I love it. The action of the writing is a pleasure for me.

Do: Yes.

L: I love the ...

Do: I would like to do this. I will try this. As I said, we have books that are very old and we have to go and look at them very delicately because they would break. Yes ... thank you.

L: Well we have ... I'm showing you where I am, look can you see, many books. I love having books around me.

Do: I would like to see books. And each book is written in your language.

L: Yes, but then it is translated into other languages also, if it is a book which many want to read then it is translated into all languages.

Do: That is very interesting. And if you had a book, it would be something personal that you could keep for yourself.

L: And you can hold it.

Do: Yes. We cannot hold our books.

L: No, but you can hold much more because you can hold the contents of many books within your very being. You're very lucky.

Do: Yes.

L: You're very lucky, because you have all the knowledge within you.

Do: Thank you for talking to me.

No: I am No. I am a girl.

L: Hello No the girl. Your name is strange in this language.

No: Is it?

L: Yes. It is the opposite of no ... yes.

No: I do not understand that.

L: If I say to you 'Do you like animals?' what would you say?

No: I like animals.

L: But would you say yes or no.

No: I do.

L: Ah, in our language we would say yes. And then if there was something we didn't like we would say 'No'.

No: I think I understand.

L: I'm sorry if I confused you.

No: No.

L: Ah, you see, you used it.

No: Yes.

L: And the other ....

No: Oh [realising] yes. Very strange.

L: Sorry, I'm playing with you.

No: No, that's all right. Colours ...

L: Colours?

No: Why do you have no blue people and red people? And green people. Why are they all the same on your planet but different? No green. No blue. No red. Is that ... what's the word I'm looking for ... is that boring because there is no colour?

L: As in anything, if you have never experienced it you don't know what you are missing.

No: Your animals are all different colours.

L: Yes. And some have different patterns [showing her first a zebra then a Dalmatian dog] we have striped animals and spotted animals ... do you have that?

No: Yes. We are all the same colour, our people - if you are different colours does it make you different towards others.

L: Unfortunately here the people are not able to see past the image of the body and to see a being encased in a vehicle. Here there is much tension and anger and even hatred in some areas – there are people who hate others just because of the colour of their skin. It's very wrong.

No: The other thing as well is the different shapes and sizes. You all look so different.

L: Yes.

No: We all look the same but we know who we are because we all have an individual ....

L: Signature.

No: Yes, that is it.

L: We are not advanced enough to be able to read a signature here.

No: I see. Thank you.

Fo: I am Fo [pronounced Foe] I am a boy.

L: Hello Fo.

Fo: I have many questions. But I cannot think of what I want to ask ... numbers ... you have a love of numbers?

L: Er ... no. I have a love of words but I am not very good with numbers. But I can try and answer questions. You will not find me very advanced in numbers. I can try.

Fo: I see. No ... I just wondered really ... I was looking at the use of numbers to calculate and looking at the various methods that you have of calculating. And it seems now that you do it by machinery, you have machinery that does it. But we do all of that, as you say within our heads, and we can do it very quickly. Is there a great inaccuracy in numbers – if you ... how can I explain ... if you do not all think the same ...

L: Aah, yes, you each check each others calculations don't you. I have been told that.

Fo: Yes. Is there much inaccuracy?

L: Very much, also ... there are two problems here at the moment with numbers – our children ... when I was a young child I learned to do calculations in my head, and to have an understanding of basic numbers – the children here now, when they learn, are not learning the use of numbers, they are learning the use of the machine and of course with a machine if you press the wrong button your calculation isn't right.

Fo: You have to know what to put into the machine, yes.

L: So this is a problem for young people here now, they often have no numeracy skills – but the other problem is because this is a very material world where everyone is interested in wealth, they are interested in the numbers because they want to own ... [struggling to explain the manipulation of statistics and balance sheets to a child whose world does not suffer from materialism] ... a lot of the commodities here, gold for example ...

Fo: Gold? Mineral ...yes ...

L: So the interest in numbers here is a commercial interest in materialism, the problem being that the numbers can be manipulated ... it is hard to explain ... you can manipulate numbers and there are many who like to manipulate inaccuracies ...

Fo: We could not do that because when we think of calculations we have many of us who check these calculations. And it is when we all come to the same conclusion, only then we put this number forward.

L: There are many numbers you have here that you can doubt – now that's not possible where you are.

Fo: We do not have doubt. Thank you for speaking.

Angd: This is Angd. I am one of the elders.

L: [Laughing] Angd, I loved that, maybe at some time we can do it again. I loved it.

Angd: Whenever you wish. It is good for the children because it advances their education. I hope you did not find them too annoying.

L: No, the reverse.

Angd: I hope you have a better insight into our people.

L: Yes I do. I am really touched by this. May I send them some images through you?

Angd: Yes, you can send them whatever you wish to send them. They would enjoy that, and we will put it there for all the children to use.

The next day I sent the children a selection of images of flowers, animals and birds from around our planet.

***

So Many Different Faces

The Thirteen have faces similar to our own and IVO's faces have become acceptable as what we expect from our 'classic alien', but if you were to look at a Council Meeting where all of the Member civilisations are represented you would see a great variety of forms.

In order to understand why there are so many different solid people, and such a variety of shapes and sizes, with an even bigger variation of facial appearances, it is necessary to understand how solid life evolves, and at what point solid life separates into the divide that is the animal kingdom and intelligent people.

Previously we looked at how planetary systems are formed and Jasper ended his beautiful description with the following words ... 'The forces have settled down and the new solar system waits for life to begin' and he continues here with his description of the truth of all evolution ...

Evolution

Jasper says ...

We have already spoken about how all planets are formed. All planets within them have all the constituents needed to make life exist. All life – plants, animals, biological life, germs – all constituents are there.

Let us continue now with a newly formed planet and look at how life evolves upon it. The planet is just a ball of hot rock but within the ball of rock is everything that will be needed – the building blocks of life. All stages of the processes which follow take millennia if not billions of years for each stage, so do not make the mistake of looking at each step and imagining that the next follows quickly. We are talking a vast amount of time before we reach the stage for intelligent life. So let's begin.

The planet cools down and moisture from the substance of the rock condenses and forms pools of liquid (sometimes what we would call water but not necessarily) on the surface. The pools are stagnant and as happens with stagnant water small particles of life starts to form. If you look into a pond today you will see that there are microscopic organisms forming there. At the start of life on our example planet the rock pools formed single cell life forms. Let us look at one such pool and follow the evolution of what occurs, remembering again that time is moving the processes along very, very slowly.

The pool has rudimentary single cell life within its water. It has certain gasses in the atmosphere and certain sustenance within the water allowing the single cell to live. Many millions of single cells exist there for endless millennia until some divide. In time the small creature divides and divides again until it is a creature which can now swim in the water. Over time the multi cell creature evolves until it is quite complicated compared to what it was originally (imagine here a fish). In time natural evolution means that there are eventually too many such creatures in the pool – living, eating, reproducing in the pool. The food supply is starting to run out.

Certain of these rock-pool dwelling creatures learn that if they can just slightly pull themselves out onto the outer rim of the water they can eat algae and other microscopic plants that grow near the water's edge. In time the creatures find that they can pull themselves up onto the edge using certain muscles, and eventually the muscles become stronger and eventually evolution will make the fish sprout limbs that enable it to pull itself onto the edge of the land itself. This little creature still does not have the confidence to leave the water, so as well as using the land it returns to the water. It has become an amphibian. Some of the fish are quite happy with the pool and stay there as fish. The amphibians move on.

The amphibians also evolve as they see that the plants around them have evolved. They can eat the plants and also the insects who evolved also from the single cell within the water pools. Through natural evolution the insects learned that they had to become bigger and fly to get away from the natural predators evolution had given them to contend with.

The amphibians walk across the land and come across other rock pools which have evolved species slightly different to their own, similar but slightly different. The two species meet and over time mate and form a completely new species. Again and again this happens.

Also for those who remained in the water, each pool has evolved a different kind of fish and other water life forms and when heavy rains flood and joins the individual pools they too combine and produce still more varieties of water living creatures.

The amphibians meanwhile see plant life higher up than they can reach and just as their ancestors before them evolved into reaching out of the pool, so they evolve to reach higher up for their food, they evolve to having longer limbs, still walking on all fours, and eventually some will evolve to becoming bipeds and walking upright whilst reaching (and sometimes climbing) for their food. Each new natural design of life form leaves its ancestors behind until the planet is populated with a variety of life forms: water creatures, quadruped animal life, biped animal life and creatures that had to learn to become airborne to escape predators or to reach food, a variety of insects and birds. Also their forms change as their environment changes. In cold areas they will grow hair or fur or have thicker skin.

Out of all the living creatures that inhabit the planet there is always one which becomes the most intelligent. One has learned to utilise its surroundings to the best of its abilities. It is this one that is selected to become the ' thinking being'. It is this species that is selected to branch away from the animal reincarnation cycle and to be granted a spirit.

So, at a point along the timeline of evolution of the planet one of the evolved body shapes is ready for an intervention from the hierarchy of the etheric existence - and for the first time a spirit is placed within a certain form - which then becomes the intelligent life of the planet. All other forms remain as animals, birds and can never evolve into anything more intelligent. Their incarnation cycle is always on a different level and will never raise to another. There is never a cross over.

Now this intelligent solid person can evolve on its own pathway with its body changing with the elements and environmental conditions of the planet and the spirit housed within the solid vehicle becoming more advanced as, over generations and generations, it becomes more knowledgeable and understanding of why it is there at all. [Ends]

You have already been told of the Thirteen who in some ways resemble our own bodies and you had already accepted the appearance of the people of IVO as being from another world. I felt it was necessary to explain how evolution takes place as we are going to meet now other civilisations, Members of The Alliance, whose forms are, in some cases, vastly different from our own. It would be possible to think of some of them as 'talking animals' but it would be a stupidity now that you know how they evolved to become intelligent people walking a planet. They are more advanced than the people of this Earth and to them our own appearance could look unusual – except that all full Members of the Alliance are much too intelligent and advanced to look at the outward appearance of anyone and judge them on that alone.

Solid life adapts itself to its surroundings and its environment. I have never been shocked by the appearance of any beings from other planets that have spoken to me. I have never been afraid of them or surprised by them. If they come from a world with a heavy gravitational pull then they will be small and wide, a lighter gravity and they will be tall and very thin. That just makes sense, doesn't it? If they come from a cold planet they would have more hair and a thicker skin than if they came from a warm one. Most solid life is of a humanoid shape – it's just the easiest body to use and solid life evolves into the most convenient form. Head shapes and features are really irrelevant and all advanced beings see past appearances very quickly.

The Overseer of The Alliance has made sure that I have 'met' many of the Member Civilisations of The Alliance and if I have not been able to speak to them in person then others have come forward and described certain other civilisations to me. I am pleased to be able to continue now with more information of just a few of the civilisations that we share this dimension with.

Alrahn

[Pronounced al-rarn] These people are humanoid in shape, like us. The environmental conditions mean that their skin is a bluish grey. They live the first part of their life under water. As a race they are great builders and explorers.

The Straalia

[Pronounced strar-ay-lia] The world of the Straalia was damaged by global warming and their ice caps melted. Their land masses are now almost completely below the waterline with the exception of a few peaks sticking up above the sea. They live in large cities built above the water on stilts. They do their farming and food gathering underwater in domelike structures, and they also grow food on the bottom of the sea.

The Straalia are humanoid, with faces similar to ours on the Earth, although their bodies differ slightly to ours, they have wider shoulders and their bodies taper downwards. They also have a more pronounced, angular, bone-structure which gives them the appearance that their faces are faceted.

The Brutarn

[Pronounced broo-tarn] On 20 March 2010 I spoke to Brell of The Brutarn. He told me that they were The Brutarn of the Brutarn Nebula and explained that he was from a solar system 42 light years away from our Earth. Their system contains one hundred and forty two planetoids, only twelve of which are occupied, the rest are either too hot, too cold or have a hostile atmosphere.

The Brutarn stand seven feet tall and are not humanoid. They are highly intelligent. They stand tall and thin with extremely long arms which can reach the floor from a standing position. They can walk on four limbs or two. Their bodies are covered with a fine hair. They and are gently by nature. When I tell you that they resemble an animal here, a sloth, do not make the mistake of thinking of them as animals. They wear clothing, of course. They are not aggressive. Their skin colour varies from a very brilliant white to browns of various shades, depending on the region that they come from within their system.

Because Brell thought that I might be thinking of him as an animal he took the time to explain their evolution to me, which was really interesting. He explained that they had evolved, long ago, from ancestors who walked as primitives. Their limbs are long, as I have said, their head and neck system is joined – as in our own case the body and the head merge completely. Their heads, though, finish in a taper and the structure of their body is such that in ancient times their heads were facing upwards so that their primitive ancestors were able to take vegetation from high level. Now their heads tilt forward, like ours. They still have the elongated nose and small eyes on the side of their head. Their hands and feet have only three toes and one thumb on each, and they are longer than ours and jointed with one extra joint. So, as our fingers are jointed, theirs have an additional joint. This is by way of wrapping around, rather than grasping, this again is an evolution from where their ancestors used to climb extensively. They also used to have a tail and this has long, like our own, gone. They are a highly evolved race.

They learned space travel long ago and travelled very extensively within their own solar system. They ventured further into space and encountered other life forms, other beings, many times. A contingent from The Brutarn attempted to visit our Earth before the time of the dinosaurs. They were coming to The Great Meeting, but they fortunately had not arrived when the domes were destroyed and had to turn around.

They developed a method of growing organically that which they need, very similar to the technology of The Thirteen. The Brutarn also use craft that are grown in structure. Their buildings are also organic in their nature. They are grown and nurtured and engineered into shapes. They resemble a tree (in appearance only) with a very wide girth, towering into the sky. These buildings have networks of chambers within and window openings to the atmosphere. They grow to a great height. Because these buildings are living they are able to move with the elements and they move with the air currents, making them very stable.

The Brutarn speak by telepathic means. They are now vegetarian by nature, only eating that which grows. In their past they were carnivores like us, but they have been able to engineer protein into their vegetables and fruit and so nourish their bodies without the need to eat meat.

The etheric levels and solid levels of their people mix freely and their ruling councils consist of both etheric and solid.

The Equlane

[pronounced eck-wa-lane] The environment on the Equlane's home world is so cold and hostile that their bodies are covered in a thick fur-like hair. They are not able to travel very far from their own world as extreme heat is uncomfortable to them.

The Quillern.

[pronounced quill-urn. A conversation held through Ernest on 16 March 2010]

Q: Greetings. I come from a silver … sorry … I come from a civilisation called the Quillern.

L: I am very pleased to speak to you. You are a member of the Alliance I imagine.

Q: Yes. That is why I have … that is why I have … been given the task of speaking to you. We …. We … sorry I did rehearse this …

L: Don't worry, I know it will get easier as you use this language.

Q: We come from a … you say … solar system that is on the further side from The Thirteen from you. So you are on one side and we are on the completely opposite side, the same location. We come from very far.

L: I understand, yes. [The dimension is a spherical shape, imagine a pencil pushed through the centre of a tennis ball – the ball representing the dimension – and The Quillern would be at the point of entry of the pencil and our system would be at the point of exit, opposite]

Q: And we would not have been able to send our delegations to the Alliance meetings if it had not been for the transportation tubes. The natural evolution of your planet is very similar to our own, but our planetary systems did not suffer the interferences that your own system suffered. We followed an evolution from the water, we came from beneath the seas and long ago in our history we became capable of moving both on land and within the seas. We are ... you say ... humanoid I our stature. We stand approximately the same in height as you do. But our skin is like that of a fish. It does not have skin like you do, our skin is silvery in appearance. But it is made up of a number of plates '.. you say ...

L: Scales.

Q: Yes, yes. So our form is biped. We look very similar to you do. Our skin is silver grey in nature. We grow a kind of hair upon our head which is thicker, more coarse than your own, but without close scrutiny we would be almost the same as you. The features are the same as your Earth people, the only difference is that our fingers and our toes are webbed between them.

L: Yes, from the water, yes of course.

Q: And between our arms ... our arms ... have webs beneath the arms. We still swim freely and breathe freely. As I have said we look the same as you, but beneath the ears on each side of our head we have a membrane that is a gill, we can breathe through this. It is barely visible, but we can breathe beneath the water. We dress mush the same as any other would really, we wear clothing like you do. We walk. We talk infrequently.
L: You speak telepathically.

Q: Yes. We have long since developed this ability.

L: Do you have a collective consciousness?

Q: Yes. We have a collective consciousness. Our life cycle is very similar to your own except that we live much longer. Our reproductive system is the same as your own, we have children. We have young but we have many young and our young are born multiple and the difference between our culture and your own is that our young leave us very early. They leave the comfort or ... I do not know what you would say ... they leave the confines ...

L: Of the family unit.

Q: And they live in communities. So when they are young they move away from us. They live together, they develop ... they develop their ... mental capacity at a very early age and they hone their physical skills, on their own, away from us. And then when they have grown sufficiently, they return and integrate with the rest of us. It follows a cycle very similar to many animal and fish species on your Earth.

L: I think it is very sensible, because it means that the time of the adult is not taken with the rearing of the child and all are working to full capacity.

Q: Yes. Some return to the depths of the water to live when they are young. Some live within vegetated areas. It depends on the climatic conditions. Our planet is very similar to your own, we have seas, we have icecaps but the general atmosphere is very warm and you would say tropical in most areas. And we have areas of very dense undergrowth, we have mountain ranges like you do, we have small areas of barrenness ... deserts ... but these are of natural construction, not forced like your own. We have vehicles ... craft ... that are powered by the force of the mind power. We are able to move them with the power of our own input. We travel extensively in our own system with craft that are adaptations of smaller craft. They are spherical in nature, varying in sizes depending on the use. They are structured inside with segments, they have chambers within them. They are spherical in nature, they can carry few or many depending on their size. They also are silver opalescent in their appearance. They look very much like a pearl. Like the craft of The Thirteen, they are grown in an organic way, we also learned long ago how to manipulate the genetic growth of ...

L: Plant life.

Q: Yes ... so the vehicles ... craft ... that we use to travel vast distances are grown and they grow ... like the ... inside of an ... orange .. something that is segmented. So the cavities form inside and they grow naturally. And we are able to influence the growth by input of an energy input, like you would say ... electricity ... is this correct ... electricity?

L: Yes, I understand.

Q: When the craft is growing by the input of these energy bursts we can fashion the shapes of the inside, we can influence the way that the structure moves. So we can form caverns, cavities inside. We have travelled far, like The Thirteen, but certainly not on such long journeys as they have, but our craft also have a self-generating structure. We live in cities above the ground. We live in cities that are also of a spherical nature. They are like bubbles. And we grow these large bubbles and where the bubbles touch each other and intersect these sections are opened. So we build ...

L: So they are like domes?

Q: Yes, but we build many on top of each other and on the sides of each other. So then where the bubbles intersect it is opened ...

L: It is a walkway through, so you build a network of spheres.

Q: Yes, this is correct. And the spheres, the cities, are normally built by the side of the water and the structures extend into the water.

L: How beautiful.

Q: So that we can pass from inside the structure, into the water without venturing into the atmosphere. So that is an insight of what we are like. Your Earth has gone through such trauma and we are full of sorrow that someone who could have followed the same pathway as us has been so tampered with. I am pleased to meet you.

L: I am very pleased to meet you. I do not know your name, do you have a name? Do you use such labels?

Q: I am Qui [pronounced Quee] of Quillern. I am in solid form, but we also have a hierarchy, we have those who are not solid who we integrate freely with. I will try and speak to you again.

L: I would look forward to that. Thank you for this.

Q: It is welcome to you. I think the term is good ... bye.

L: Goodbye for now.

Q: Yes.

The Bacaan

[pronounced ba-carn. 2 February 2007]

Bantaal of the Bacaan said ....
All life on this planet you inhabit is organic – what you call flesh and blood. All things that are organic have a similar cell structure. All life on this sphere was developed from single-cell structures.

I come from a civilisation where walking life is not based on organic. It is possible for the spirit of life to exist in other structural forms that are not organically based, like yours. If you were to be able to probe these distant planets with your instruments you would see nothing there. It is because you are not looking for the correct form of life.

The basis of all life on this Earth of yours is carbon-based. Carbon is the building structure on which all is made. There are minerals on your Earth and within your Earth that have no 'life' as you call it. But this is not so on other spheres.

On my home planet the structure is silicone based. This is a mineral structure that is available on your Earth but has no 'life' here, it is an

221

inanimate structure. Silicone makes up many structures and formations but they have never had the breath of life introduced into them.

So it is possible for other spheres to be constructed in completely different ways and the balance of materials to be completely different. It is not necessary for each to be structured in the same way – it is what the environment dictates. On this Earth of yours you breathe oxygen-based air mixed with carbon dioxide. Carbon dioxide is a killer to you but on other planets this is reversed, rather like the plants here, they breathe in reverse and the bi-product of the material is oxygen.

When you travel distances as an etheric form it does not matter and you are able to visit anywhere. In this vast structure of the universe keep your mind open and expect the unexpected. You would never be able to visit these places in the organic form you have now. That is why it is necessary for beings to evolve beyond the limitations of the physical body so that they can have the ways unlocked to them. They would be able to visit places which are completely untouchable to them in their solid form.

It is rare, but there are life forms which are completely crystalline in structure, and they are very beautiful. I know how much you enjoy enlightenment – you are using your mind to expand the world you know and now you must realise that there are more worlds to expand your knowledge into. If you use your mind openly you will be able to accept all things. The spirit is pure energy and the body that it occupies can be constructed in many ways.

If you were to look upon the form that I possessed when I walked I would resemble your ice crystals. I carry the form of a quadruped, but constructed in faceted materials, each layer of facet being a very thin microscopic thin layer, making up the structure, We all walk in this way. We are of very delicate construction and would not interact with your cumbersome organic form. I am but a traveller. I will walk on from you now.

I said 'I am humbled that you came, and Bantaal replied 'Do not be humbled by anything. We all come from the same beginnings.' I saw Bantaal's form, he showed it to me, as he had walked before he became etheric. He walked on all fours and his whole body, legs and head were made out of tiny thin shards of glass-like layers. He was opaque and the sun shone through his body and made him appear to be lightly tinted into pastel rainbow colours. He was quite beautiful and extremely fragile. Crystalline beings are rare and cannot interact with other heavier life forms, it is highly dangerous for them.

Life survives and flourishes in many forms – and all of them are beautiful in their own way, but Bantaal (who speaks to me often and has become a friend) is special. He comes a great distance to speak to me. His planet is the last surviving planet of such beautiful crystalline people. They cannot attend the Council Meetings of The Alliance in solid form and so neighbouring civilisations have to represent them there. Fortunately all the Members of The Alliance are aware that if others were to set foot upon their world when in solid form the Bacaan would perish. Even those who visit there when they are in etheric form get the feeling that the perfect form of these beautiful fragile people might shatter even with such etheric interaction, such is their delicacy.

The Scarab People

Just as The Bacaan cannot mix with other solid civilisations there is another civilisation who historically could not do so either, but for a very different reason. Teelagh, a Higher Being, explains. ..

Teelagh said ...
I have travelled this dimension and seen many civilisations and watched the interaction between them all as they journey through space. Thankfully this dimension has, in the main, advanced enough now for most of those who exist within it to see past the vehicle which the spirit uses to carry it They know that the vehicle was 'designed' to enable that being to exist in comfort and productivity in that being's home environment.

I know that this Earth has not yet advanced enough for the people who walk upon it to walk together in harmony. Many who walk on this world still see the colour of a persons skin rather than the being encased within it. I have seen people on your Earth recoil from someone who has a body which is distorted in some way or someone who has a facial disfigurement. I know that there are certain races who have an animosity towards other races because of where they live. Thankfully your Earth is one of the few places left in this dimension where such ignorance and stupid intolerance exists but a very long time ago there were many worlds such as yours.

The Scarab People have been pictured on the walls which remain from Ancient Egypt and they did walk this Earth long before the Great Meeting and continued a relationship with this Earth after that. They are great explorers and travellers, highly advanced and technologically adept, they have always enjoyed journeying to other worlds and whenever they have interacted with others they have always educated or helped other worlds in some way. Now they are easily accepted and welcomed on most worlds where the hosts are without any thought for the appearance of their visitors. But this was not so in the past.

Long, long ago when The Scarab people had to appear to those of a primitive elevation, such as the like of your own Neanderthals, the Scarab People were aware that those who saw them would recoil, certainly the children of the primitives were afraid of them. Such was their compassion and understanding for those that they wished to help, that they developed a type of body suit which resembled a form more acceptable to the primitives, an exo-suit, which they would encase themselves in before encountering those who were less advanced. It is sad that they had to do this, but a credit to them that they had the understanding to do so.

The Scarab People are bipeds with a body similar to the Earth frame, but their head differs in that it has two feelers on top and two feelers lowering from the mouth. Their mouth is small and they have the large compound eyes you would call 'insect eyes'. Their hands have pincers instead of fingers.

The Scarab People are a race of kind, compassionate and highly intelligent, advanced people and any civilisation visited by them today are most fortunate. Thankfully, gone are the days when they had to disguise their appearance. I wonder if your Earth would ever be ready to accept such beings without judging them by their appearance. If you are beginning to understand that Members of The Alliance who slightly resemble Earth's animals are most definitely not animals, then it should be easy for you to understand that the Scarab People and others are most definitely not insects.

Perhaps one day you will have the opportunity to see for yourselves what these different people look like, and then you might all stop taking such an interest in what you foolishly believe is the 'perfect human form' and stop striving to improve your appearance, often at the expense of improving your mind.

Awkwell

[pronounced awk-well] The Awkwell are humanoid bipeds but their young walk on all four limbs until their backs straighten. Even then they do not grow to more than five feet tall. They are vegetarian and as a race they are mainly farmers and growers.

The Regarten

[pronounced re-gar-ten. 21 March 2010]

D: Greetings. I am Dayvos. [pronounced day- voss]

L: Hello, I am Lillie and I am pleased to speak to you.

D: Greetings. I am of The Regarten people. We are explorers. We have travelled far and wide in all that we can find, of course there are areas that we have not found, yet. But we are great explorers and travellers. We like to gather knowledge. We feel that we have never learned enough. We are distributors of knowledge also. We have visited other worlds and we have taken knowledge that they have not had. We are not, do not misjudge us, we are not ones who interfere. We feel that if we have the knowledge then we should share with others and we have visited many civilisations where for just one simple piece of knowledge it has ...

L: Advanced them?

D: It has held them back.

L: Oh, I see, because of the lack of knowledge, I understand.

D: Yes. We pride ourselves in the production of natural things. We are, I suppose you would say, by nature farmers. We grow many varieties of plant life ... is this right?

L: Plant life, yes, it is right.

D: Our whole society is based upon that which grows. Even the structures in which we live, are grown.

L: Ah, similar to The Thirteen.

D: Yes, very much so, and we also are great I suppose you would say ... meddlers.

L: [Laughing] How charming.

D: We like to ... we have very enquiring minds, we make intricate machinery that sometimes is completely useless, and we went through a period of making complicated paraphernalia that had very little purpose.

L: We would say you were inventors.

D: Yes, inventors. But we found that the science of making machinery from that which was inanimate was very limited and they would wear. So we simplified our methods and we like to teach others how to use the resources that they have – so we now would rather grow than make. We can manipulate the growth of organic matter that fashion into ... whatever we wish, basically. Our craft that take us from world to world are organic in nature, they grow ... they grow.

L: Again like The Thirteen.

D: Yes. We travel at immense speed. We use the polar magnetism that all bodies produce, all planetoids, all solar systems contain magnetism and we use this ...

L: To pull you towards it.

D: Yes. Gravitation. We use this. We use this. So we are able to travel far and wide and we have done so. When we travel vast distances whole generations exist and demise upon the vehicle. But now of course we have the introduction of the transport systems the Alliance have brought to us. We are bipeds. We are very similar to your own genetic makeup. There are subtle differences with us. We are the same in basic height as you are. Our facial features are very similar to your own. We have a protruding ... structure above our eyes. Like a forehead that protrudes.

L: Oh, yes, I see, I understand.

D: Do you understand?

L: Is it a bone structure, like a frill?

D: No, no, it is like a ... the bone structure above the eyes protrudes further.

L: I understand, so it is like a cliff hanging over your face, I'm sorry to be impolite but it shows that I understand, how wonderful, good.

D: We have hair on our head that grows further than yours, you would say like a mane I suppose. So it grows from the head down onto the neck and part of the back and finishes there. That is our main difference. Invariably we are light skinned like you. Our hair colour changes from dark to brown, to white, this is the only difference between our own people. Of course we all recognise each other.

L: Yes. Do you have a collective consciousness.?

D: Yes, we have a consciousness. We also, like many others communicate via the mind. But we do still speak, we speak to our young because they do not develop the power of communication until they grow. Their brains have to develop to a state where they no longer need to speak. It is very much a ... noise ... when the young speak amongst themselves.

L: Lovely.

D: We live in cities that we grow. We grow our vehicles. We farm extensively. We enjoy the fruits of our labour. We enjoy the variety. We have vast festivals where others bring their produce.

L: So you are also very sociable.

D: Yes, we exchange, we constantly compete in a friendly way to grow something different and we have festivals where we enjoy eating and drinking the fruit of our labours and we exchange new ideas. We bring ideas from other worlds, we bring our fascination of all things that grow. We are constantly looking for more and constantly exchanging that which we have with others. We have found that in the past we were able to take our knowledge to worlds that have very meagre growth and we were able to produce plant life which could thrive in a particular environment. We have been to many worlds where they have been dying because their nutrition is diminishing. We have ... as I have said we are basically farmers, but we have the ability to produce meaningful, edible food in the most hostile of environments. We have been to planetary systems where the ground has been all but useless, devoid of all nutrients. Thereby we have produced plants that take their nutrition from the air itself. We have been to environments where there has been conflict and the earth has been devoid of any nutrients because of disturbance. Again we have been able to produce. We are able to produce also plants that will grow in hostile atmospheric environments. So, we love to grow. We just enjoy what we do. We are farmers.

L: Farmers and explorers! What a wonderful combination.

D: Yes. We, like many others did eat the creatures that walked, in the past. This has been the way with many civilisations, it is part of the evolution as we see it. But now we have all of the nourishment which we need, from that which we grow. As I have said we have grown our whole culture on being able to share this with others and we gain enjoyment from what we do. We really ... it is not worship, but we really ... respect that which we grow. We have a respect for all that grows. And we enjoy it. We live much longer than you do.

L: Yes, I'm sure you do.

D: We have a healthy disposition. We find that the food that we eat is very nutritional. We have helped many by taking to them the seeds of that which we grow. If we had our way we would make the whole of creation a vast farm. We cannot stand to see wasted land. We find it very difficult to understand that civilisations such as yours have vast communities that have no food.

L: And no water. No fresh water.

D: It is the life blood of all. But you see even plants can be grown that possess moisture. Is there anything else you wish to know about us?

L: I have no questions thank you for now.

D We are of collective consciousness. We exist in solid form and we have elders who exist in ...

L: Who are etheric.

D: Yes.

L: And you mix freely?

D: Yes, we consult each other. We like to think that although of course we have no religion, or need for such, we do not worship any unseen, unheard, unknown being, but we feel that our elders watch over us and they guide us. So in this way we help each other. We feel that our non-solid beings guide us in what we do. We aspire to become an elder. We grow materially and we demise. And we become elders, we become teachers of others. We enjoy teaching.

L: Yes, I can hear that in your voice, in what you say.

D: But we have plenty of what we need, but without being wasteful.

L: Are you able to give me some idea of your location? Of your system, and how many planets within your system?

D: There are seven planets in our system. Not all planets are inhabited, but all planets have vegetation.

L: Yes, I imagined that to be so.

D: We farm the entire system. We waste nothing. That which is not consumed is returned to the earth as nutrients. We waste nothing. There is no starvation on our world. There is no famine. There is no want for nutrition. All are equally treated. But our society is such that we all work together. We enjoy what we do. We enjoy seeing that which we have grown, we enjoy consuming and enjoying that which we have produced. We have elders as I said, we mix freely ...

L: And your location ...

D: Sorry, yes ...

L: Are you able to ... I know I will not understand the distance but if you could give me a location, are you in the area of The Thirteen, The Nine ... ?

D: We are closer to The Thirteen than to you, we are on the far side of The Thirteen.

L: Ah, so you are closer to The Quillern?

D: Yes, probably equidistant from The Thirteen.

L: Oh, OK, I think that is all I will understand.

D: Yes.

L: But I do have some understanding now of where you are, thank you. And you use the tubes?

D: Yes, the tubes are ever growing. We find that we can reach many areas now and as I have said it is our wish to visit all. We do not know if we will have the time ...

L: But you plan to.

D: Yes. We hope that the whole of creation would turn to be green. This is the colour of life. So, that is what we are. We will speak again I hope. Goodbye.

L: Goodbye for now.

The Fwenille

These people are extremely fragile. They cannot endure heavy contact. A simple handshake would cause severe damage. They are biped humanoids who grow to five or six feet tall. They spend their entire life with minimal contact with others outside of their own world.

The Nine

I refer many times to the walls of Seti I's tomb in Egypt and here I must do so again as The Nine are represented in that historic record also. They were represented at The Great Meeting and many of The Nine perished there.

The Nine are unusual in their form in that their civilisation have a variety of head shapes. They were not the original occupants of their system of Nine Planets, they evolved elsewhere. A number of different civilisations, long before the time of the Great Meeting (long, long before our time of the dinosaurs), banded together and formed a new civilisation which occupied a system of nine planets. The original occupants of The Nine Planets had already evolved to being fully etheric and it was with their permission and help that this newly formed group populated the system of nine very beautiful planets. The originals have now moved elsewhere leaving a fully unified population existing as The Nine. The Nine now consider themselves one people and long ago stopped even noticing their variety of faces.

The Nine are pictured on the wall of Seti's tomb with the head shapes of a 'ram', two different 'bird' heads, one with a longer 'beak', one a short snubbed 'beak shape', a 'baboon' head, and a 'humanoid face' like our own which resemble the ancient Egyptians in many tomb paintings. This is how they looked at the time of The Great Meeting and much time has passed since then (dinosaurs walked the Earth for 150 million years) which means that The Nine have evolved since then into face shapes which are much more muted and softened so that although you can identify their origins their 'animal like' faces are much less pronounced.

It was Eshe of the Nine who gave us the description of the pyramid craft used by The Nine in our section on space travel and here she gives us a description of one of their planets ...

The Nine's First Planet

[Eshe - 26 August 2007]

Eshe says ....

We are in a pyramid craft above a planet which is similar to Earth. This is The First Planet. All of the nine planets are similar, certainly in the way they are governed and their town planning is the same, and so describing one is enough to give you a good idea of all.

As we look upon it we see land mass, blue oceans, the brown and green of the land and two polar ice caps. It is bigger than your Earth and whereas on your planet the land masses have separated, here there is one big land mass with sea all around it. We are still in the darkness of space as we view the planet and then it gets lighter as we go through the different colours as we lower towards the planet, until we see blue sky and clouds and start to lose the curvature of the planet as we come down. Now we see the greenery as we drift down slowly and land.

The crew are streaming out of the craft and being met by their friends and families. They are all humanoid with a variety of different facial features. We see head shapes and faces which I can only describe as resembling some of your own Earth's animal head shapes – birds, baboons, cats and even some who look like your own paintings of ancient Egyptian Earth faces. A mixed race of people forming one civilisation. They are all smiling and laughing. The crew have brought with them small gifts for the children who come to meet them. The crew is a mix of male and female. They are taking their baggage away on trolleys which hover and float and they walk away from the airbase towards the city.

You can walk to the city or use a form of 'transport'. You select your destination and travel there in a split second - in most advanced civilisations the use of molecular reconstruction is commonplace and so it is not unusual for people to transport themselves over short or long distances in this way.

Once in the city we see tall glass buildings which tower so high above that you cannot see the tops from below. They look like a collection of glass tubes fixed together. Inside the buildings they have 360 degree vision out of the windows, in fact this is an advanced technology which makes you feel as if there are no walls (or windows) - that you have a completely clear view of that which surrounds the building. Sometimes in the recreational areas it seems as if there are no floors or ceilings either and you have complete spherical vision. To move between floors we use a 'beam of light' technology. You step into the beam and are transported to the floor of your choice.

The buildings are for a variety of purposes similar to those you would imagine. There are places to eat, places to live, places to enjoy the entertainment of music and art and other places to gather together for recreational purposes. The streets between the buildings are clean and the buildings themselves glisten in the sunlight. Everything is very fresh.

This area houses also the buildings which undertake the organisational areas of government. There is a form of commerce. Once they become adults the people all work, until they are older, and they work for a form of credits. There is an allocation of resources and each person has an allocation of food, clothes and leisure items. When they join an away party for rescue work elsewhere their allocation is transferred to the manifest of the craft which they serve upon.

The way the cities are laid out is of particular note. There is a large central area of countryside within which is an educational facility, an Academy for all ages, a Museum which houses all of the history of The Nine and the history of The Nine's exploration of other worlds, and a Healing Centre, although ailments are few. Around this large circular area of greenery you find a ring of the cities - in this way each part of the city can make its way into the open countryside with ease and use the facilities there.

Farming on a large scale takes place out of the cities. The farm lands are the size of your countries and very well organised. Everything is used, nothing is wasted and because of the food that they eat and the clean energy which they use the people are very healthy. The planet's weather is controlled. They can manipulate rain so that their crops are always watered adequately.

Their Healing Centre is of interest. You would call it a hospital. We walk along the pathways through the countryside until we come to a section of buildings which are several domes huddled together. They are open at the sides and as we enter we see dimmed lights and it feels very peaceful. There are operating rooms for severe problems but this is often not necessary. If operations are performed they are non-invasive and the patient leaves immediately surgery is finished. There is no fear. In the outer area doctors perform minor repairs as people are waiting. There is no pain, no wailing. As soon as you step into the environment you are instantly calmed. We see a woman there with a young boy and we see his leg is broken and bent. He is quite happy and just sitting waiting – pain relief comes from the atmosphere itself. We see a doctor come over to the boy and he manipulates the leg back into its normal position and we see him using his healing hands and mind power to mend the break. The boy is calm throughout and when the doctor is finished he gets up, unperturbed, and runs off and out of the building.

They do not call them Doctors, they call them Healers. The place is full of Etheric Healers who are in the etheric layer and they add their energies to that of the Solid Healers. They call the Etheric Healers 'Elders'. They are there but you cannot see them – their energy is there. There is a concentration of energy in the building which comes from the Elders and if you had a minor ailment it would be enough to go into the building for it to heal. This is how those in the waiting room are instantly calmed. There is another area with really old people there who have thin bodies and bones. We see a pool of liquid, thick like mercury, which is milky white with pearl rainbow colours shining from it. This is a rejuvenating, revitalising liquid and it is enough to lower the old people into it. These people are older than you could imagine – these people have a very long life span. The rejuvenating liquid can also be found in large pools on the outer edge of the countryside and the people go there and bathe together in them for relaxation and pleasure.

The people look happy. They go to work and they live their lives in the same way that most advanced civilisations do - without war, violence, greed or jealousy. Their children play like any other children. They are cultured people with a love of music, art and literature the same as all intelligent people and they have long since advanced past the primitive need for any type of worship or religion. [Ends]

The Nine have a special role in this dimension. They are the most advanced technologically of all of the civilisations and because of this and their compassionate nature they are 'The Emergency Services' for the dimension. The network of the tubes has now spread far and wide and this, along with their own advanced technology allows them to arrive at any system quickly to aid in times of natural disaster. Through The Alliance they can now be alerted as soon as there is a problem. The Alliance members in the locality of any problem planet also step in to assist with supplies and aid. A unified Alliance spreading out across the whole dimension means that assistance can be given as soon as a situation arises. Here is an archive piece of information from The Nine where Eshe describes an emergency mission.

A Rescue Mission by The Nine

[Eshe, 12 December 2008, with a description of an Away Mission. This describes in great detail one of their works of rescue. This is from The Nine's archives]

Eshe says ...
I am accessing in the archives 'File Name: System No 873, Planet No 2. Loss of Environment and Climatic Disaster.'

Looking from the pyramid craft as they descend towards the planet and as they approach it shows that the planet is totally covered in ice with the exception of a thin band around the middle and the occasional mountain tip sticking through the ice elsewhere. The seas are frozen over and the whole planet is covered in a carpet of blue/white ice. Their sun is still operational and they can detect the heat from it, so whatever has happened came from something other than a cooling of their sun.

A thermal picture on the viewing screen confirms what was seen visually. It shows a sphere where from its poles towards the centre the equipment registers blue/white and pale colours and yet the heart of the planet shows red and orange. They analyse from above the planet for a long time. The fear is that if they land they could be frozen there and not get off.

The Nine's scientists are seated around a conference table aboard the craft and they beam up people from the planet to join them. Please understand that it is unusual to have a planet such as yours where it would be unexpected for help to arrive in this way. These people were well aware of The Nine and of their missions and were expecting them. They are humanoid and have faces the same as those you have on the Earth. They look extremely unwell.

Their scientists and officials explain that their planet has taken a very long time to degenerate to this dangerous stage which has been caused by a collision from space and that they have slowly moved their civilisations until they are now sited in the band around the middle. They were a highly evolved society with their technology and over this period of time they had had to abandon their cities and now did not have enough resources to sustain themselves.

They show The Nine a graph of the different sectors of their population and it shows a massive depletion. Many civilisations are dying out. Their core sample drilling equipment has also shown them that the core of the planet itself is also cooling. The Nine decide to concentrate on two areas, firstly the atmosphere and secondly the core, and say that they must raise the core temperature first as the planet is too cold to attack just the atmosphere. They decide to bore into the planet at different points to access the core. They explain that they must do this slowly as if the temperature rises too quickly the planet will explode.

The plan is to work at these different points and cause a chain reaction. They explain that this will take a very long time. Short-term they plan to help the people by clearing the dust cloud which has formed around their planet and by building solar collectors which will enable them to sustain themselves. They will make sure the planet does not freeze any further and this will halt the deterioration. Evacuation is not an option.

The Nine launches a series of filter satellites which systematically orbit the planet, filtering the atmosphere as they go. Clear lines show behind the satellites immediately as they move around. The Nine beam down masses of drilling equipment to various locations. These machines burn away the ground using laser technology, coiling down in a circular motion and spinning very fast, cutting away the rock. Then they insert heating elements into the bore holes.

Days, weeks and months pass and from above it is possible to see the vegetation changing and the atmosphere is clearing. Looking at the thermal picture it shows warm spots appearing all over the planet. In time the thermal picture changes to show it fairly even all over. As the planet warms steam starts to emit from the holes, forming clouds in the near-clean atmosphere, which in turn produces warm rain. This falls upon the planet. Slowly the ice melts and it is possible, eventually, to see land masses starting to appear from under the ice. The Nine explain that the steam jets will diminish when all the ice has melted. They explain that they will leave their satellite filters which will continue to work, and will burn up in time and do not pose any threat.

The Nine also leave various pieces of large machinery to help the inhabitants rebuild their cities. They promise also to monitor from afar to make sure there are no problems but they now leave the people to their own planet. This mission is complete. [Ends]

Natural disasters upon planets are not unusual. Many civilisations have evolved their solid forms to compensate for historic changes in temperature, land mass reductions, freezing planets or water planets. Life does not give up in those circumstances. It changes to compensate. If a planet starts to become too cold then solid life forms will move underground to survive, too hot and they move into the seas to stay cool. Life fights to survive at all costs and mostly manages to do so. The advancements of civilisations now mean that such ecological disasters are few and any problems can usually be rectified, often with the technological assistance of The Nine and a helping hand from other Members of The Alliance.

The Sarmalanian

[Pronounced sarma-layn-ian]
The Sarmalanian are an example of a civilisation that were greatly helped by The Nine, to the point of their very existence being saved. If you were to be passing their system on a space craft and observed them and the way that they live you could think that they were not a very advanced race. You would not see modern towering cities and land vehicles and flying craft. They have never been interested in space exploration although they have always welcomed visitors with warmth and kindness. But it is a mistake to think that just because a civilisation have avoided technology as a way of advancement they are backward in some way. Not so. There are many civilisations who prefer a simple, natural way of life and yet they are highly advanced in their evolution. The Sarmalanian are just such a race.

Sadly the Sarmalanian suffered from a virus which was so virulent that it spread and killed a very large number of their population. The nearest we would have here to that would be an influenza virus. The Nine were alerted to their plight and sent a taskforce there to neutralise the virus and stop it spreading. It is also interesting to note that the virus was started by the cooling of their solar system of five planets. Their star was beginning to cool and as the temperatures dropped on their planets (particularly the one which was inhabited) this caused the virus to mutate and spread amongst them. As well as halting this terrible virus The Nine were able to regenerate the star itself, and the environment was able to start the process of returning to how it should be.

Having used their technology to repair these people and their world The Nine took away with them all signs of their technology as it was obvious that these people did not wish for it and wanted to return to their simple, natural way of life. The Sarmalanian are Full Members of The Alliance and when their delegates wish to attend Council Meetings of The Alliance they are collected in the craft of their 'neighbours' who give them a lift to the meeting. All Full Members of the Alliance are intelligent and advanced enough to know that technology is not necessarily a sign of an advanced race. How interesting to think that the Sarmalanian are Full Members of The Alliance and that as they were speaking to me, with strong telepathic messages, the solid people walking our own Earth did not even know there was an Alliance, and the Earth is a very long way behind the advancement of the Sarmalanian.

The Sarmalanian stand over 6ft tall, with a stocky frame similar to our bears here, a light covering all over their bodies of almost white 'hair' or 'fur' and a kind hairless, humanoid face like our own.

The Berdark

[pronounced burr-dark]. Not all civilisations choose to build structures on the surface of their planet. The environment of many planets means that the conditions are too harsh to enable anyone to exist exposed to the elements. The Berdark are cave dwellers. They are between 5 and 6 feet in height. As they advanced their structures built within caves became more intricate until now they have vast, sophisticated cities underground. Their evolution means that they have very poor eyesight and they cannot tolerate bright light. Their bodies are covered with fine hair.

The Cauyarl

These people spend most of their life under water and so are, of course, excellent swimmers. They are biped amphibians who grow to seven or eight feet tall. They have vast underwater cities.

The Abglyn

[pronounced ab-gleen] The Abglyn are a civilisation of people who have suffered greatly because of their own ways in the past, long before they were part of The Alliance and long before any other civilisations were in contact with them. What happened to them is their own fault, they readily admit that. But it does not make their story any the less distressing and harrowing to hear.

[21 March 2010. The speaker was a very thin, skeletal, emaciated man whose appearance was like that of the poor people released from the horror of near starvation and malnutrition in the concentration camps at the end of World War II on our Earth. Ernest said that as this man spoke

through him Ernest could feel the mans own body fighting to stay alive –
an unstable heartbeat as if the body was struggling to stay alive]

C: Greetings.

L: Hello. I am very pleased to speak to you.

C: Yes. I am pleased to speak to you also. We have studied the
communications your Earth transmits, so that we know, or hope that we
know, how to communicate with you.

L: Well you are doing very well so far. I am aware when I speak to such
advanced people that it is necessary for you to go back in your history to
find what it is like to communicate in this way. It must be difficult.

C: Yes, as so many others we communicate by thought patterns, we do not
speak like this. Although we can, we do not choose to. We find that we can
say all that we need to say with the mind. My name is Cal.

L: Cal?

C: Yes. I have been looking at your phonetics and some of our words, or
most of our words, do not interpret. So ...

L: You found the nearest.

C: Yes. C .. A .. L ..

L: Cal.

C: Yes, and our people are called The Abglyn.

L: Ab – gleen.

C: Yes. But even to add to the difficulty the pronunciation, the
interpretation ... would be A .. B .. G .. L .. Y .. N.

L: Ok, yes I understand.

C: That is the people, who we are.

L: OK the Abglyn. Lovely.

C: We are bipeds, we walk upright as you do. But our bodies are fragile,
we are humanoid in construction but our bodies are very ... you would say
... skeletal. We do not grow to great mass, our bodies are very ... slight,
slight in their nature. We do not put on body mass. This is a genetic

deficiency because we have, years ago in our history, we had great conflict between us and other adjoining worlds. We are a system of four planets Four planets circling around a star. Four planets that originally of which three were occupied. Now only two. We are a peaceful people. We banished all conflict long ago. We learned a terrible lesson. We became advanced, as many have done, and we grew in advancement. We were aware of others on other planets close to us and eventually we developed methods of travel between us, primitive by all standards but they grew to advancement. And transportation between worlds became commonplace. It was interesting to see how all of the inhabitants had evolved along the same line. We had much in common. Our stature then was as you are now. We were, in many ways, like to people of the Earth in appearances. We were friends for a long time and the history is so far away now that we do not know exactly what caused the conflicts, but of course it does not matter now. Thus we entered into periods of prolonged conflict between us. And as I have said it is so long in our history now that we do not even have records of what was. All traces of the cause have gone. We now live with the consequences. It came to an all out war between the three planets that were occupied. It could have been greed, it could have been any reason. The conflicts consumed our resources at an alarming rate and it went on for centuries in your time. Endless times.

L: Generations?

C: Yes. Whole generations lived and died in warfare and knew no different. Culminating in the almost complete destruction of one world, completely. We changed sides constantly, between the three of us and it came to a situation where two of us opposed the one and the destruction was total. And, too late, we realised what we had done. And we tried to make amends, we rescued them, the very few survivors from the world that we had destroyed. Even to this day it is not possible to set foot upon it. Such was the contamination from the conflict. As a consequence, we blighted our own evolution and it is a deficiency in our body structure. The contamination caused to our material bodies – we do not grow to great stature.

L: Oh, how sad Cal. Like a constant reminder.

C: In some ways we feel that it is right and just that we are reminded of this. So much time has passed now, we have become accustomed to the way that we are. We are a peaceful people now. We have seen at first hand what misunderstanding and conflict can cause. And we have travelled far and wide through many universes, we have advanced methods of transportation. We have met many others and we have tried to impart our knowledge upon them to stop them falling into the same traps that we did.

L: Yes, what a warning.

C: We banished all methods of conflict from our own people on our home worlds and we are severe with any of our kind who show any signs of aggression. We must keep the peace. Our existence is so fragile. But this is the same with all existence. We were also going to attend The Meeting.

L: Oh, how sad. So you have that also in your history.

C: We saw it as a way of moving forward. We hoped that what we could bring to the conference with our knowledge of disasters, we could be a great lesson to those who would listen to us.

L: So The Meeting was after your warfare? [Placing it before dinosaurs here]

C: Yes, so long ago.

L: Yes, exactly, now I can put it into a timeline, yes.

C: When we were travelling towards The Meeting we had this feeling of hope for our people. And we hoped that the peace that we had learned would be shared with others. But we did not make The Meeting, we were told of the great disaster, the great conflict, and sadly we turned for home. And we stayed, confined to our own lives, for much longer, until we were contacted by the Alliance.

L: Oh, Cal, what a terrible, terrible thing. How sad.

C: Now we are finally full members of the Alliance Council, and we are listened to. And we hope that we can bring peace to others. We did try to suppress our history because we were ashamed, but we feel that the lesson that we have is to tell others where we have failed.

L: I am a big believer in the truth, and telling all, but it is hard to do so, Cal, I can understand that.

C: Warfare and conflict is the biggest waste of all. We are all the same, although physically we look different. We have to learn the same things and if we can stop others from reaching the point of destruction that we reached, then we feel that we have fulfilled our place here.

L: I can see that you are great teachers.

C: Yes. So ... we occupy two planets. Our cities are wonderful. There are structures that reach high into the upper sky. They are crystalline in structure. The crystals we manufacture by a chemical reaction – we grow crystals. So sometimes entire buildings are grown using this method of production. The crystalline structure, the various components bond themselves together and make for great strength.

L: And yet I imagine they look so beautiful, and fragile in appearance.

C: Yes, they appear to be, but they are strong. We travel space, but now we use the tubes, this has made our movement much easier. We still have craft that we use to move from one to another, these are powered by the source of energy, the star. The craft are made to absorb this energy and convert it to useful energy. This is the way that all machinery works on our worlds.

L: All solar, yes I see.

C: Solar, yes. We live like you do. Our societies are very similar. We live in units of elders and youngers. We bear young as you do. But our success rate with offspring is not always as good.

L: Because of the genetic problem?

C: Yes, our females bear many children but many do not survive.

L: Oh, how terribly sad.

C: We would hope that in time this would be cured and many scientist from with the members of the Alliance are working upon it, but a lesson to us is that in time you learn to live with what you have.

L: Can I ask you a question?

C: Yes.

L: Your solid beings who walk – is there any pain for you? Because of the genetic problem?

C: There would be pain ...

L: Yes.

C: But we have learned to control all things through our mind. Our bodies are healthy ... our bodies are healthy and we live to a long age. It seems to me that the problem is with the starting of life. Once life has began and our offspring begin to grow ...

L: Then they can flourish.

C: Yes, but the problem is with the ...

L: With the start.

C: Yes. But we have learned to control all things with our thoughts ...

L: Oh, good, I would hate to think of you being in any pain.

C: And the pain is stopped by the power of our own suppression. We live like you do. We farm, we grow that which we need to eat. We grow much in the way of vegetation, and nearly all vegetation is edible in one way or another. We grow and we prepare. We cook ... is that what you say?

L: Yes it is, it is. Where you combine foods to make something else, yes.

C: Yes, we heat it to change its properties. We drink the juices of the fruits and the roots. It is a lesson to us that although we still bear the marks of what we have done everything else is as normal – the food is abundant, it did not suffer. But it has been so long now and we are thankful that we are here. The lesson we have is that you must learn to live with what you are. But we flourish, we are happy, and we are happier now that we have others in the Alliance to share with We are pleased. We have a society that allows none to suffer. We would not allow such as your Earth where some have the abundance of what they grow and others have none. Our society makes sure that all are fed and cared for, always. We care for one another. We grew, as many societies have grown, into a collective consciousness. We have an elders system of, you say non-solid.

L: Etheric.

C: Yes, etheric. And our governing bodies are made of etheric and solids and we use the knowledge of the elders combined with the abilities of the solids to continue our existence. Both worlds co-exist together, they are almost identical.

L: Yes, I look forward to that here.

C: We have built on the remains of what was left and we decided that we would unify and make all things the same thereby taking away any need for conflict in the future. All conflict is destructive. All uncaring is destructive. We must all exist as one no matter who or what we are. And we feel that we are growing closer towards this. You could ask whatever you wish of us.

L: I have no questions now thank you.

C: Our life cycle is very similar to your own. We have probably one hundred revolutions [their equivalent to years]

L: A lot shorter than many of the civilisations I have spoken to.

C: But you see we know, we learned long ago, that the material existence is short, but once we have proved ourselves, we have eternity. So, yes, we understand that material life must end ...

L: But you know it continues, yes.

C: Yes, there is a sadness when those close to us ... no longer exist in solid form, but we do not lose them, they are always with us. Just one more I did not care to think of – it is where we are situated. We are midway between The Nine and The Thirteen but we are far away from you. We are ... hard to explain really ... we are far away. I would need to show you astral charts.

L: Don't worry, what you have told me is about as much as I can understand anyway. Thank you.

C: I will hopefully speak to you again. Goodbye.

The Abglyn, at the point of their warfare, were like us. They resembled us in every way.

***

And there you have just a few of the 5,192 civilisations who are Alliance Members. There are many others and I hope I have been able to give you enough details with this representative selection for you to see how life exists in many different forms and evolves to suit its environment.

Here are just a few more members by name: Gulille, Jahl-Agal, Juyrem, Kuy-La-Miel, Lertana, Mewsadren, Oghwelah, Powkastram, Q-lakrew, Rewdasil, Sifagone, Tefadoh, Utrewquel, Vipelqua, Wiosutarn and Xasterain.

THE ROLE OF THE ALLIANCE

The Alliance Council

The civilisations we have introduced to you in the previous sections are all Full Members of The Alliance and have representation on The Alliance Council where decisions are made to protect all solar systems and uphold the Laws of Existence of this dimension.

As I have already said all 5,192 solar system within this dimension are now Members of The Alliance and a small percentage (like the Earth) are still only Associate Members. I hope that is a sobering thought. It amuses me that today's works of science fiction, and indeed any fiction which ventures away in its storylines from this planet, sees Earth as the most advanced of all, and presumes that if there were to be some sort of federation of planets or organised force for the universes, that Earth would be the advanced civilisation running the whole thing, with the Headquarters of the Federation here on the Earth. The Earth is not even close to being considered for Full Membership. The journey to that status is a long one.

The actual Headquarters of The Alliance has historically been on the planet of The Thirteen but now the Alliance has grown to the extent that the facilities on that planet, though vast, are too small to house the whole Alliance Council and so they meet on various planets with technology linking them so that they appear to be in one location.

Most Member civilisations are represented at those meetings and those members form the Alliance Council which is made up of a mix of etheric and solid beings, both layers mixing freely. Full discussions take place concerning many issues concerning the dimension, all Members are heard and all ideas are considered before decisions are finally made and any necessary action taken.

The Overseer Of The Alliance

There are many on this Earth who would be shocked if I were to reveal here the identity of the current Overseer of The Alliance, as part of his origins are from here, The Earth. When this dimension was at the point of preparing for its transition and The Great Meeting was taking place here to discuss those preparations, certain individuals were fortunately outside of the domes when the attack took place. The Overseer was one such individual. Having witnessed that terrible atrocity he had to exist in the etheric layer and wait for life to restart here and also help what was left of the dimension to once again reunite and work towards the present day Alliance. He has travelled to many worlds and helped many civilisation become what they are today.

He is a Higher Being and as part of the plan to recover from what Hilas, Avadna and Unksal did to the Earth he agreed to walk here in material form. And walk he did, in many incarnations. His final walking incarnation was as a Native American Indian. Those who treated him, and his people, so badly might not have done so had they known who he really was and who he would become. He instigated and was, for a while, Overseer of The Earth Council prior to talking up his current position as Overseer of The Alliance and Overseer of The Dimension. And whilst being compassionate and fair to all throughout this dimension, he never forgets the Earth, and he never forgets the Native American Indians - he still calls them his people. The Indians in the etheric layer know the deeds and actions of The Overseer well ... and one day soon his people still walking the Earth will be proud to know the truth of who he really was, who is really is and where he is now. This dimension owes a great debt to him.

The Journey To Full Membership

It is hard to imagine with the state of the Earth today how the solid people of the Earth will ever become Full Members of The Alliance. There are so many steps to take on this journey. Here are some of the major ones:

The solid and etheric layer must integrate and mix freely.

The people of the Earth must learn to stop considering their own welfare and consider equally the welfare of each and every living creature on this planet.

All must understand and follow all of the 1-28 Laws of Existence.

All must learnt to integrate with other civilisations from other worlds.

The people of the Earth must learn to stop considering their own welfare and consider equally the welfare of each and every living creature in this dimension.

When We Are Ready They Will Come

It will be a big step towards the evolution and advancement of the Earth when the Earth can once again accept visitors from other worlds. At the moment The Alliance do not think that the people who walk in the solid layer of the Earth are ready. They anticipate coming to make contact with the Earth and there is a set procedure for how The Alliance do this.

Put away all thoughts and fear of alien invasion, alien abduction or aliens attacking the Earth. Interplanetary violence and aggression has long since gone from this dimension. All forms of warfare and aggression has gone from most planets, leaving just a few pockets of violent behaviour – the Earth being one of them. All Full Members long ago learned to live in peace.

When they decide we are ready to receive them The Alliance will make contact. They will first speak to all government channels to ask them to warn the people of the Earth that they will be communicating. This will allow the governments to announce to their people that people from space will be contacting them, and thus prevent panic. Then, once the governments have told the people of the world to expect the contact The Alliance will break into all technological broadcasts and speak to the whole world, on all frequencies, in all languages, so that all can receive their 'hello' transmission at the same time.

They will not land for a long time. They never land until they are invited to do so. They will continue to speak to the Earth from a Space Station far away from our atmosphere. They will then start to help the Earth in many ways, offering advice and technology to improve the welfare of all upon the planet. They will only help with humanitarian projects and never do anything to assist in weaponry or help with any segregation or acts of aggression.

They will stay off world for a very long time. As long as it takes for this world to learn, to improve and to work towards being able to integrate with the other 5,191 civilisations who are our neighbours.

The Alliance already speak to the etheric layer here and when they come to communicate with us they will be able to immediate integrate with them and speak to our own etheric layer, because they are much more advanced in our etheric layer than we are in the solid layer.

In time we will all be just one big happy family. Do you think we will ever be ready to be a part if that family? Could we be ready a hundred years from now, fifty years, even ten years from now? Can you see that from where we are today?

I hope so because they plan to come here within the next five years.

Message From The Overseer Of The Alliance

The Overseer said ...

When I walked the Earth I always knew that there had to be more to just existing. Man cannot begin to understand another until he has accepted the differences and learned to live with them. Until mankind has learned to accept that, all has a right to exist and thrive. Working together for the greater good is the only way to lift ourselves up and become better. We none of us will ever become perfect, that is not the way. But learning to respect and understand others is the way for peaceful harmony for all.

I have moved on many times since I walked upon the Earth and have learned that there is a place in existence for all. I now have encountered representatives from every corner of this dimension. Good people who have learned from their mistakes and now exist in harmony and peace.

Looking back on the Earth it is hard to imagine that peace will ever come to the Earth, when even the most insignificant things still have such material value. But this phase will pass and mankind will one day be ready to join the rest of existence. Then we will move forward together.

We are patient and we will not discard the stragglers such as you, we will help you to make the pace with the rest of existence. The Alliance will not be complete until all of existence works and exists together. But that day will come, I am sure of that, and The Alliance will do all within its power to help you to take your place beside us.

Grains of sand are nothing on their own but together they become stronger and eventually, given the ages of time and existence, the grains bond to become solid rock. This rock is what we will be. Help yourselves and we will help you.

Overseer of the Alliance

THE HIERARCHY OF ALL EXISTENCE

Imagine existence as a school, a place of learning, for that is what it is. In school you start in a low level class and as you learn more you move up a level into a new class. On and on you move and, if you have made full and good use of whatever education system is at your disposal, with the completion of each level you have more useful knowledge at your disposal and many skills to take you through life.

Existence is like a school, in that it is a place to collect knowledge and make use of it, but unlike a school you do not move up a level simply because time has travelled a certain distance. You would not move into the next level just because you are a year (or even a generation) older. In the journey of existence it is possible to stay on the same level for a very long time, lifetimes in fact. Because until you have learned all that has to be learned at that level you stay where you are, repeating the lessons until you 'pass' and only when you have collected, understood and put into practise all that is available at that level, do you move into the next level. Moving through existence is like a journey and all levels are necessary for all.

Elementary Level – Etheric and Solid People

You start in the etheric layer. When it is your turn you move into the solid layer and start solid life as a solid person to walk the planet. The closest to explaining this stage of evolution is to imagine cavemen before they discovered fire. Primitive man. The lessons to be learned here are simple yet necessary, such as how to survive and yet consider others. Once lessons here have been mastered (and I speak of many, many generations of solid life) then you advance to ....

Intermediary Level – Etheric And Solid People

You are currently at the lower stages of the intermediary level. Once at this level you continue the reincarnation cycle. At the end of each solid lifespan you die and return to the etheric layer. The process of reincarnation continues with lessons to learn in both solid form and etheric. You continue to re-visit the solid layer until eventually it is decided that you have learned enough in the solid layer and have no need to return to it. At that point you continue to learn in the etheric level as an etheric person until you can move on to ....

Intermediary Level – Elevated Beings In The Etheric Layer

The reincarnation process continues throughout our own dimension and all dimensions below us. Eventually a decision is made that you have learned enough lessons in the solid side and have no need to return there. Your advancement from then will be made in etheric form. This is a great achievement and one that all should work towards. It is then that you become an Elevated Being. Elevated Beings in the etheric layer have much true knowledge and certain skills and abilities. They are mentors, knowledge-givers and sometimes healers. They learn from those above and teach those below them in the hierarchy.

NOTE: From this point in elevation all existence is etheric, there are no solid levels necessary for personal advancement.

Higher Beings

These are beings who have attained and shared much knowledge and whose actions have touched and helped many, whose motives are pure and whose actions are always compassionate. They have many skills and abilities. Jasper is a Higher Being. On extremely rare occasions Higher Beings can walk in solid form, usually because there is some task which is necessary and can only be performed from the solid side. Jasper is a Higher Being and was a Higher Being each time he walked upon the Earth. There are others.

The Next Dimension And Randah

There are many other civilisations in the next dimension. They are all etheric and all are Higher Beings with various levels of their own. Randah are the civilisation from the next dimension who have been given the task of keeping a watchful eye over this dimension. They are highly elevated, powerful yet compassionate beings. There are many other civilisations in the next dimension. There are many more dimensions above and below our own.

The Next Dimension And Anubis

There is a figure who appears on the walls of many tombs in Egypt who is a Higher Being from the next dimension, his form is as the hieroglyphs portray him – a jackal-like head on a biped body. He is Anubis. Although he is etheric now that form was as he was when he walked in our own dimension. He exists still and is the Overseer of the Next Dimension working with Randah. Over time Egyptologists have wrongly interpreted all references to him and all folk-lore surrounding him should be disregarded. It seems that even long ago the historians and experts were shallow enough to see a painting of an unusual form and misinterpret its origins.

The Supreme Being – Amun Ra

Just as the image of Anubis has carried through time on the walls of what was buried below ground in Ancient Egypt, so Ra appears in many ancient hieroglyphs. Ra shows himself as the 'bird-headed' form as he last walked. When he walked he was over seven feet tall and a magnificent being in all ways. He is magnificent still. Ra is The Supreme Being and presides over all dimensions. All are responsible to him, and he is responsible only to one other. Ra was never a god. There is no god. Ra is part of the hierarchy and uses Randah to watch over this dimension from the one higher. Ra works closely with the Alliance and is a frequent visitor to their meetings. He is a constant communicator with the Overseer of the Alliance. No decisions of consequence concerning Alliance matters (where they affect the welfare of us all) are made without Ra's consent. Although Ra is far distant from us here in elevation he will one day show himself upon the Earth. He will come not as a god, but as a knowledgeable, compassionate, magnificent being. When we here are ready he will come. It will be within the next ten years.

Ra operates from an area known as The Void. The Void is an area which transcends time and space – like an infrastructure of tunnels which allow Ra and his group (a one hundred strong group who travel and work with Ra) to travel to all universes and all dimensions at great speed. Ra's Group of Higher Beings are thus referred to as being 'Of The Void'. Ra and his group have the freedom to travel to all dimensions, unlike the laws for others there are no restrictions on where Ra's Group can go. They also use other methods of travel including the Pathways.

As I have already said Ra is answerable to only one other ....

THE POWER

There is no god, there is no devil. The hierarchy stops at one pinnacle point. It stops at The Power. The Power is not a god, it is not possible to even explain what it is, for 'it' is the only way to describe The Power. It is not a man, not a woman, it has no form and it is most certainly not a god. You cannot pray to it, talk to it or ask it for help or assistance. You cannot worship it, you need not fall upon your knees and call to it – it will not hear you. Religion is man-made and has no connection with The Power.

As you journey through existence you are on a journey that takes you closer to the energy of The Power, but at all points along that journey you alone are responsible for the speed and distance that you travel through this hierarchy. Personal accountability and responsibility prevail at all times. You are responsible for your own actions and once you break a law you are accountable for every consequence which occurs as a result thereafter. If you were to take the life of another and that other had been destined to make a great difference to mankind in some way - then you are responsible for the taking of that life and what did not happen in the future because you did so.

The Power has set down laws, the rules for our journey. These laws have been given to all. When we leave the etheric layer to walk the solid layer we bring the laws with us. All of our memories of previous lives are withheld and we come here to start afresh, but we each carry the basic instincts. These are the laws and each one of us does know them. They are the rules for the journey and only by following them can you move through the various levels of existence.

The laws have been tampered with in the solid side in many ways, by many man-made 'authorities', but here are the laws that we all carry within us. When we return to the etheric layer we are judged based on how we followed these laws whilst on the solid side and punishment is meted out according to those which we have broken, taking into account the prevailing circumstances at the time when they were broken.

THE THIRTY TWO LAWS OF EXISTENCE

Elementary Levels
1. Learn to feed and nourish your own existence.
2. Learn to live and respect all others.
3. Protect that which is your own and respect that which is not.
4. Teach and share knowledge with others.
5. Respect that which is beyond your understanding.
6. Worship nothing and be worshiped by none.
7. Value and respect all that lives.
8. Honour the memory of life that dies and moves on.

Intermediary Levels

1-8   Adhere to 1-8 and in addition ...

9. Help all as you would wish to be helped.
10. The taking of any life is a crime.
11. Do not take that which does not belong to you.
12. Respect all solid and etheric differences be it outward appearance and form, status and position, current location and origins and all related ways.
13. Do not attempt to create life outside of the natural cycle.
14. Do not impose your will or belief upon others.
15. Respect all existence as if it is your own. Look down on none and look up to none at your own level, treat all as equal.
16. Respect those whose level is above your own.
17. Allow no being to perish if you can help them, share what you have.
18. Respect but do not worship your own physical body.
19. Value no material thing over any living thing.
20. Respect the land on which you walk and know that it is not yours to keep and abuse.
21. Value all life in the solid layer but respect also the cycle of life and be ready to move into the etheric level without fear or doubt of its existence. Be aware of the curtain between the layers and be ready to cross it when it is time to do so.
22. When in solid form learn all that you can about the needs of others and understand them.
23. Better yourself and be the best that you can at whatever you do no matter how lowly.
24. Accept death of the solid existence and embrace etheric existence.
25. Do not profit or benefit by exploiting the death of others.
26. When etheric existence is reached be prepared to meet all of your failings in solid life and accept any judgement without question.
27. Accept etheric existence as the way forward and if eventually you are judged to be worthy – move forward as permanently etheric. Whether temporarily etheric (as part of the reincarnation cycle) or permanently etheric, once you become etheric let go of that which holds you back from material existence. When you are in the solid layer allow those who have departed from you and joined the etheric layer to move forward in their own layer and allow yourself to progress in your own, ready to join those who have already departed.
28. Once etheric, comfort and stay close to those you have left behind until they can accept your passing but also be ready to progress in the etheric layer. In the solid layer release those who have departed as soon as you are comfortable but be mindful that both sides have a duty to continue their existence.

Advanced and Higher Levels

1-28   Not forgetting 1-28 and in addition ... ...

29. Teach others, help all existence to move forward so that you can also move forward
30. Learn all knowledge, seek new knowledge from every corner of existence
31. 31   Constantly strive to move forward being ever mindful of those that you affect above and below you.
32. Strive to be part of the greater understanding.

Your future

So, what about you as you are reading this in the solid layer. Maybe you are wondering how quickly you can move through all of this and advance yourself to the higher levels. Well, the journey takes much longer than you can imagine because there is one more movement of levels that we have not yet discussed. In the case of the journey through existence it is not the arrival that is important, it is the journey itself. And to all intents and purposes that journey will never end. Just be assured that each level achieved is much more rewarding than the one before and know that the thirst for knowledge, once you are on the correct route, is never quenched.

The Transition

Once every single person and being in the dimension has learned all that there is to learn at that level and they exist in a completely unified dimension where all care for all – then the whole dimension moves to the next and a new dimension is formed at the lowest point as each dimension moves along one. Are you beginning to imagine how long your journey is?

Coming Back To Earth

It must seem strange to be given a set of laws which you were not aware of until now. Well, let me tell you that everyone who comes to this Earth from the etheric layer is aware of them.

This book started out by talking of us here on the Earth, and if you have not been too seduced by talk of space craft, planetary systems and dimensions I hope you can think back to the two layers of our own planet – the etheric layer and the solid layer. The etheric layer is the primary layer and for a 'short time' those who need to come to the solid side are born into this solid world. When they arrive here as innocent babies they come without any memory of previous lives, without any plan of where they are to be born, they take the first available egg and arrive here ready to grow and learn.

But creation is very clever and the only 'tools' these babies bring with them are The Laws of Existence. Like the operating system of a computer they are already within each baby, each tiny human being, as a knowing. An instinct. So you see ... you do know right from wrong. And if each individual were left alone and was not tampered with by others who impose their own ways, false laws or greed upon them, then this world would soon become what it should be – a place where all can live together in safety, peace and harmony and where all are fed, clothed and have enough to survive. Because the natural instinct is to follow the Laws of Existence. Surely all reasoning minds can see that it is the greed and uncaring nature in the solid layer that has escalated out of control to make certain things 'acceptable'. The taking of life is wrong – warfare is wrong, murder, in all of its forms including suicide (assisted or otherwise) and abortion, is a crime that will be answered for in the etheric layer. The creating of life is wrong, when did that become acceptable?

If the governments and authorities in the solid layer are currently unaware of these laws, then who imposes them? Despite the relaxed 'laws and punishments' in the solid side, usually governed by commercialism, the punishments are very real in the etheric layer. And the etheric governing body who are responsible for judgement in the etheric layer are never swayed by commercialism. They judge on true facts and nothing can be hidden from them. They do not impose the punishment, that is for a higher authority, but they do make the decisions on what each person who has moved on from his last solid life is guilty of. They are the Earth Council.

THE EARTH COUNCIL

All 5,192 Members of the Alliance (Full or Associate) have a Council in place which governs their own home worlds. Elevated and advanced civilisations have a Council which consists of a mix of etheric and solid members as both layers mix freely, whereas those (like Earth) who are less advanced start with a Council taken from the etheric layer only.

Our own Earth Council has a maximum membership of 21 members. The number of Council Members fluctuates as various members leave to take up positions elsewhere and as others join to take their place. Usually the Earth Council operates with eighteen serving Members. Those who have sat upon the Council and moved on are often retained as Council Elders for advice. There are also many Council Advisors who can be called upon by the Council at certain times, when their speciality is needed, Jasper is a Council Advisor.

I am privileged to have been asked to become the solid voice for the Earth Council, so that I can pass on to you any information they feel that you need. Once the solid side is elevated enough to communicate and mix freely with the etheric side then of course the Earth Council will consist of both solid and etheric members, until then they will need to speak through us.

Council Members are selected carefully. It is hard for you in the solid layer to think that an Elevated Being is the sum of all of his or her incarnations, I know that you need a solid identity to focus upon when you think of someone. And so although each Council Member is much more than his or her one incarnation, I will describe to you the most 'famous' identity of some of the current serving Council Members. Sadly, for legal reasons in the solid layer I cannot currently name them. The Council Members understand that in many cases the commercialism they left behind when they joined the etheric layer still 'owns' their names. They will gladly tell you who they are in the future, and would do so now, but they understand that at this time I cannot. So, remembering this was only one of their many incarnations, let me describe them to you:

The Industrialist

An American industrialist and pioneer. A man of great vision who had great wealth and power. He and his group of helpers now specialise in assisting those who cannot come to terms with finding that once they are in the etheric layer all are equal. His group work on combating all of the problems that materialism in the solid layer creates for both layers. He would like to see the solid side of the Earth moving towards Ethical Commerce for the good of all.

The Scientist

A brilliant mind. A pacifist and a visionary. He and his group of some of the greatest minds from the sciences learn from other members of the Alliance and are working towards being able to rectify Earth's problems by use of the sciences. He would like to see science put to work to improve the situation, health and welfare of all in the solid side, with the exclusion of none. He abhors the use of science to develop weaponry and any destructive technology.

The Visionary

He is saddened that so many think of him as a painter. He walked as a visionary and inventor who could also paint. It is the shallowness of today that sees the price tag on his paintings and works of art rather than the advanced knowledge contained within his work. A man who possessed knowledge that was far in advance of that which was 'of his time' and he struggled during his lifetime to come to terms with what he had. He now knows even more and where he is shares it with many. He can learn from other worlds now and his knowledge grows with every passing second. He can one day share it with us on the solid side too. When we are ready we can have it.

The Western Statesman

A truly great man who lead his people to peace at a difficult time. He is fair, honourable and just. He was a leader of men and continues to be so. He and his friend, the Member which follows, work tirelessly together to do what they can to repair the damage done in the solid layer, which carries into the etheric layer.

The Russian Statesman

Another great mind. A compassionate and honourable man who devoted his life to his people and the peace of the world itself. He has been wrongly portrayed in the history books in many ways, both those written in his own language and other languages. One day the world will find out how he sacrificed himself and his career for peace. Both he and the previous Member work with a large team in the etheric layer who one day hope they can help the solid side towards a time of peace and a life without fear for all nations - without exception.

The Asian Statesman

A role model for humility and compassion. He lived his modest life trying to campaign against injustices for all and hoping to unite a worsening divide between two people who should have been brothers. He now works along with the two following Council members to bring true spirituality, humility and hope to the etheric layer, where all are equal and without divide. He will continue this work with us on the Solid Layer when we are ready.

The Religious Leader.

He walked here in a position of authority in one of the leading Earth man-made religions. Away now from the commercialism of this solid layer he has the complete truth of existence itself and helps those who arrive in the etheric layer expecting angels, a god and all the trapping man-made religions promise, to come to terms with true spirituality. Once they leave behind these fantasy heavens and false expectations they realise that what is there, in being less, is much, much more.

The Singer Songwriter

He says that he started out as a musician and poet with defined ideas and ideals. His fame grew and his wealth with it. He now helps others find true spirituality away from religion and material greed. He feels he was always 'searching for something' in the solid side and now knows he has truly found it.

The Greek Philosopher

He walked in Ancient Greece and many 'academics' use his work today, despite it having been wrongly translated and misinterpreted repeatedly, almost now unrecognisable from his original manuscripts. He (along with the next Member) joined Tovan 375 and the craft of The Thirteen when they were passing the Earth and when he arrived at the system of the Thirteen joined the Alliance to work as an Ambassador for them. During his time as an Ambassador he has visited many civilisations throughout the dimension, helping many of them to improve their knowledge and understanding until they were able to become Full Members of the Alliance. He joined the Earth Council recently which he considers 'coming home' and will assist the Earth to become Full Members.

The Pharaoh

He accompanied the philosopher and journeyed with him, also as an Ambassador for the Alliance. He is a great architect and builder of cities and his time travelling has expanded what was already a great mind. He too has returned home to the Earth at a time when we should be working towards a greater understanding of all things. His knowledge will, in time, benefit both layers greatly.

The Medicine Man

One of three Native American Indians currently serving as Council Members. He is a great spiritual healer and heads a group of healers who work to help those who are troubled and died in despair. Today's warfare and total disregard for human life means their task is a vast one. Far from the 'savages' history portrays most Native Americans are spiritual and wise. If they have followed their ancestors teachings they soon elevate into positions of Elevated Beings when they rejoin the etheric layer. They have long been misunderstood and those who consider themselves superior to them soon find out the truth when they arrive in the etheric layer. The truth of who they really are is soon to be told.

The Indian Chief
He walked as the son of THE Indian Chief who has now moved on to become The Overseer of the Alliance which means his father holds the most important position in this dimension. He is like his father in his strength, his integrity and his compassionate humanitarian ways. His family suffered much during their time in the solid layer and their descendants suffer still. One day father and son will return to their descendants and explain the truth of who the North American Indians really are. Maybe then the world will stop looking down on them and realise what it has missed by repressing such a group of potential teachers and spiritual leaders.

The Earth Council's role is very involved and judgement is just one of their tasks. They (with many elevated helpers) oversee the judgements all must face as every single act each person carried out whilst they were walking is relayed for judgement: How they treated others, what they did with their time walking, did they make a difference – negative or positive, did they break any of the laws which are subject to severe punishment, how many of the lesser laws did they break. Where there any mitigating circumstances. They then pass the individual to the Higher Authority who make the final decision on what comes next.

The Overseer Of The Earth Council – Ray
Our current overseer walked long ago in ancient Egypt as a Pharaoh named Smenkhkare [pronounced smen-car-ray] who prefers to be called Ray. He is not the Smenkhkare who the Egyptologists date around the time of Akhenaten. He shares the name but Ray preceded Nefertiti and Akhenaten by many generations. History has not found him (as is the case with many Pharaohs) and many of the dates, orders and dynasty details 'read' from the ancient inscriptions are misread.
But even if history has not found him Ray was a Pharaoh in Ancient Egypt. He has recently returned from an endless trip of knowledge-gathering and he comes to the Earth Council having spent time as Overseer of the Alliance. He too has the feeling of having 'returned home' at a time of great enlightenment for the Earth.

I have asked Ray to give us some words for this book ...

Message From The Overseer Of The Earth Council

Ray said...

For so long the Earth has spun on erratically, sometimes in control, sometimes far from it. History has moulded and damaged the earth and stopped man from being himself. Many have manipulated mankind to suit there own selfish means. Interference and meddling have halted understanding and progression.

Belief and non belief have collided head on and caused the way forward to be barred and painful. But now mankind does not need to move on without guidance, care and understanding.

We are here for you and although we may be unseen we are here. We are here to untangle the ways of the past and straighten the ways forward. The Council numbers many. Each and every member would appear familiar to most, but we have all left behind our own persona.

We are the members of the Earth Council and our concern is only for mankind. We will help you to move forward and become ready for the next step of joining the rest of existence on equal footings.

RAY
Overseer of the Earth Council

Message From Lillie Whittle

Lillie says ....

I would like to think that many read this book for a second time, a third time and many more times again after that. There is so much knowledge here, so many messages, so many true facts, so much science - and it answers most things.

I hope many use it as a reference book and yet I have avoided indexing the book. Every single piece of information in this book is important and I hope everyone reads it all. I would hate to think people might just dip into it for a certain piece of information and miss the rest of the knowledge.

And I hope that after the first few readings it is the start of the book that becomes the more important, not the sensational space facts, but the words of those simple people who spoke to you from the etheric layer. I hope you are able to see that the main fact which should be taken from this book is that those who are no longer walking on this solid surface are just behind the curtain waiting for us all to be together again. They are safe and well and they understand it all now.

I hope you do too, and I think you will take more from the book each time you read it. It has been a privilege to write. It has been a privilege indeed to have been given this information to pass on to you. I hope you learn from this work. There is more to come, I am learning more and more each day and I will pass a lot more on to you. Jasper is a good teacher.

The biggest privilege of all is that I am able to work with Jasper. We are great friends. He is a Higher Being and he knows everything there is to know about everything important. I am so grateful to be able to help him bring this work to you.

This book is not mine, it is his. I cannot ever put into words the enormity of what a gift I have been given in Knowing Jasper.

Lillie, July 2010.

Message From Jasper

Jasper says....

I said at the beginning of this volume that there were SOME things that you needed to know.

I was wrong.

Now I say to you that you need to know ALL things.

I hope that you have carefully read and understood all that has been written here. I do not expect you to understand it all. Some may get nothing from this book. But I have tried.

I hope that you will find something different in these pages every time you read them. I hope that you can begin to understand that there is more to existence than your mind (with its current material limitations and restrictions) can comprehend. An open mind is ready to learn but a closed mind can never even start to expand. It becomes stale and eventually useless.

Life carries on - the only barriers that will stop you on your journey of existence are those that you put there yourself.

Yes, you do need to know ALL things. It will take time and your journey has only just begun. I will keep teaching you for as long as the short time that I will be here permits.

This volume is just the first page in the vast library that is yours to learn.

Jasper

NOTES